# Tell It Well:

## Communicating the Gospel
## Across Cultures

# Tell It Well:

## Communicating the Gospel Across Cultures

by

John T. Seamands

BEACON HILL PRESS OF KANSAS CITY
KANSAS CITY, MISSOURI

# Contents

# Preface

Recent research has revealed some startling facts concerning the unfinished task of world missions. Out of a total global population of approximately 4 billion, about 2.7 billion people are yet to be evangelized. Either they have never heard the gospel or have not heard it sufficiently to make an intelligent decision. Out of this vast multitude only about 15 percent may be considered culturally close neighbors who can be reached by existing Christians within the context of their own language and culture. The remaining 85 percent, though they are geographical neighbors, are, in fact, culturally distant peoples who can be reached only by evangelism that crosses cultural and language barriers. This 85 percent represents roughly 17,500 different ethnic and sociocultural groups, speaking over 5,000 languages and dialects. All this highlights the necessity and urgency of training committed Christians around the world for effective cross-cultural communication of the gospel.

During the past few years several good books have been published which help to prepare us for this gigantic task. Of major importance are: *Message and Mission,* by Eugene Nida; *What's Gone Wrong with the Harvest?* by James Engel and H. Wilbert Norton; and *The Contagious Congregation,* by George Hunter. Each one has its particular significance and contribution.

In this book I have tried to approach the subject from yet another standpoint. I have intentionally avoided the temptation to be highly technical and theoretical. I have sought throughout to be as simple and practical as possible, and yet maintain the degree of academic quality required by such an important subject.

I have written with several groups of readers in mind. There is, first of all, the professional missionary preparing for full-time service abroad, who will be engaged in cross-cultural evangelism and church planting. Illustrations are taken from a variety of countries and cultures to equip this person for effective communication of the Christian message to people of other faiths. Then there is the layperson engaged in business or official work in some foreign country, who is a committed Christian and desires to witness for Christ to those whom he contacts in his profession. At the same time we realize that our own backyard has become a mission field, for the U.S.A. is becoming more of a pluralistic society, ethnically and religiously, all the time. There are Muslims, Hindus, and Buddhists in our midst; Chinese, Koreans, Vietnamese, Arabs, Mexicans, Asian Indians, and others. We have a tremendous opportunity and responsibility to win these people for Christ and teach them to be responsible members of the Christian Church. In order to do this, Christians in America— laity and clergy—need to know something about other religions and how to witness intelligently to followers of these faiths. Some of the basic principles discussed in this book will be helpful to those who are witnessing among secular-minded or unchurched people of our own culture.

Besides the section dealing with principles and methods, I have included a description of the present religious climate around the world, and a discussion of the challenge that is confronting the Church these days from the non-Christian religions. I have also tried to explain basic differences between Christian revelation and the world religions, in order to emphasize the uniqueness of the gospel and particularly the person of Christ. We must know our world and know our message before we can learn the methods.

If the material in this book will enable even a few missionaries and laypersons to become effective bearers of the truth and witnesses for Christ, the author will feel that his labor has not been in vain.

—JOHN T. SEAMANDS

# Introduction

The gospel involves *communication* because it is essentially *news—good* news at that! The *most important* news! It is the news that God has not left us in our sins, but has loved us so much that He gave His Son to live and die and be raised again that we might be redeemed from all sin. It is the good news that *God is not against us because of our sin, but is for us against our sin.* So the gospel is *not a venerable record,* but *a vital report.*

News must be told. It cannot be kept secret. It is the very characteristic of news that it must be proclaimed. That is what we do with the daily news of the world—get it out as far and as fast as possible, by every available means: television, radio, telephone, cable, magazine, newspaper, and word of mouth. This is what we must do with the eternal news of God—proclaim it to all men by all means.

The gospel involves communication of *the truth—*what God has revealed as truth, not our ideas of what is truth. We must be faithful to the biblical message. As ambassadors of the Kingdom we have no right to tamper with or alter the truth. We must "tell the truth, the whole truth, and nothing but the truth." It is the truth that sets men free.

The gospel involves *effective* communication of the truth. *What* we say is important, but *how* we say it is just as important. For we are not only *proclaimers;* we are also *persuaders.* We preach for a verdict; not just to *inform,* but to *transform.* Jesus was the Master Communicator, for He not only spoke the language of the people, but also framed His teachings in forms which had optimum information value as well as truth. His words were *truth with impact.* Those who heard Him "were astonished at his teaching" and declared, "No man ever spoke like this man!" (Matt. 7:28; John 7:46).

When Peter, newly anointed with the Holy Spirit, preached to the multitudes in Jerusalem on the Day of Pentecost, all those who heard him "were cut to the heart, and said to Peter and the rest of the apostles, 'Brethren, what shall we do?'" (Acts 2:37). Governor Felix and King Agrippa trembled when they heard the persuasive witness and preaching of the apostle Paul (24:25 and 26:28). Communicating the gospel is always to bring man into a definite encounter with God, an encounter that requires response, that calls for a man not only to hear but also to believe and to act.

For communication to be effective it must be *adapted to the background and needs of the listener*. Jesus was an expert at this. To Nicodemus the Pharisee He spoke about the new birth; to the sinful woman at the well He spoke about the Living Water. To the rich young ruler who idolized his possessions, He said, "Go, sell [all] . . . and come, follow me" (Matt. 19:21); to the woman taken in adultery He said, "Neither do I condemn you; go, and do not sin again" (John 8:11). When preaching to farmers, He talked about the soil, the seed, and the harvest; when addressing fishermen, He spoke about fishing for men.

The apostles, in their preaching, followed the example of Jesus. When they were proclaiming the Good News to their own people, the Jews, they started with Abraham, Moses, David, and the prophets of the Old Testament, and then proceeded to the Christ of the new covenant who fulfilled all the ancient prophecies.

But when they preached to the Gentiles—as Paul, on Mars Hill in Athens—they started with the Creator of all men and quoted from their philosophers and poets. To the Jews they spoke of Jesus as "the Lamb of God"; to the Greeks, they described Him as "the Word of God" (cf. John 1:29, 1).

Sadhu Sundar Singh, the beloved Indian Christian, used to tell about a high-caste Hindu in India, who fainted from the summer heat while sitting on a train at a railway station. Someone ran to the faucet, filled a cup with water, and brought it to the man in an attempt to revive him. But in spite of his condition, the passenger would not accept the water because it was offered in the cup of a man belonging to another caste. Then someone noticed that the high-caste man had a cup on the seat beside him; so he grabbed it, went out and filled it with water, returned, and offered it to the man, who now readily accepted the water with gratitude. Then Sundar Singh would say to his audience, "This is what I have been trying to say to you missionaries from abroad. You have been offering the water of life to the people of India in a foreign cup, and we have been slow to receive it. If you will offer it in our own cup [that is, in an indigenous form], we are much more likely to accept it."

There are many ways to report the news—through mass media, or the written page, or by the spoken word. Whatever the means, the reporter must be sure the news is accurate. In the same way, the messenger of Christ will present the Good News (the gospel) in many different forms to different people, in accordance with their cultural and religious background, and in accordance with their own needs. But whatever the form, the content will always be the same.

A television newscaster was once speaking to a select group of ministers. In deep earnestness he said to them, "You preachers have the greatest news in all the world. Be sure you tell it, and *tell it well!*"

That is what this book is all about: telling the Good News in a telling way.

# PART 1

# The Gospel in Relation to Other Religions

# 1

# The Religious World
# of Today

Not long ago, a Christian missionary in Sri Lanka (formerly Ceylon) received a visit from a Buddhist priest who came to borrow some books on Christianity. "I didn't know that you were interested in Christianity," said the missionary.

"I am not," was the reply, "but my job is to train young monks who will go as missionaries to the West; and I think it's a good idea that they should know something of the religion of the natives before they get there."

We may smile at this story, but it should cause us to pause and reflect, for it is indicative of the religious climate of our day. It is symbolic of the many changes that have taken place in the last two or three decades. The Christian messenger of today is living in a vastly different world from that of his predecessors.

Before we can become effective communicators of the gospel, it is essential that we understand the religious environment of our contemporary world. We need to be aware of the changes taking place in the world religions, the ways they are challenging the Christian faith, and the various forces contending for the hearts and minds of people everywhere. Such an awareness will enable us to preach a gospel that is more relevant to the needs of our hearers. Let us look at some of the facets of the present religious scene.

## 1. "The Field Is the World"

These words of Jesus found in Matt. 13:38 are very pertinent to our present world situation. The entire geographical world has reverted to a mission field.

Formerly we used to divide the world into two distinct camps—
the Christian West and the non-Christian East. This appeared to be a
neat and simple division, since the Christian faith was confined largely to Europe and the Americas, while the great world religions such
as Islam, Hinduism, Buddhism, and animism, held sway in the
Middle East, Africa, and Asia. But now the Church of Jesus Christ is
established, at least to some extent, in every part of Asia and Africa,
and Christians are to be found all across the world. At the same time
Christianity has suffered several major setbacks in the Western countries, and some are even talking of a post-Christian era in Europe
and the United States. It is quite evident that there are no real Christian nations anywhere in the world, but there are genuine followers
of Christ in almost every land.

There is no geographical domain over which the Christian faith
any longer holds sovereign influence. On the one hand, the "home
churches" of the West do not hold an uncontested position in their
own culture. Many persons have no connection with, and no respect
for, the Christian Church. They do not accept the norms of Christian
behavior as their pattern for living. On the other hand, the "mission-
founded churches" of the East are set in the midst of situations
strongly influenced or even controlled by the non-Christian religions
of the world. This means that every Christian congregation, regardless of location, is in an environment that is definitely missionary
in character. The frontier between Christian and non-Christian is
therefore not geographical but spiritual. The line of demarcation is
that of faith and un-faith. The mission field is not simply "over
there" or "across the seas," but is everywhere and at our doorstep.

We seem to be getting back to the situation of the Early Church.
Not since the early centuries has the Christian faith and its mission
been so sharply demarcated from, and without the support of, its
cultural environment. The Early Church was conspicuously alien to
its environment in the Roman Empire. It had to create its own culture within the pagan culture which surrounded it on every side. It
had to confront the various claims of Greek and Oriental philosophy,
syncretistic mystery religions, and cults of family, city, and state. Is
not this the situation today, where the Church has to contend with
contemporary secularism, materialism, and pagan life-styles?

The Early Church did not withdraw from this confrontation but
endeavored to use it as an occasion of declaring its faith. The great
Christian theologians and preachers challenged the spokesmen of the
pagan philosophies and religions, while the rank-and-file Christian

laypersons seized every opportunity to witness in the marketplace. The Church of today must recapture this spirit.

There is one difference between the situation of the Early Church and our situation today. The Early Church was just in its beginning, and therefore pure, with no sad history in the background. This made the Christian movement powerful and effective. But today's organized church is largely responsible for the present hostile environment. It has to contend with its own failures and sinfulness. The greatest hindrance to the advancement of the church is from within its own ranks, not from without. Millions inside the church give only nominal and superficial allegiance without genuine commitment to Christ and the Christian faith. Western culture has become de-Christianized.

For the past few centuries the world missionary movement has been in one direction—from West to East. Christians from Europe and North America have been sending their messengers to the countries of Africa, Asia, and the Orient. But in recent years the movement has begun to flow in the opposite direction as well—from East to West. So we hear of the Hare Krishna movement, Zen Buddhism, the Black Muslims, Bahaism, Transcendental Meditation, and Yoga, right here in the United States. Hindu temples and Muslim mosques have been and are being built in some of our major cities. Thousands of our young people have been "converted" to these various religious movements in the past two decades; the United States is fast becoming a pluralistic religious society. The options in the field of religion are becoming more numerous.

This means that the confrontation between religions is no longer confined to the Eastern countries. It is now all around us. No longer are Christians only in India and Pakistan and Sri Lanka rubbing shoulders with Hindus, Muslims, and Buddhists. Christians in England and Canada and the United States are regularly meeting followers of Krishna and Mohammed and Buddha. Today in England, the birthplace of Methodism, there are more Muslims than there are Methodists.

There is, however, a bright side to the present situation. The religious confrontations all about us offer new and exciting evangelistic opportunities. No longer is it necessary to go to India to witness to a Hindu, or to the Middle East to witness to a Muslim, or to Thailand to witness to a Buddhist. Followers of these faiths are right in our midst—as delegates to the United Nations, as businessmen, and as students. The latter number into the tens of thousands on our university campuses. Thus, we have a mission field in our front yard.

Recently a committed Christian couple in Lexington, Ky., in the course of their business met a young Hindu salesman from India. They invited him to dinner one evening; and, while seated around the table, they shared with him their personal faith and experience in Jesus Christ. They found the young man very open to the gospel, and before midnight this couple had the privilege of leading him into a personal experience with the Savior. A few months ago I had the joy of baptizing the new convert into the Christian faith. The latest news is that this Christian couple have now been able to lead the young man's sister into a saving relationship with the Lord. This all happened, not in far-off India, but right here in Kentucky!

It is a sad but true fact that few of our church members here in the homeland are prepared for this confrontation, and thus are unable to seize the evangelistic opportunity that is all about them. Since many are not fully committed to Christ themselves, they have nothing to offer the people of other faiths. Others know little or nothing of these other religions and don't know how to witness intelligently to Hindus, Muslims, Buddhists, etc. Our pastors and churches will have to do a better job in preparing our people, spiritually and mentally, for the missionary task that confronts us.

## 2. The Resurgence of Non-Christian Religions

Another very significant ingredient of the contemporary religious environment is the resurgence of the non-Christian religions. A few decades ago these religions appeared to be dormant, silent, on the defensive, more or less accepting the superiority of the Christian faith. But in recent years, particularly since the coming of independence to the Afro-Asian countries, the Eastern religions have become vocal, aggressive, and quick to claim universal validity for themselves. They have been copying many methods employed by the Christian Church, and carrying on their own missionary programs. It is evident they have taken on new life.

Although a neat grouping with anything like clear-cut distinctions cannot be made, it may be convenient to consider this resurgence of the Asian religions as of three main types.

*a. Revival.* As a result of political independence, the people of Asia have been reaching back into their own history, culture, and their own indigenous religious faith. They have sought for new religious foundations to help build up their political systems and to help maintain unity in their countries. Opposition to the political, cultural, and religious domination of the West during the days of colonialism has led Asians to return to the "faith of their fathers" with renewed zeal. This has resulted in a "revival movement" particularly within Buddhism, Islam, and Hinduism, brought about primarily by forces making for change from *within.* It is the *old* come back to life, claiming for itself a new resistance and relevancy to the environment. Thus we see a renewed emphasis on the celebration of religious festivals, the building of new temples and mosques, the production of religious literature, and religious education for the youth.

A main characteristic of the revival movement has been the tendency toward establishing state religions, that is, making the religion of the majority the national religion. In Burma, for example, for a short period in the 60s, Buddhism was declared to be the state religion. In Afghanistan, Pakistan, and the Middle East, Islam is considered to be the state religion. India has succeeded so far in maintaining freedom of religion, and separation of state and religion, but there is an aggressive segment of Hindu society that would like to see "India for the Hindus." In each case the majority religion is equated with patriotism—"To be a loyal Burmese, you must be Buddhist; to be a genuine Pakistani, you must be Muslim"; etc.—and the loyalty of the minority groups is questioned.

At the same time, as a result of this strong feeling of religious nationalism, we have seen serious restrictions placed upon the entrance of Christian missionaries, and, in some cases, complete prohibition. In 1966 the government of Burma ordered all missionaries to leave the country. Malaysia permits Christian missionaries to serve within its borders for a limited period of 10 years. Several Muslim countries have stopped the entry of missionaries, while others have drastically curtailed the activities of missionaries. It is difficult for a missionary to obtain a visa for service in India these days; the number of missionaries in that country has declined steadily in the past 20 years.

A vivid illustration of this type of religious resurgence is found in the recent events in Iran. There the reins of government have passed from king to *mulla;* Islam is clearly a state religion, and Islamic law is the law of the land. The leadership is seeking to establish a theocratic government based on the will of Allah.

*b. Reform.* Another form that the resurgence of the Asian religions is taking is that of reform. In this case change is brought about from *without,* and is due primarily to the stimulus of factors in the environment. The change results in the acceptance and incorporation of new ideas and practices and the discarding of certain former ideas and practices. In consequence there is reformation, where the emphasis is more upon the *new* than upon the *old,* and sometimes on the new as against the old.

The major force behind this reform movement is the impact of Christianity itself, with its high ethical standards, its emphasis on God's holiness and love, and its concern for the value of the individual and for social justice. This has resulted, in the first place, in a dramatic religious housecleaning, whereby the non-Christian religions have abolished some of their grosser practices, such as headhunting, cannibalism, infanticide, temple prostitution, *purdah* (seclusion of women), and polygamy. Then again, it has resulted in a degree of Christianization, whereby the world religions have incorporated a number of Christian values, such as the equality of women, concern for the poor and oppressed, unselfish service of mankind, etc.

In India, temple prostitution used to be a fairly common practice among certain segments of Hinduism. Parents would dedicate a daughter to a certain goddess, and the girl would carry on her trade in the name of religion. The caste system was also one of the strongholds of Hinduism, practiced for centuries with the sanction of religion. But after independence in India, and with the forming of the new constitution, Hindus themselves took a strong stand against "untouchability," promoted the concept of equality for all, and outlawed the practices of temple prostitution and polygamy (for Hindus). In recent years they have established orphanages, hospitals, leprosariums, and dormitories for children of low-caste parentage. Many Hindus are now exhibiting a strong social concern.

Krishna is one of the most popular gods of Hinduism. He is even becoming a favorite among some American and Western youth who have become followers of the Hare Krishna movement. There are many Hindus who have been claiming for some time that Krishna and Krista (Indianized name for Christ) are equal or just different names for the same person. However, when one studies the lives of the two persons, it is quite evident their character is not the same. Two of the most common stories told about Krishna is how he once stole butter from a housewife, and on another occasion how he stole the clothes of certain milkmaids *(gopis)* who had left them on the bank while bathing in a pool. When the girls begged for their clothes, Krishna made each one approach him with open arms in a posture of supplication.

Now when one compares these stories of the "Lord Krishna" with the life story of the Lord Jesus Christ, Krishna, the playboy, doesn't make a very good showing in the presence of Christ, the holy Son of God. So in order to give more credibility to Krishna as a person worthy of our respect and worship, Hindus have sought to give a new interpretaton to his escapades. They insist that the story of the *gopis* is not to be taken literally, but as an allegory with spiritual meaning. It is really teaching (so they say) that any person who comes into the presence of God stands naked or stripped of all his status, prestige, and achievements. He stands as a mere man in the presence of Deity.

According to the Koran, a Muslim man is permitted to have four legal wives, on condition that he treats all of them equally. Some modern Muslim scholars contend that this provision really serves as a deterrent to polygamy, for the simple reason that it is impossible to treat four wives with complete equality.

All of these illustrations point to the fact that there is a definite reform movement going on within the non-Christian religions today. They are becoming more Christian in their outlook and concepts. In one way this only makes our mission more difficult, because some non-Christians feel that the gap between their faith and the Christian faith has now been narrowed, so "conversion" from one side to another is completely irrelevant.

*c. Restatement.* The third form of resurgence within the non-Christian religions is a renaissance movement due to changes brought about by forces acting both from *without* and from *within.* The process is more that of *interaction* than reaction. For here the religion and the environment act in turn as both stimulus and response. This interaction leads to such a radical shakeup of the foundations that the result is a restatement or repatterning of some of the major concepts of the religion. In the process, the old faith acquires a new meaning, new resilience, and new vitality. Let us look at a few examples.

All through the history of Islam, the concept of *jihad* (the holy war) has been an important idea in Muslim politics. It has often encouraged Muslims to take up the sword in an effort to defend the faith and rid the world of the "infidel." But in modern society, world opinion is strongly opposed to taking up arms in the name of religion. Religion, it is argued, should lead to peace, not to war. So modern Muslim scholars are now interpreting *jihad* from a spiritual viewpoint. They insist that *jihad* refers to the battle between the forces of righteousness and unrighteousness that takes place within the heart of every man. This, of course, is a concept that can find ready acceptance anywhere in the world.

The teaching of Buddhism is founded on the "Four Noble Truths" expounded by its founder—to exist is to suffer; desire is the cause of all suffering; to get rid of suffering, one must get rid of all desire; the way to overcome desire is to follow the Eightfold Path of duty. This will lead to *nirvana* (the extinction of life). But the common people all over Asia today are engulfed in "the revolution of rising expectations." That is, they are no longer willing to accept their poverty and degradation as the "will of the gods" or "the result of their *karma*" (deeds committed in a previous life). They want the basic necessities of life: food, housing, employment, and education. They are full of desire for a better life, a life that is free from the chains of hunger and insecurity. It certainly doesn't make much sense to say to such people that desire is the cause of all suffering and that they need to get rid of all desire. This has no appeal for the masses. So among modern Buddhist scholars, *nirvana* is not being described negatively as loss of desire and existence, but more positively as a state of perfect bliss and contentment. This makes the Buddhist teaching more relevant to the contemporary situation and more acceptable to the common man.

In Japan, after World War II, the old form of Buddhism that centered around the ancient shrine and the professional priest soon lost its appeal among the general populace. In its place there arose a variety of new forms of Buddhism that produced magnificent buildings of modern architectural design, and emphasized involvement of the laity. These so-called new religions all claim to be "the true Buddhism," but none of them looks anything like the original. They have formulated their own doctrines and offer a utopia of material prosperity and well-being.

\* \* \*

There are signs of this religious resurgence all across the world these days. Note, for example, what is happening in the Buddhist world. Buddhist leaders are copying many methods used by the Christian Church. They are translating their Pali scriptures into several of the major languages of the world. They conduct preaching services, youth rallies, and scripture quizzes. They organize Sunday schools and branches of Y.M.B.A. (Young Men's Buddhist Association). They have adapted some of our hymns, such as, "Buddha, lover of my soul," "Buddha loves me, this I know, / For the Dhamma tells me so," and "Sweet hour of meditation."

In Sri Lanka there is a Buddhist missionary training center in the capital city of Colombo, and its leaders often solicit funds "for the spread of the gospel of Buddha to the pagan of Europe." There is another large training center in Rangoon, Burma, where they are training Buddhist monks in Hindi and in English, in preparation for missionary service in India and the English-speaking world. The Shin sect of Japanese Buddhism is supposed to have more than 300 missionaries in Europe and North America at present.

Islam is also on the march today. The aggressive Ahmediyya sect has its mission headquarters in Rabwah, Pakistan, from whence they have sent forth several hundred foreign missionaries into various countries of the world. This group produces a mass of literature which seeks to confute the basic truths of the Christian faith. They claim that Jesus did not die on the Cross, that He escaped and fled to Kashmir, where He died and was buried (in Shrinagar). The Ahmediyya missionary in Lagos, Nigeria, challenged Billy Graham to a public religious debate, when the latter was conducting a campaign in that country a few years ago. Then when Billy Graham went on to Nairobi, Kenya, the Ahmediyya Muslim missionary stationed there challenged him to a public healing contest. "Let us take 30 incurable patients," he proposed, "and by lot you take 15 and I'll take 15. Let us see who can heal the most!"

In Cairo, U.A.R., the Supreme Islamic Council carries on a very aggressive missionary program for the continent of Africa. Training camps are turning out hundreds of lay missionaries in a concerted effort to win the uncommitted animist tribes in central and southern Africa. Tireless printing presses flood the continent with cheap copies of the Koran and pamphlets that proclaim the word of Allah. In Libya, a tax-supported Islamic center with a $20 million budget is directing propagation of the Muslim faith in 35 other countries. Two dozen Islamic organizations are cooperating in plans to construct a powerful radio station in Mecca, Saudi Arabia. To be known as "The Voice of Islam," the station will seek to counterbalance Christian broadcasting in Africa. The same group plans to launch a global broadcasting campaign to spread the Islamic faith.[1]

It is apparent that Islam is on the march in a manner un-matched, perhaps, since its conquest of North Africa and the Near East in the seventh and eighth centuries. Bolstered by a near-monopoly of the world's oil supplies, and the financial power that oil provides, Islam is equipped with an unprecedented array of political and economic armaments, in addition to its intrinsic religious zeal. Islam is now considered the second largest religion in Europe. In Western Europe alone, there are 8.7 million Muslims; in Britain, not less than 1 million, more likely 2. In 1976 the Islamic Council of Europe announced its aim of establishing a mosque of reasonable size in each major city in Europe. Since then, the $7.5 million Central Mosque in London, seating 2,900 people, has been opened, and plans announced for a $20 million structure in Rome, the center of the Catholic church, that will "rival St. Peter's Cathedral in splendor."

England seems to be a special target for Islam. One Muslim leader declares it is "ripe for conversion." There are now 300 mosques in the country, some of them former Christian churches, and a reported 22 English-language newspapers propagating Islam. In 1976 the world's first festival of Islam was held there, at a cost of $2 million. It was opened by the queen and lasted three months. A statement declared: "Unless we win London over to Islam, we will fail to win the whole of the Western world." A Muslim training center has been opened, and at a press conference held in London in December, 1978, Islam's intentions were made clear by the headline: "Muslims Launch Missionary Crusade for Britain and the Rest of the World."

In the United States, it is estimated that the number of Muslims has increased from 1 million to 3 million in the last decade; and Muslim leaders claim that Islam should now be considered a major national religion. Of this number about 1 million followers are said to be of Arab descent, while most of the rest are blacks converted to Islam, mainly through the Black Muslim movement. That organization is now called the World Community of Islam in the West, and refers to its followers as Bilalians, in honor of Bilal, the first black convert to Islam. At the last count there were 133 chapters of Mus-lim Students' Associations in North America, and 84 mosques, one of the newest being a $1 million structure going up on a main street in Toronto. Islamic publications in North America are increasing, with one periodical claiming a circulation of 740,000.

Islam, supported by petro-dollars, is now becoming involved in social programs in the U.S.A., with aims that are clearly stated as religious. A Model Communities Program funded by $50 million from Saudi Arabia is planned for urban centers across the country, concentrating on improving ghetto housing, providing jobs, schools, and religious centers. If successful, program funds can be increased to $150 million by 1981.

## 3. The Challenge from the Non-Christian Religions

As a direct result of this religious resurgence around the world today, the Christian faith is being challenged by the non-Christian religions to a greater extent than ever before. The challenge is coming to us in several different forms, some belligerent and some conciliatory.

*a. Criticizing our failures.* These days non-Christians are highly critical of Christians in the West, and seem to delight in pointing out our failure to live up to our own standards. They remind us of our high divorce rate, the ever-increasing crime rate, the pornographic filth that floods our bookstalls and theaters, Western imperialism, our obsession with free sex, two world wars that originated in "Christian Europe," and U.S.A. involvement in the war in Vietnam, etc.

In his book *Asia and Western Dominance,* the Hindu writer K. M. Panikkar has a chapter on "Christian Missions," in which he discusses the failure of the Christian movement to convert Asia. He suggests five reasons for this failure:

(1) "the missionary brought with him an attitude of moral superiority and a belief in his own exclusive righteousness";

(2) "the association of Christian missionary work with aggressive imperialism introduced political complications";

(3) "the sense of European superiority which the missionaries ·perhaps unconsciously inculcated produced also its reaction";

(4) "the wide variety of Christian sects, each proclaiming the errors of others, handicapped missionary work";

(5) "the growth of unbelief in Europe . . . broke whatever spell the different sects of Christianity had among certain classes of Asians."[2]

A few years ago, a Buddhist scholar, Vijayawardhana, wrote a scathing attack on Christianity in a volume entitled *The Revolt in the Temple*. The following two quotations are samples of his remarks:

> It is strange, but significant, that Christian missionaries seldom talk of the propagation of their religion except in terms of war. 'Winning for Christ,' 'warring against heathendom,' 'fighting for the cross'—these are but a few of the sanguinary figures of Christian speech. It is indeed ironical that the cause of the Prince of Peace, as Jesus is often claimed to be, has to be espoused by such militaristic missionaries. . . . Even Christian hymnology has not been proof against the ravages of the bug of militarism, and otherwise sweet-tempered young women and inoffensive old ladies are heard not infrequently bawling out lustily: "Onward Christian soldiers, marching on to war" and so on and so forth.[3]

> Christian civilization of today is gradually forsaking the religion in which it has lived for nearly fifteen centuries. A great European country, Russia, has openly and officially rejected its ancient faith and espoused Atheism. Slogans are everywhere displayed which declare religion the chief enemy of human progress and welfare. . . . Christianity, or what remains of it, is fast dying. What is now left of the old theology in the circles of the educated and intelligent? . . . The Christian religion is dissolving before our eyes.[4]

*b. Challenging our claims.* Many non-Christians are contesting the Christian claim to uniqueness and final truth, and also the right of Christians to convert others to their faith. Dr. Malasekara, learned professor of Pali at the University of Sri Lanka, wrote in *The Buddhist* magazine:

> Conversion is an ugly word. To us in this country it has all manner of undesirable associations, of force, of bribery, and corruption, of denationalization, of the exploitation of poverty and ignorance and greed, of disease and helplessness. Attempts at conversion breed strife and ill-will; the days when Buddhists and Hindus tolerated proselytisation are gone. They will meet the challenge to their faiths with vigor and determination. They will no longer accept the claims of any religion to be the sole path of righteousness or happiness.[5]

Dr. M. B. Niyogi, a staunch Hindu and former chief justice of the Nagpur High Court in India, declared that "since conversion muddles the convert's sense of unity and solidarity with his society, there is a danger of his loyalty to his county and state being undermined."[6]

The sad part is that there are some "Christian" leaders who would agree with the critics of Christianity. Arnold Toynbee, the outstanding British historian, suggested that "we ought to purge our

Christianity of the traditional belief that Christianity is unique."[7] Prof. J. G. Davies of the University of Birmingham, one of the most extreme spokesmen for the new secular theology, says categorically: "Individual conversion as it is usually understood and attempted by the 'revivalists' is neither a concept nor an activity that I find acceptable. . . . Really, I would prefer that the term 'conversion' be eliminated from the Christian vocabulary."[8]

One might expect outside critics to speak thus, but surely not those who claim to be within the fold!

*c. Claiming universal validity for themselves.* Some non-Christian leaders are not only contesting the Christian claim to uniqueness, but at the same time are making extraordinary claims for universal validity on behalf of their own religions. Professor Vijayawardhana of Sri Lanka, after declaring Christianity a "dying religion," wrote about his own Buddhist religion:

> Although the Buddhist way of life still embodies an ethical creed far in advance of the world's development today, it does offer in the present anarchy of ethics a creed to live for, and a principle to live by. The creed is righteousness, translated to the ideal of the brotherhood of man; the principle, justice.[9]
>
> When the day comes when men of all creeds and colors accept as their religion the common brotherhood of man and obey the Buddhist teaching that they should love one another and hold as their highest ideal the continuous search for, and love of, truth, mankind will be well on the way to the millennium.[10]

A few years ago, Maharishi Mahesh Yogi, Indian guru and spiritual leader of the TM movement in the West, boldly declared before an audience of 5,000 New Yorkers gathered together in the Felt Forum of Madison Square Garden: "This afternoon I can announce convincingly that this Transcendental Meditation will definitely create world peace for thousands of generations." He went on to say that "wars, famines, and earthquakes are all signs of tension. Meditation eliminates tension and thus eliminates the problems."[11]

In a little booklet entitled *The Impact of Islam on Human Progress,* Prof. Mahmud Brelvi of Pakistan extols the virtues of Islam and quotes from many writers, Western as well as Eastern, to prove that modern science, Western law and culture, Western architecture, Western poetry and art, sociology, Western thought, and Christian theology all owe a heavy debt to Islam. He praises "the magnanimity of Islam," the extensive "social revolution" sparked by Islam, and "the contribution of Islam to global welfare."[12]

Leaders of each world faith are now claiming the superiority of their religion over all the rest.

*d. Inviting us to compromise.* In contrast to the preceding stance, some religious leaders across the world take a more liberal approach in their attitude toward Christianity. Rather than making extraordinary claims for their own faith, they readily accept the validity of all religions as well as their limitations. They suggest that no religion has the final word, and that all religions are on an equal footing. They therefore invite Christians to renounce their claim to absolute truth and to accept this conciliatory attitude toward all religions.

This invitation, which comes particularly from Hindu spokesmen, is based on two widely accepted modern concepts. The first is the political concept of "peaceful coexistence," an idea adopted by Prime Minister Jawaharlal Nehru of India as the basis for his foreign policy with China. Pandit Nehru said to the leaders of China: "If you desire to establish a Communist government, that is your prerogative. In India we prefer to have a democratic republic. Now if either one of us seeks to impose his system of government upon the other, it will only lead to tension and war. So let us recognize each other's government and live side by side in a state of 'peaceful coexistence.'"

This concept is then carried over into the religious realm. For example, the Hindu says to the Christian: "I happen to be a Hindu by birth and preference; you happen to be a Christian. Now if either one of us seeks to impose his religion upon the other, it only leads to misunderstanding and strife. So let us recognize one another's religion and live side by side in a state of 'peaceful religious coexistence.'"

The second basis for this invitation to compromise comes from the attitude of science toward truth. Science, it is said, never claims to have arrived at final truth. It is constantly making new discoveries about the universe and enlarging its horizons of truth. It scraps old theories for new ones all the time. For science, truth is only relative. In the same way, it is argued, people are constantly discovering new facets of philosophical and religious truth about God and the meaning of life, so no one should claim to have absolute spiritual truth. To do so is a clear sign of bigotry and false pride. How much better, it is suggested, that we recognize that all religious truth is relative and that we join in a common search for additional truth.

*e. Inviting us to cooperate.* This is another conciliatory appeal that goes even further than the preceding invitation to compromise. Stated simply, it goes something like this: "The greatest enemy of mankind today is irreligion—secularism, materialism, and atheism. So let us cease arguing among ourselves which is the superior religion; let us stop trying to convert from one religion to another. Instead let us join forces in a crusade against the common enemy of secularism, and seek to win modern pagans back to religious faith and practice." Some would even suggest that we join together in worship services and in programs of social uplift.

Christian people must face all of these challenges and invitations squarely and honestly. In response to the criticisms leveled against our behavior, we dare not attempt to cover up or rationalize our failures. We must sincerely confess our sins before God and our fellowmen, come to the Heavenly Father in genuine repentance and humility, ask for full and free forgiveness, and then by the grace of God try to live out the Christian life in love and holiness. Non-Christians must see that to be a Christian is to be different from the world and to be like Christ in motive, attitude, word, and deed. We must take a stand against the moral evils and injustices of our day, and seek to change not only individuals but society as well. We must try to strengthen the foundations of family life and to renew the spiritual life of the church. Nominal Christians must become genuine Christians.

In response to the challenge against the biblical claim to ultimate truth and the call for spiritual conversion, evangelical Christians must unashamedly declare that these matters are nonnegotiable. The uniqueness of the Christian revelation is not a subject for debate; it is a question of what are the facts. If the Bible is the inspired, authoritative Word of God, and if God has acted decisively and redemptively in history through the incarnation and crucifixion of His Son, then Christ alone is the Way, the Truth, and the Life, and no one comes to the Father except through Him. At the risk of being called "narrow-minded bigots" and "religious imperialists," we dare not surrender what is not our own. We must take our stand firmly on the Word of God. (In Chapter 4 we shall deal in greater detail with these matters.)

### 4. The Growing Spiritual Vacuum

In spite of all the outer show of resurgence by the non-Christian religions, there is unmistakable evidence of a growing spiritual vacuum in certain areas of our contemporary world. Amidst outer demonstration there is inner decay.

The spiritual vacuum is quite strong among university students across the world. Through the scientific approach to life, they have developed questioning minds and want to put everything in a test tube before they will accept it. They are becoming disillusioned about religion in general; some are even accepting the Marxist attitude that "religion is the opiate of the people." Thus many students are jettisoning the "faith of their fathers" and becoming agnostic or secular minded. They feel that no matter how much their traditional religion seeks to modify its basic concepts and to modernize its practices, it is still irrelevant and meaningless for 20th-century civilization. In a recent government survey in Japan, 65 percent of the students said they followed no particular faith whatsoever.

The spiritual vacuum is also strong among the lower economic masses in urban centers around the world. Urbanization is a characteristic phenomenon of our day. People are moving from rural areas into the cities to find employment, education, entertainment, and a better way of life. As a result, large metropolises are developing in every country. Tokyo, Japan, has a population around 11 million; Seoul, Korea, 8 million; Mexico City and Sao Paulo, Brazil, each have a population of between 8 and 9 million. Bombay and Calcutta in India each have close to 7 million people. Now when these migrants resided in the villages, and were making a living as tenant farmers, they were quite aware of the forces of nature and were more God-conscious. They realized that no matter how hard they worked in the field, if the Creator did not provide the rain and sunshine, their crops would not grow. But once they move to the city, they get lost in the cement jungle and become more conscious of the ingenuity and creativity of man as they observe the thousands of cars, the maze of highways, the skyscrapers, and the sprawling factories. They seem to forget the Creator and become more machine conscious. And so they become secular minded—and church dropouts.

Then there are certain entire countries where a spiritual vacuum has been created by various environmental factors—political, historical, or sociocultural forces. South Korea, for example, is one of these lands. For certain historical reasons there is no particular non-Christian faith which has a strong hold on the people in general. Samuel Moffett, veteran Presbyterian missionary to Korea, writes: "Most Koreans will tell you they have no faith whatsoever. The cities are a religious vacuum." The late President Chung Hee Park, when asked what his religion was, answered, "My father and mother were Buddhists, but I am nothing."

Japan is another example. It is a highly industrialized nation, with the highest standard of living in all Asia, competing in the markets of the world. Its people, generally speaking, have become very materialistic and secular minded. Throughout Latin America there is a vast spiritual void; for though 85 percent or more of the people are supposed to be Roman Catholic, actually only 10 percent are practicing Catholics involved in the life of the church. In many countries in central and southern Africa, where the majority religion for centuries has been animism, education and modern technology are fast undermining many of the old traditional beliefs and practices. Even in several European countries there is a tragic, widespread spiritual vacuum, with the vast majority of people having no connection with the Christian Church and making no commitment to Christian values and standards.

There are two important facts to remember about any spiritual vacuum. The first is that it offers the Church a tremendous evangelistic opportunity. When people are without a strong commitment to any particular faith or ideology, they are usually more open to new ideas, and thus to the Christian message. They are approachable; they are winnable. In many areas of the world today the Church is seizing the present opportunity for evangelism and is experiencing spectacular increases in the number of conversions and local congregations. By a conservative estimate, 55,000 people around the world become Christians every day, and at least 1,400 new Christian churches are organized every week.

The gospel is swiftly filling the spiritual vacuum in South Korea. Since 1940 the number of Christians in the republic has doubled every decade. In 1940 there were only about 300,000 Christians, but by 1950 the number had increased to 750,000. In spite of the heavy casualties and massive destruction suffered during the war with Communist North Korea (1950-52), by 1960 the number of Christians had again doubled to become 1.5 million. In 1970 the figure stood at approximately 3 million, and today in 1980 it has crossed the 6 million mark. There are 2,800 churches in the capital city of Seoul alone. It is estimated that over 40 percent of the R.O.K. Army is now Christian. Bishop J. Waskom Pickett has called South Korea "a Christian nation in the making."

Throughout Latin America the evangelical movement is witnessing phenomenal growth. In 1900 there were only about 31,000 active, baptized members in the Protestant churches, according to *Latin American Church Growth.*[13] This book estimates that by 1966 there was a total evangelical community of more than 10 million. The number is probably doubled today. Both in Brazil and Chile, evangelicals account for 10 percent of the population. An Associated Press survey estimates that as many as 40 million persons in Latin America —where the total population is more than 280 million—have ties to evangelical congregations.[14] The Pentecostal groups in particular are winning large numbers of people who have moved into the cities from rural areas. These low-class factory workers have cut their family and church ties in their hometowns and appear to be especially receptive to a vital Christian message. Converts from this section of society are forming large congregations and erecting spacious sanctuaries. There is one church in Santiago, Chile, that can accommodate a congregation of 15,000, and another in Sao Paulo, Brazil, that can seat 25,000.

On the continent of Africa, south of the Sahara, an almost unprecedented growth of the Christian Church has been taking place in the last few decades. At the beginning of this century, Africa was a Muslim continent to the north, while traditional animism held sway in the center and the south. A few pockets of Christianity existed in such countries as Mozambique and Angola, besides the white Christians in the southern regions. The entire Christian population was possibly only 4 million. Africa now has around 150 million Christians, representing 41 percent of the total population of over 360 million.

In Kenya, for example, the 2 million Christians of 1950 became 4.5 million by 1960, and 8.5 million by 1975. Each year over 300,000 Kenyans are converted to the Christian faith, and roughly 300 new church buildings of varied sizes and quality are being constructed in the country. If one considered as a standard of measure those who declare themselves Christians, it could be said that 70 percent of Kenyans profess to be Christians.

David Barrett, missionary sociologist, who has been doing extensive research in population and church growth in Africa, estimates that by the end of this century there will be 350 million Christians on the continent of Africa, or 50 percent of the total population.

From all these statistics it is clear that the present spiritual vacuum in many parts of the world is offering an unusual opportunity for evangelism and growth to the Church of Jesus Christ. And greater opportunities may lie ahead. One can only surmise what the situation may be several years down the line when China, with its

850-900 million people, opens up again to the preaching of the gospel. After 30 years or more of Communist rule and an imposed atheistic philosophy, the country has been swept clean of the old Buddhist and Confucianist faiths. That means the Chinese people on the whole have no religious faith. The Christian Church, however, as recent contacts have shown, is still alive and well. Its numbers may have been decimated, but the Church itself has been purified and vitalized. So if freedom of religion is again granted to the people, the Christians will come out of hiding and, joined by committed Chinese Christians from all across southeast Asia, will form a mighty evangelistic force to move into the spiritual vacuum. It could turn out to be the greatest missionary challenge that has ever faced the Christian Church in its entire history.

At the same time, however, we must point out that there is a negative side to the spiritual vacuum. It not only provides an open door for evangelism and church growth, but is also fraught with potential danger. For people will not remain in a spiritual vacuum for a long time. As Dr. E. Stanley Jones often warned us, "Nature abhors a vacuum, and human nature abhors a vacuum. "If the gospel of Jesus Christ does not move into the spiritual vacuum fast enough, then some man-made "ism" or ideology will move in. People are made in such a way that they have to believe in something; they must commit themselves to something or someone. This means that there is a certain urgency about this whole business of world evangelization. We must not—we dare not—delay. A people who are open to the gospel today may not be open tomorrow. If we don't act now, it may be too late.

Two areas of the world have already proved the reality of this potential danger. Brazil is one of them. With the largest population in South America, complete religious freedom, and millions of people untouched by the Catholic church, it offers a challenging opportunity for evangelical Christianity to lead these people into a personal experience with Christ. As someone has said, "The door to evangelism in Brazil is not only wide open; it's off its hinges!" Now it is true that the evangelical movement in Brazil is doing much to fill this spiritual vacuum, and thousands are entering into a saving relationship with Christ each year. But at the same time it is not moving fast enough into some sections of Brazilian society, and so another "faith," spiritism, has entered the scene as a viable option for many.

Spiritism is said to be "one of the fastest growing religions in Brazil today." There are two main divisions of the movement. The better educated usually follow the teachings of the French spiritist, Kardec, and emphasize the philosophical aspects of the movement. But by far the largest number of adherents include the middle and lower classes, caught up in the emotional expression known as *Umbanda*, which emphasizes trances and spirit-possession. The following is a description of their ritual, given by a U.S.A. missionary who attended one of their "services."

From the street it looked like any little church building. But when I stepped inside, the difference became immediately apparent.

An indefinable air of anticipation hovered over the place. Through a side door, my eye caught the movements of women dressed in long, well-starched white gowns, and men in white shirts and slacks. Half the room was closed off from view by a faded green curtain. Though almost filled, I managed to find a seat on the front row.

I was alerted by a sudden sound like the warning buzzer at a basketball game. Singing began . . . an unfamiliar type of invoking hymn, repeatedly inviting the *spirits* to come upon the willing, waiting disciples. As they sang, the drapes parted, disclosing 40 or 50 white-clad marchers moving in a circle before a strange, nondescript altar, on and over which were representations of various saints and spirits, including St. George on his white charger, who, I learned, is one of the favorites.

Presiding over the service was a solemn, very rotund, green taffeta-gowned matriarch called the "Chefe do terreiro," meaning "Chief of the grounds." As the song ended she led in a chanted prayer, and I was startled to recognize part of it as the Lord's prayer . . . a thing so sacred in these clandestine rites.

Then it began! Starting around the circle, the "chefe" pressed on the forehead of each participant, whirled him once around, and then let him fall in a trance to the floor. Jolted back to reality by the sudden crashing to the floor of a rigid body, I sat for the next 45 minutes as a dejected observer while men and women took turns screaming, falling, shaking, flailing in convulsions, and at times making sounds like animals.

This was the night to receive the spirits of the old Indians from the primitive tribes of Brazil. Other occasions call for the spirits of old Africans who are thought to return to occupy each worshipper.

This visitation from the "Indian spirits" and "African spirits" has its objective in offering to its believers special consultations with a spirit for healing. Special effects were achieved by the "possessed" donning straw hats and smoking crude black cigars. People in the audience would parade to the front for help . . . many well groomed . . . some led or carried small children.

All had the look of people who had tried "everything" and were now in desperation, willing to try even this.

I was suddenly ashamed and burdened—ashamed that somehow we who are entrusted with the Good News have never gotten to these spiritually despondent ones . . . and burdened with the desire to unshackle all these deluded spiritists from this depressing bondage. [15]

Brazilian sociologists now indicate that up to 40 percent of Brazilians participate at one time or another in spiritist ceremonies. Even more believe in the reality of the forces involved in spirit worship. [16] It is indeed tragic that such a large number of people in Brazil are going to these extremes in order to find the answer to life's problems, when they could find perfect satisfaction in the person of Jesus Christ.

Japan is another clear example of what happens to a spiritual vacuum when the Christian Church fails to move in at the appropriate time. Prior to World War II, Buddhism and more particularly Shintoism (emperor worship) were the two most powerful religious movements in the country. The Japanese considered themselves a special nation with a divine destiny. They looked upon their emperor as divine and paid homage to him at Shinto shrines. But suddenly at the close of the war, the whole religious philosophy of Japan fell apart. Their armies were defeated and their cities lay in ruins. The emperor stood before the microphone and before the whole nation renounced his claim to divinity. The people soon discovered they were without a faith. A feeling of frustration, hopelessness, and insecurity swept over the land.

Sensing the situation, Gen. Douglas MacArthur, commander of the Allied Occupying Forces and a professing Christian, issued a call to the Church in the U.S.A. to send 1,000 missionaries and tens of thousands of Bibles to Japan. Now it is true that many prewar missionaries did return to Japan, and certain outstanding evangelists like Dr. E. Stanley Jones and Dr. Larry Lacour conducted many successful evangelistic campaigns across the country. It is also true that there were several outstanding converts to the Christian faith, such as Captain Fuchida and Admiral Sato, who commanded the air and submarine attack on Pearl Harbor at the beginning of the war in the Pacific. But these efforts were not on a scale large enough to be commensurate with the overwhelming spiritual needs of the nation. As a result the so-called new religions moved in to fill the vacuum. At one time there were 378 of these groups registered with the Ministry of Education. [17]

Doctrinally the new religions were syncretistic, with the great mass of Japanese folk religion providing the basic materials. They drew heavily also from Shintoism, Buddhism, and Christianity. Functionally they were crisis religions, seeking to restore emotional stability, confidence, and meaning to life. They all promised prosperity, health, peace of mind, and security.

The new religions have not won many devotees among the intelligentsia of Japan, nor the university students, but they have attracted millions of followers from among the masses. Today it is estimated that over 20 percent of the entire population belong to one or another of these new religious movements. Industrialization has killed much of the social solidarity that was once a part of Japanese society. The new religions, through policies of friendliness and sympathy, have made their believers aware of themselves as persons working in concert with other persons toward the accomplishment of desirable and seemingly attainable goals. And they offer the people a sense of identification and community.

Two of the new religions in particular have been very successful in winning followers. *Rissho Kosei Kai* boasts a membership of several million. Its headquarters in Tokyo occupies an entire block and includes a worship center, a hospital, two high schools, an office and printing press, a kindergarten, old folks' home, and playground. The grand temple is a modern building with eight stories, capable of accommodating 35,000 people. *Soka Gakkai* had only 5,000 members in 1951, but today is the fastest growing new religion in Japan, boasting a membership of over 15 million. Just a few years ago it completed its magnificent new headquarters at the foot of Mount Fuji, outside the city of Tokyo. With unusual architectural design and all modern electronic facilities, the center cost around $100 million. Both *Rissho Kosei Kai* and *Soka Gakkai* claim to be "the true Buddhism," taking pride in their strong lay movements, and encouraging their followers to go out and win new converts.

It is indeed tragic that when the spiritual vacuum arose in Japan at the close of World War II, the Christian Church was unable to move in fast enough and with sufficient vitality to meet the crisis. We lost one of the greatest evangelistic opportunities of this century. The new religions may have won the allegiance of millions of people, but they are very superficial in character, demand no strong break with the past, and are unable to effect genuine moral transformation. They may offer a certain degree of emotional and psychological consolation to the masses, but they are powerless to satisfy the deep spiritual needs of the people.

## 5. Summary

From the preceding discussion it is quite evident that the religious picture of our contemporary world is indeed a complex mosaic with many facets. We are living in a highly pluralistic world. A great variety of forces are at work; many voices are calling for attention; many isms are competing for the hearts and minds of men.

The whole world has reverted to a mission field. The Christian Church everywhere is set in the midst of a pagan environment. The confrontation between the world religions, and between faith and un-faith, is found on every continent.

The non-Christian religions are experiencing a resurgence of new life and activity. Sometimes this resurgence takes the form of a revival of the old traditions and practices. Sometimes it expresses itself in a reform movement, whereby it discards the old and incorporates new concepts and practices. At other times the resurgence results in a radical process of reformation, as the religion in question seeks to become modern and keep up with the spirit of the age.

The non-Christian religions are challenging the Christian faith with new boldness and vigor. They are criticizing the glaring inconsistencies between the profession and the practice of Christians. Some are contesting the Christian claim to final truth and the right to convert, while others are attempting to establish their own claims to universal validity, and are seeking to convert outsiders to their faith. Still others are inviting us as Christians to unite with them in a common search for truth, and to join forces with them in the worldwide struggle between religion and irreligion.

In spite of all these resurgent movements, there is a growing spiritual vacuum which has developed across the world, as many are revolting against all religion and moving toward humanism and secularism. This is particularly true of university students, the masses in large metropolitan areas, and in countries where Communism reigns supreme. The spiritual vacuum offers the Christian Church a tremendous opportunity for evangelism, but at the same time it is fraught with potential danger. For if the Church does not act effectively and with adequate resources, people will reach out after some other "faith" to help fill the inner void.

Only a Church that is spiritually alive, deeply committed to its Lord, empowered by the Holy Spirit, faithful to its calling and message, and sensitive to the total needs of people—only such a Church can be adequately prepared for the challenge of our day.

# 2

# The Christian Faith
# and Other Faiths

Two Christian missionaries were walking together along a road in India near their mission center. Both were men of sincere conviction and earnest devotion. Suddenly they came in sight of a new Hindu temple under construction, and one of them said with a note of disgust: "Ah! I hate to see that. Another fortress of the enemy!"

"Well," said the second missionary, "I'm not so sure. I would be more inclined to say: Another witness to man's search for God—and thank God for it!"

This raises some important questions. How should we, as Christians, view the non-Christian religions of the world? As enemies of the gospel, or as allies in the common fight against evil? What is the relation of the Christian faith to other world religions? Is the gospel a unique revelation, in a class by itself? Or is it just one among many religions?

Before attempting to discover methods and principles of communicating our faith, we must first determine the nature and quality of our faith. For our attitude toward the gospel will largely determine the method of mission we adopt. For instance, if we believe Christianity is just one among many viable options, we will be quite satisfied with interreligious dialogue and sharing of our views with others. But if we believe the gospel is the unique revelation of God to man, we will endeavor to confront everyone with the radical claims of Christ.

Let us, therefore, look at the various theories which have been propounded to describe the relation of the Christian faith to the non-Christian religions—all the way from the most conservative to the extreme liberal views.

## 1. The Fundamentalist Position

This view regards the nōn-Christian religions as false and wholly evil. The world religions are "of the devil," or the products of depraved man under the control of Satan. Therefore, the relation between the Christian faith and the other religions is that of truth versus error. Christianity is never to be *compared* with any other religion; it is always to be *contrasted*. It is impossible for Christians to regard the world religions as allies, or to join with them in any cooperative enterprise in the field of religion. It is a waste of time for us as Christians to study the world religions. If we do study them, it should be in the spirit of a general studying a map in order to defeat the enemy. There is nothing in the other faiths which can be used as a bridge for the gospel.

Some who hold this general attitude would also admit that in the non-Christian religions there are *some* elements of good, but maintain that these are so inadequate, or so closely interwoven with error, that the Christian must seek to destroy completely the religious systems in which they are found, and to replace these with Christianity.

Though this position jealously guards the uniqueness of the Christian faith, it suffers from certain glaring weaknesses. In the first place, it is not accurate to say that the other religions are void of any truth whatsoever. The Hindu concepts of the supremacy of the spiritual over the material, and the certainty of the moral order (whatsoever a man sows, that he will reap), are indeed worthy of recognition. Within the Eightfold Path of Buddhism there are many noble ethical practices. Islam, of course, has taken from Judaism and Christianity the concepts of the unity and sovereignty of God. All of these provide bridgeheads for presenting the gospel. Any religion that consisted of 100 percent error would find it impossible to persist. It would be self-destructive. The only way error or evil can live is by becoming a parasite on some element of truth or the good.

This fundamentalist position usually leads to an attitude of condemnation and hostility toward other religions and the cultures which they represent. It is bound to arouse resentment. Furthermore, if the Christian messenger refuses to study and understand the religion of his hearers, how will he be able to relate the gospel effectively to their background and needs?

## 2. The Fulfillment Theory

There are many who are not satisfied with the extreme, dogmatic attitude of the fundamentalist, and so have sought a more conciliatory approach through the fulfillment theory. They gladly recognize that each one of the world religions possesses some degree of truth, some more than others. But at the same time these religions contain certain elements of untruth; again, in varying degrees. The world religions go part of the way on the road to truth and thus are somewhat of a preparation for the Christian message. On the other hand, the gospel is final and absolute truth; it goes all the way. Thus the relation of the Christian faith to other world religions is that of complete truth to partial truth mixed with error.

Toyohiko Kagawa, the great Japanese Christian, sought to describe this view by the use of a Japanese analogy of the various pilgrim paths that lead to the summit of the sacred Mount Fuji, with their stations along the way which are climbed annually by thousands of pilgrims. Kagawa claimed that some religions become tired and stop at the third, or fourth, or sixth station. Buddhism (his former religion) might even reach the ninth station. But it is only Christianity, he affirmed, that leads to the top.[1]

Furthermore, the fulfillment theory strongly maintains that the Christian faith "comprehends" and "fulfills" all the partial truths found in the other religions, while at the same time purging them from their errors and supplementing them with truths and values that they do not in themselves possess. In them, we see "broken lights"; in the gospel, the full radiance of God's glory. This means that much as *Jesus* came long ago, not "to abolish the law and the prophets . . . but to fulfil them" (Matt. 5:17), so *His gospel* comes today to the laws and prophets of other religions. As the gospel is brought to the people of non-Christian religions, it comes to hearts more or less—however little in some instances—prepared for it by their former religions. This preparation should be viewed discriminately but gratefully by the missionary as the gracious work of God.

This view of the Christian faith, as the fulfillment of all that is best in other religions, has been upheld by a long succession of Christian thinkers. For example, Dr. J. N. Farquhar, a missionary to India, endeavored, in his book *The Crown of Hinduism,* to apply this theory to the relation between Christianity and Hinduism. After examining in detail the beliefs and practices of the Hindus, he concludes that "Christ provides the fulfillment of the highest aspirations of Hinduism . . . He is the Crown of the Faith of India."[2] He claims that Christianity fulfills the Hindu scriptures, the Hindu family system, Hindu asceticism, caste, and the worship of idols. Dr. Kenneth J. Saunders, a colleague of Dr. Farquhar, and Baron Von Hugel, the great Catholic scholar, have made similar attempts to prove that Christianity may be regarded as "the Crown of Buddhism."[3] A few Christian writers have even maintained that Christianity can be regarded as "the Crown of Islam," though this is more difficult to prove, for Islam is later in date than Christianity and at certain points expressly denies some of the main teachings of the Bible.[4]

The fulfillment theory appeals strongly to many minds. It offers a way of approach to non-Christians that is more courteous and less provocative than the fundamentalist position. It avoids the wholesale condemnation of systems of religious belief and practice which contain much that appears to be unquestionably admirable. It opens the door for dialogue with non-Christians, as well as for common social service. It encourages the study of other religions; not simply with a view to criticize them, but with the expectation of finding points of contact for the presentation of the gospel. At the same time this view affirms with undiminished confidence that the Christian faith is the one and only perfect faith for the whole of mankind.

Now so far as the relation of Christianity to Judaism is concerned, the theory of fulfillment can be accepted with complete confidence. Jesus Christ, in Matthew's Gospel, declared openly to the people: "Think not that I have come to abolish the law and the prophets; I have come not to abolish them but to fulfil them" (Matt. 5:17; see also 3:15; Mark 10:19; 12:28-31; Luke 11:42; Rom. 12:18; Gal. 5:14). But with regard to other world religions, the idea that they are "fulfilled" in Christianity is open to serious criticism. We need to ask such questions as: Are the other religions partial revelations, like the Old Testament? Are they going in the same direction as the Christian faith? There is much evidence to conclude that they are sometimes going in tangents or even in opposite directions. Furthermore, though we might admit that the gospel fulfills the highest *aspirations of individual non-Christians,* can we claim that Christianity fulfills the non-Christian *religious systems?* The theory of fulfillment tends to ignore the fundamental differences of spirit and ethos that distinguish the non-Christian religions from each other, as well as from Christianity. As Dr. Hendrik Kraemer has pointed out, to look for the fulfillment of the world religions in Christianity is as unscientific as to look for the fulfillment of a rosebud in the full-blown flower of an orchid. In large measure, the great non-Christian religions are "all inclusive systems and theories of life," each with its own distinctive quality; and no one of them can be included in any of the others.[5]

3. The Theory of Discontinuity

This view was expounded at the International Missionary Conference held in Tambaram, India, in 1938, by Dr. Hendrik Kraemer of Holland, who wrote, in preparation for the conference, _The Christian Message in a Non-Christian World._ He argues that the Christian revelation is in its essence so entirely different from all other religions that there is, and can be, no point of contact between the one and the other.

Kraemer follows Karl Barth and Soren Kierkegaard in maintaining that there is an "absolute qualitative difference" between God and man, between the truth revealed in Christ and truths discovered by man, and consequently between the gospel of Christ and other religions. The gospel is a revelation from God to man; it "falls from above, like a stone into water." Here we see the "givenness" of the gospel. This divine revelation is a self-disclosure and is supremely in the Incarnation, in the person of Jesus Christ. The Bible deals primarily with the redemptive acts of God in history, not just human experiences or ideas. Religious experiences or ideas are present and important, but in no sense are they central. Kraemer entitles this view "Biblical Realism."

As for the non-Christian religions, Kraemer maintains that they are the products of human religious consciousness, reflecting the speculations and gropings of man. They present human ideas as philosophies, views, and experiences. They are based solely on human effort and wisdom—often admirable—never on revelation.

Like Barth, Kraemer describes all other religions as "unfaith," "not acts of response to God, but acts of resistance to God." There is, therefore, a radical _misdirection_ that runs through all these religions.

Thus, the Christian faith, as a divine revelation, is unique (Latin, _sui generis_), in a class by itself. It possesses absolute, final truth. Kraemer speaks of this as the "otherness" of the gospel. If we take the "revelation" claimed in different religions, we have to confess that they do not piece together or form an intelligible whole. The Vedas, the Koran, and the gospel do not make a coherent scheme. They do not even answer the same questions. The claims of the various religions are clearly conflicting.

The relation between the Christian revelation and the world religions is therefore one of "discontinuity"; and this is so utter that it is impossible to make any kind of comparison between the gospel and any other religion. "There is no point of contact," Kraemer insists; "there are no bridges from human religious consciousness to

Christ."[6] The non-Christian religions are in no sense a preparation for the gospel and are quite irrelevant for the purpose of bringing to men any true knowledge of God or salvation. Theologically speaking, nature and reason do not afford preambles or lines of development toward the gospel of grace and truth as manifest in Jesus Christ. That is, human reason does not take man part of the way in his quest for truth, and then grace comes along and takes him the rest of the way. Grace has to start from zero.

Furthermore, the gospel is *not* the fulfillment of religions, nor indeed can be. Kraemer insists that we must look at the world religions, not piecemeal or in isolated sections, but as complete philosophical or religious systems. (He calls this the "totalitarian" or "holistic view.") Kraemer might be willing to admit that the gospel does fulfill some of the basic God-directed aspirations of *individual* non-Christians, such as the longing for forgiveness or fellowship with God; but he strongly denies that the gospel fulfills all the individual aspirations that arise from their religious systems—for example, the Buddhist longing for *nirvana* or the Hindu longing for escape from *samsara* (cycle of birth and rebirth). Such aspirations are part of the radical misdirection inherent in these religions.

It is important to recognize that Kraemer's insistence upon the "absoluteness," "finality," and "otherness" of the Christian revelation does not mean that these qualities are ascribed to any one type of Christianity which exists in the world today. "Empirical [historical] Christianity," says Kraemer, "stands under the judgment of the Revelation in Christ."[7] The gospel as found in the Word of God is pure and final, while many expressions of Christianity have been, and are, fraught with heresy and impurity, such as the Inquisition, the Crusades, the teachings of Sun Myung Moon, etc. There is, of course, a uniquely close relation between Christianity and the gospel that does not exist between other religions and the gospel. But it is only for the gospel that we can claim absolute finality, not for historical Christianity.

It is also important to bear in mind that the exponents of discontinuity insist vigorously that their view does not involve condemnation of, nor contempt for, the non-Christian religions or their cultures. They are appreciative of anything that is good or of value in these faiths. Furthermore, they do not deny that God has been working in the minds of men outside the sphere of Christian revelation. There have been, and may be now, acceptable men of faith who live under the sway of non-Christian religions—products, however, not of these religious systems, but of the mysterious action of God's Spirit.

In all his reasoning and efforts to formulate his position, Kraemer takes his standpoint within the realm of the Christian revelation. He finds his authority in the Word of God itself. He readily admits this is a "prejudiced position"; but he points out that the only alternative is to start with the "prejudiced position" of human reason and its finite ideas about religion and God, and this is unacceptable. Human reason stands under the authority and judgment of God.

Hendrik Kraemer, of course, has had his critics like anyone else. Some contend that his theory of discontinuity produces an aloofness between the Christian messenger and the recipients. Kraemer answers that the connection we seek is not between religious systems, but between persons. The Christian, by his outgoing friendship and love, can find many "points of contact" with non-Christians. By identifying himself with the problems, needs, and aspirations of people, the missionary can win his way into their hearts and lives.

Others contend it is wrong to claim that Christians alone are witnesses to a divine revelation, while other religions are exclusively the product of a human "religious consciousness." They argue that man's religious consciousness is really the universal manifesting of a human response to God's continual endeavor to reveal himself to man. And if so, is not every religion founded on what is, in some sense, revelation? To which Kraemer would reply: "If all religions are the results of revelation from God, then why do we not find a general unity running through all the religions? Why are there so many discrepancies and so much confusion? God cannot contradict himself."

Still others contend that Kraemer's distinction between the pure gospel and imperfect Christianity leaves us wondering what is the absolute element in the gospel, and how it can be made known to our human minds in its absoluteness. It seems to be indefinable and elusive. They ask: "What is the essential Gospel? Kraemer claims to know it. But isn't it only his interpretation of the Gospel?"[8] Kraemer readily admits the difficulty of a partial and imperfect understanding of the Christian revelation and therefore a defective grasp of its standards of evaluation and judgment. But he reminds us that Jesus promised us the gift of the Holy Spirit for this very purpose—to "teach [us] all things" and to "guide [us] into all the truth" (John 14:26; 16:13).

Whatever we say about Kraemer's theory, we must admit that he has presented his position in a most logical and convincing manner, and has taken his stand solidly on the Word of God. His views demand our sincere consideration.

### 4. The Liberal Position

In general, advocates of the liberal position maintain that God's revelatory action in Christ is but one slice of the whole loaf of God's revelation in the history of religions, and this Christian portion cannot claim to be the whole of universal revelation and salvation. Truth is relative, not absolute. Christianity, like other religions, is only partial truth and has its limitations. It has something to offer the other religions, but at the same time the other religions have something to offer it. So there must be common sharing, give-and-take. Instead of seeking to win people to our point of view, or to "convert," we should join in dialogue and a common search for truth. The result is to place Christianity as a religion among the religions, not above them in a category of its own. Christianity may be quantitatively, but not qualitatively, different from the other faiths. It must abandon its claim to possess the only saving revelation of God to the world.

Illustrations of the liberal point of view may be found in the writings of several well-known authors. Prof. William Hocking of Harvard held that "our present Christianity does not include all that other religions have," and that it needs the contributions which other religions can give.[9]

Albert Schweitzer, the famous missionary to Africa, wrote: "Western and Indian philosophies must not contend, in the spirit that aims at the one proving itself right in opposition to the other. Both must be moving toward a way of thinking which shall . . . eventually be shared in common by all mankind."[10]

The well-known British historian Arnold Toynbee wrote in his book *Christianity Among the Religions of the World.* "We ought . . . to try to purge our Christianity of the traditional belief that Christianity is unique. This is not just a Western Christian belief, it is intrinsic to Christianity itself. All the same I suggest that we have to do this if we are to purge Christianity of the exclusive-mindedness and intolerance that follows from a belief in Christianity's uniqueness."[11]

One of the most publicized expressions of this view appeared in the book entitled *Re-thinking Missions* (1932),[12] which contained the report of a Laymen's Commission, appointed from the U.S.A. and Canada, to inquire into the working of Christian missions in the

Orient. The report names Jesus, along with Buddha and Mohammed, as one of the great founders of religions who have been teachers of men.

These great leaders "spent themselves speaking to their own people and have left behind them an impulse which has moved on steadily across boundary after boundary." It describes as the old view the idea that "there was but one way, the way of Christ." The business of missions is not to "transmit the letter of doctrine but to fulfill the religious life of the Orient." What Christians believe to be the authentic, historic facts of the New Testament appear to be regarded as "the symbolical and imaginative expression" of Christianity. We are to consider ourselves not as the bearers of a definite message, but as "brothers in a common quest with the non-Christian religions." We are to find and "stand upon the common ground of all religion." The Christian Church must not do what the Early Church did, "aim at destroying or displacing the whole structure" of other religions. Christianity and the other religions must join in a common quest for truth and experience which are not offered in any final and absolute way in Christianity. The missionary "will look forward not to the destruction of these religions, but to their continued co-existence with Christianity, each stimulating the other in growth toward the ultimate goal, unity in the completest truth." The aim of missions is thus defined: "To seek with people of other lands a true knowledge and love of God, expressing in life and word what we have learned through Jesus Christ and endeavoring to give effect to His spirit in the life of the world."[13]

*Re-thinking Missions* was condemned by most church leaders and supporters of missions at the time, but its spirit still seems to be alive in various circles today.

Dr. William Ernest Hocking, professor of philosophy at Harvard University, was chairman of the Re-thinking Missions Commission. A few years later (1940), he published a book entitled *Living Religions and a World Faith*, in which he developed his own theory of the relation between the world religions. He maintained that our goal is indeed a world faith; but no religion is qualified to be such, not even Christianity, because it does not include all that the other religions have.[14]

There are three possible approaches to a world faith: (1) radical displacement, whereby one religion supplants all the others; (2) amalgamation, which throws all religions into one pot and mixes them up; and (3) reconception. Professor Hocking rejected the first two approaches and strongly advocated the third. He maintained that each religion has its own distinctives, its radical essence, its essential characteristics. Each religion should rethink or *reconceive* its own beliefs in the light of the essential beliefs of the other religions. This will produce a new world faith embodying the essential features of all, but different from any one of them. This will take time, Hocking admitted, so in the meantime we must be content with a peaceful coexistence of religions and with cooperation in worship and service. Furthermore, "the search for essence is progressive. It comes to no final stopping place; for every Reconception, there is conceivably a better one to be had."[15] This change, however, is not in the truth itself, but only in our apprehension of the truth.

In recent years a new and subtle type of liberal theology has arisen, called "Anonymous Christianity," espoused particularly by Roman Catholic theologians. It takes various forms, but they all come out at the same place.

In his book *The Unknown Christ of Hinduism,* Dr. Raimundo Panikkar of India argues that Hinduism puts God at the center of its system, seeks to know God and be one with Him. Since Christ is one with God and part of the Trinity, then is not Christ inherent in Hinduism?[16]

Karl Rahner, leading Catholic theologian in the U.S.A., argues from a slightly different standpoint. God's saving will is universal and efficacious. He wants all men to be saved. This means that God is working everywhere with all men, even in and through the non-Christian religions. It gives all human beings the real possibility of a relation leading to salvation. Those who follow Rahner now say that there are two ways of salvation according to God's plan. There is the normal way in which a person meets the grace of God in his own religious situation, and there is the special way in which he receives salvation through the gospel of Christ in the New Testament. Thus we need not "take Christ" to the followers of the world religions; He is already there, though unrecognized. And these followers are, therefore, already Christians, though they don't realize it. They are "anonymous Christians." We need not seek to "make" Christians out of these people; all we need to do is to help them see that they are already Christians.

The following proof texts are used to uphold this position: "This is good, and it is acceptable in the sight of God our Savior, who desires all men to be saved and to come to the knowledge of the truth" (1 Tim. 2:3-4). "And without faith it is impossible to please him. For whoever would draw near to God must believe that he exists and that he rewards those who seek him" (Heb. 11:6).

So it is argued that since there are men in other faiths—even men with no religious affiliation—who possess these minimum qualifications of faith, it can be said that there are "anonymous Christians" all over the world. The missionary task of the world then is to witness in an explicit way to God's grace which is implicit everywhere; i.e., we are simply to make plain what is hidden.

Other theologians argue from John 1:4 and 9. "In him was life, and the life was the light of men . . . the true light that enlightens every man." This means Christ is working beyond Christianity, everywhere, with every person. Thus we find striking similarities in other faiths to the teaching of Jesus and the apostles. For example, in Hinduism we find four such areas: (1) intuitive wisdom, (2) devotional self-giving, (3) consciously chosen discipleship, and (4) service in the spirit of human community. These ideas find their source in Christ who is manifesting himself in Hinduism. Thus he whom our Hindu "brethren" call the Supreme Reality under a different name is none other than the timeless Christ.

It is quite evident that all these forms of the liberal position are contrary to the truth expressed in the Christian Scriptures. In general, this position starts with man's idea of religion, what the essence of religion is, and then goes on to judge religion from there. It places human reason above divine revelation and surrenders the uniqueness, the finality of the Christian faith. It cuts the very nerve of motivation for Christian missions.

As to Hocking's theory of reconception, it is a theological impossibility to reconceive the fundamental ideas of each religion in the light of the other religions and still maintain the essential essence of each. For example, how are the Muslim and Christian views of the person of Christ to be reconciled, when on one hand the Muslim claims that Jesus is not the Son of God, is not divine, did not die on the Cross, and did not arise from the dead; while on the other hand the Christian affirms all of these facts? Or how is the strict monism of Hinduism (that only the spiritual is real) to be harmonized with the dualism of Christianity (that both the spiritual and material are real)?

On the basis of Scripture we must also reject the theory of "anonymous Christianity." We agree that Christ through the Holy Spirit is working outside the Christian revelation with every man. But to equate the working of the Holy Spirit with a man's religious ideas (or his religion) is to confuse the issue. We must read on in John's Gospel. Not only is Christ the Light, but He is shining amidst the darkness. We can't forget the vast areas of darkness in the religious ideas of mankind. This position (anonymous Christianity), though it claims to center on Christ's activity in the world, actually surrenders His uniqueness. It leads to universalism—all are saved; all we need to tell them is they are saved—and does away with the necessity of conversion and justification. It implies that we have no business calling on people to change their loyalties from one faith to another. This position leaves the religious world the way it is; it leaves people to their own religious devices. The purpose of the Christian mission dwindles down to nothing more than helping Muslims be better Muslims, Hindus better Hindus, humanists better humanists, etc.

To be an "anonymous Christian" is a contradiction in terms. The New Testament insists upon an explicit confession of faith (Rom. 10:10), and the need for preaching the Good News implies it (vv. 14-15). Without an explicit Christianity, there would be no missionary enterprise.

There are other questions which can be raised about the theory. One such question would be whether we Christians, in our own goodwill, would be willing to be called "anonymous Buddhists" or "anonymous Hindus"? This position shows an insensitivity to the religious commitment of other peoples. Another question asks whether our concern for the anonymous Christian is but the dying gasp of a Western imperialism. Those who hold this view appear to be attempting to bring all other people under the umbrella of Christianity, whether they are willing or not.

## 5. Summary

After this detailed discussion of the various theories on the relation of the gospel to other religions, and the many implications that grow out of these theories, we now summarize our convictions on the subject.

*a.* In all our reasoning we take our stand on the revealed Word of God itself, which is our final, authoritative Guide. There is no higher standard of judgment. The only alternative is to begin with human reason, which is unacceptable.

*b.* The Christian revelation as the record of God's self-disclosing action in Jesus Christ is unique, absolute, and final. It is qualitatively different from anything else that comes under the term *religion*. It is in a class by itself.

*c*. The other religions consist largely of philosophies, speculations, and experiences of man, growing out of his religious consciousness, but do contain elements of truth found in general revelation (as the existence and omnipotence of a Supreme Being), residues of truth taken from the Old Testament (such as stories of the fall of man, places of refuge, blood sacrifices, etc.), and residues of truth from the New Testament (such as the virgin birth, ascension, and second coming of Christ, as found in the Koran).

*d*. The world religions, in varying degrees, contain many aspects of *ethical truth*, but they do not contain *saving truth*, which is found only in God's redemptive act through Christ on the Cross. How can the religions of the world produce the quality of true righteousness which, we confess, not even Christianity (when perceived as a religion) can produce? The righteousness of God is a gift of grace, not a product of religion.

*e*. The distinctiveness of the Christian faith does not lie in its ethic *per se*. At that point there are beautiful similarities with other religions. The distinctive fact about Christianity is that it is the only faith which has a Savior. Only in the gospel does one find the emphasis on what God has done rather than on what man must do.

*f*. Jesus Christ is the only Savior. He died for our sins and was raised for our justification. There is only one way of salvation for the whole of mankind, and that has been shown to be universally valid and all-inclusive in "the name which is above every name" (Phil. 2:9). There is no more serious crime against God than to substitute a humanizing ethic for a divine salvation.

*g*. The world religions are in some sense a preparation for the gospel in that they contain certain elements of truth and ethical practices which provide bridgeheads for presenting the gospel. At the same time they possess a fundamental misdirection which makes it difficult for people to understand and accept the gospel. For many, the Cross is still "a stumblingblock" or "foolishness" (1 Cor. 1:23, KJV). But the omnipresent Holy Spirit precedes the proclamation of the gospel and prepares hearts to receive Christ (prevenient grace).

*h*. The Christian faith is not a fulfillment of the world religions when viewed as integrated systems of thought. It is only a fulfillment of individual basic desires, such as the desire for forgiveness, peace with God, power for living, etc.

*i.* God is working in the minds of men outside the sphere of Christian revelation. There may be acceptable men of faith who live under the sway of non-Christian religions—products, however, not of these religious systems, but of the mysterious working of the Holy Spirit.

*j.* The Bible is a book that belongs to all of humanity, not just to Christians. Christ belongs to the nations, not only to Western countries. The gospel is for the world, for East as well as West. "The task of the Christian mission is to witness in word and deed to the universal unity of the whole reality in Jesus Christ. This is not a message against the religions but for them."[17]

## 6. Our Attitude Toward Non-Christians

In view of these strong convictions concerning the uniqueness of the Christian revelation, what then should be our attitude toward the adherents of other world religions? The following characteristics should serve as basic guidelines:

*a. Assurance mingled with humility.* On the one hand, as Christians we can be sure of the Truth in Jesus Christ; not that we have the truth, but *He is the Truth.* We can be assured of the forgiveness of our sins and our relationship with the Father. We can be convinced of the truth of the gospel and its power to transform all who believe. We can unashamedly proclaim Christ to all men and confront them with His demands and promises. On the other hand, there is no basis for boasting or pride whatsoever, for this Truth is not a man-made discovery, but a God-given revelation. Our salvation is not an attainment, but an obtainment; it is not a reward for our deeds, but a gift offered in a nail-pierced hand. The only difference between other people and us is that they are sinners and we are sinners saved by grace (because we had the opportunity to hear the gospel). This involves responsibility to proclaim Christ, not the privilege to boast about ourselves. The late Dr. D. T. Niles of Sri Lanka used to say, "Evangelism is one beggar telling another beggar where to find bread."

A Hindu gentleman once said to Dr. E. Stanley Jones, after hearing him preach: "You are the boldest man I have ever seen. You said you had found God. I have never heard a man say that before."

Brother Stanley's comment was: "That was no credit to me—not the slightest. I had looked into the face of Jesus and lo, I saw the Father! But India has not had that face to look into, and the consequence, the vision of the Father is fleeting."[18]

Dr. Hendrik Kraemer declared that our attitude toward non-Christians must be "a remarkable combination of downright intrepidity [boldness] and of radical humility."[19] *Radical humility,* because the Christian messenger is the bringer of a divine gift, not something of his own making or achievement; and what he has received for nothing, he gives for nothing. *Downright boldness,* because the Christian is the bearer of a message, the witness of a divine revelation, not his discovery, but God's act. In this light he has the freedom and obligation to maintain, in the face of the loftiest religious and moral achievements, that all men need conversion and regeneration, both non-Christian and nominal church member.

*b. Tolerance without compromise.* The Christian witness must be tolerant in his attitude toward the views of other people, but at the same time be uncompromising in the claims of the gospel. To be tolerant means to be open-minded, fair-minded, sympathetic, understanding of the other person's position. It includes the personal right to hold an opinion, express it, and to change it. But tolerance is, at best, a negative and nerveless virtue. It leads to no decision; it inspires no enthusiasm. It is courteous and gentle, but not indifferent to truth. It has no right to surrender the truth. *Toleration must be based on truth.*

Edmund Perry, in his book *The Gospel in Dispute,* puts it very clearly:

> Tolerance is simply a humane attitude and has nothing to do with the truth or falsity of another man's conviction. We can be tolerant of another person and of another religion while disagreeing with them completely. In fact, because the Gospel of Jesus Christ is the *free* grace of God, we Christians ask not simply for tolerance among the religions, but for *freedom* of religions. To the extent that we are faithful witnesses to the free grace of God we practice and demand that others practice freedom of religions. We grant that as a religion among religions, Christianity has no more or no less right than any other religion to exist, to teach, to propagate, to proselytize and practice in a given state or culture, but this political equalitarianism does not compromise for one moment or in any degree our Christian belief that the Gospel of Jesus Christ alone is unqualifiedly, ultimately and irreducibly God's word to and for mankind.[20]

*c. Love mingled with respect.* In all Christ's dealings with individuals, He showed a genuine respect for their personalities. He refrained from any attempt to force His will upon them, but sought to draw from them a voluntary acceptance of His demands. If they did not respond, He passed on. He refused to use the power of political action or of supernatural miracles in order to bring in the kingdom of God. He followed the ideal of the Suffering Servant, believing that only as a crucified Messiah would He be able to draw all men to himself. It was His love that broke down all barriers and won the hearts of men.

Dr. E. Stanley Jones once asked Mahatma Gandhi, "What can we Christians do to help India?" Without hesitation Gandhi replied, "Live like Jesus lived. *Don't adulterate or tone down your religion. Make love central.*"

As to the manner and presentation of the Christian message, we who go to a foreign land should have the inward feeling, if not the outward signs, of being adopted sons or daughters of that land, and we should offer our message as a homage to our adopted people. Respect and love should characterize our every attitude. That country should be our home, her future our future, and we her servants for Christ's sake.

This love is more than just our puny, finite love for Christ. It is the divine, matchless love of Christ operating within us and flowing through us into the lives of others. This sort of love is not natural to us, neither can it be self-generated. It has to be received as a gift from God and poured into our hearts by the Holy Spirit who is given unto us (Rom. 5:5).

# 3

# Questions
# and Answers

Many questions are being asked of us by non-Christians these days, but certain ones are asked most frequently and demand our attention. We must face these questions honestly and find intelligent answers to them.

## 1. "Are Not All Religions Equal?"

"Is there not a fundamental unity in all religions?" This view is expressed by various analogies:

"All roads lead to Rome, all religions lead to God."

"All rivers flow into the ocean; likewise, all religions lead to God."

"You can approach the peak of a mountain from any side, but eventually you will reach the top."

"There are many ways to get upstairs. You can climb the staircase, take the elevator, or climb a ladder and get in through a window."

"The soul of religion is one, but it is encased in a multitude of forms."

"All religions are springs running from the same source, and nourish different soils and different peoples" (Mahatma Gandhi).

"Why do you say there is only one way to God? You cannot prescribe the same drug for every disease."

"Supposing that from four corners in a square, four men desire to get to the center. They will go in different directions, but they will get to the center. There are different religions, but they all lead to the center—God."

57

It is easy to state such a claim (that all religions are equal) but not so easy to substantiate it. A scientific study of the various religions shows that they are *not* all the same.

*a.* In the first place, all religions are not the same in their *doctrines.*

(1) Take, for example, the concept of **God.** In Hinduism, the ultimate reality, Brahman, is relationless, actionless, blissful, Pure Essence (without attributes). Buddhism in its original form denied the existence of God. In Islam, fellowship does not exist between God and man. To suggest a Father-child relationship is sacrilegious because it suggests a lack of reverence toward the Divine. In the Christian faith, He is the God and Father of our Lord Jesus Christ, who yearns for fellowship with His prodigal sons, and who constantly acts and creates anew.

(2) Take also the concept of **man.** Buddha taught there is no such thing as soul, only a series of mental states. In Hinduism, man is not really separate from the Ultimate. The individual soul is but a part of the Universal Soul. In Christianity, man has an eternal soul (or he *is* an eternal soul); he is made in the image of God and is distinct from his Creator.

(3) Then again, look at the concept of **the world.** In Hinduism, the world is not the creation of God, but an emanation of the one Ultimate Reality. It is the result of *maya,* illusion. In Christianity, the world is the creation of God, tragically perverted by sin, yet God's working place, desperately real, and the place of responsible decisions between God and man.

(4) Finally, look at the concept of **the moral law.** In Hinduism and Buddhism, the moral law is not rooted in God. It is to be found in the law of *karma* which operates independently of God. God is lifted up above the law of *karma* and has nothing to do with it. If God is lifted above morals, the devotee gets to the place where he, too, transcends morals. He is not affected by good or evil. In Christianity, God and man are both bound by the same moral laws. Our morality is firmly fixed in the nature of God and in the historic fact—the nature of Christ. To be Christlike is the highest attainable or even imaginable goodness.

*b.* In the second place, all religions are not the same in their *goals.* In Buddhism, the goal is the extinction of life; the goal of the gospel is the fullness of life. Hinduism proclaims deliverance from *samsara,* the wheel of birth and rebirth; the gospel proclaims deliverance from the guilt and power of sin. The Islamic view of Paradise (a place of sensual delight) is certainly not the same as the Christian view of heaven (a place of moral perfection).

Dr. E. Stanley Jones declared that

to hold all religions the same is to practice mental abdication. This is not mental liberality; it is nonsense—and unscientific. Science does not wave its hand over all theories and say they are equally good and equally valid. That attitude would paralyze science. . . . Science puts its theories under life to see whether they fit the facts . . . it chooses. . . . We, too, must choose in the deepest things that concern life. I do choose. I choose Christ and His Kingdom. It is not faith that makes men believe in everything. It is a false tolerance which is real indifferentism.[1]

## 2. "What Is New in Christianity?"

"We have the same teachings in our religion."

Several years ago I was making a journey by train in North India. Before long I discovered I was surrounded by a group of Ammidiyya Muslims and was soon drawn into an animated discussion on religion. But whenever I introduced some aspect of Christian truth, my Muslim fellow passengers would say: "We have the same teaching in our Koran." Here I was face-to-face with the new apologetic of the Muslims. They would not attempt to prove our gospel is not *true*, but that it is not *new*.

Hindus also claim they have the same truths. For instance, Christ said: "Turn the other cheek; love your enemies." Hinduism says: "You are to be like the Sandalwood tree, which, when smitten by the axe, pours its perfume upon the axe that smites it." Hindus also claim that they have the idea of redemption. In the churning of the milk ocean, the serpent that was used as the churning rope suddenly vomited poison, and Shiva, to prevent its dropping into the ocean and poisoning the milk, drank it himself. But before it could reach his stomach and scorch him, his wife, Parvati, caught his neck where the poison got stuck, giving it a bluish hue.

Buddhists claim that much of the ethic found in the New Testament finds its parallel in the ethic contained in the Eightfold Path of discipline, such as purity in speech, thought, and action.

We must admit that there are several similarities between Christianity and other religions. We thank God in sincerity for all the fine things in their cultures and thinking. However, Christianity is unique, not so much in its doctrine or ethic, but unique because of the person of Jesus Christ. HE makes the difference—the world of difference. He *is* unique. He alone *is* Savior and Lord. The lack for which nothing else can atone in the other religions is just this— Christ. They have no Christ. And lacking Him, they lack life's supreme necessity.

Dr. E. Stanley Jones was preaching in one of the Indian states prior to independence. The Hindu prime minister as chairman said in his opening introduction: "I shall reserve my remarks for the close of the address; for no matter what the speaker says, I will find parallel things in our own sacred books." He had confidently believed beforehand that he would find them. But at the close of the meeting he was nonplussed, for Dr. Jones did not present "things"; he presented a Person—Jesus—and that Person was not found in their sacred books.

What is new in Christianity? It is Christ, and He is always new! That's why the gospel is "Good News."

### 3. "Why Do You Christians Claim that Christ Is the Only Way to Salvation?"

"Why cannot you state the teachings of Jesus in harmony with the teachings of other religions, without stressing what you call the 'uniqueness of the person of Christ'?"

This is a question we are asked over and over again—by Muslims, Buddhists, Hindus, even Jews. It is the question of all questions and goes to the very heart of the gospel.

From personal experience I have found the best way to answer this question is by a series of statements, as follows:

    *a.* I am in no position to surrender that which is not mine. I am not presenting claims which I am making on behalf of Christ, but only explaining the claims which He made for himself.

    *b.* Listen to the claims of Christ:

        (1) Jesus said, "I am the way, and the truth, and the life; no one comes to the Father, but by me" (John 14:6).

        (2) He further stated that He is "the bread of life," and those who come to Him should never hunger or thirst (6:35).

        (3) He claimed to be "the light of the world" and the Source of eternal life (8:12; 11:25).

        (4) He found in himself the fulfillment of the long-expected promises of the Messiah and Yahweh's kingdom, contained in the Old Testament (Matt. 13:16-17; Mark 1:15; Luke 4:17-21, 24-27, 44).

        (5) He accepted the descriptions given by Peter ("Thou art the Christ, the Son of the living God") and by Thomas

("My Lord and my God") (Matt. 16:16 and John 20:28, KJV).

(6) He spoke of His eternal existence (8:58; cf. Exod. 3:14). To know Him is to know God (John 8:19), and to honor Him is to honor God (5:23).

(7) He claimed to be the "Son of God" (10:36; 5:17-18).

(8) On two major occasions of Christ's ministry—at His baptism (Matt. 3:17) and His transfiguration (17:5)—a voice from heaven authenticated His deity.

(9) He claimed for himself power to forgive sins (9:1-8) and authority to judge the world (25:31-46; John 5:22).

These are fantastic claims. No other man—not even Buddha or Mohammed—made such amazing statements about himself.

c. Now, one of two things is true: Either Christ *is* all that He claims to be, or He is the biggest liar, the greatest deceiver in history; or, to say the least, He is suffering from hallucinations or from delusions of grandeur. There is no middle ground. Either He *is* or He *is not* what He claims to be. (Most non-Christians admit that Jesus was a great teacher. If so, then they must be willing to accept what He taught about himself. They also confess that Jesus was a good man. But if He is good, He must be good all the way through, not just in part. Then we must take His claims seriously.)

d. As for me, I have taken Christ at His Word, and I have found Him to be all that He claims to be. Through Him I have found access to the Father. In Him I have found the Way, the Truth, and the Life. He has offered me forgiveness of sins and power for daily living.

e. As a Christian I come to share with you what Christ means to me and what He has done for me. I believe He can also do the same for you, if you put your trust in Him. Then you, too, will discover that He is all that He claims to be.

f. If Christ is not all that He claims to be, then nothing matters. You can brush Him aside and forget Him. But if He *is* all that He claims to be, then nothing else matters. You are face-to-face with Christ; He is on your hands; and you must ask the all-important question: "What shall I do with Jesus who is called Christ?" (Matt. 27:22). This claim—that He is the only Savior—is not something we *concede* to Christ, but something He *confronts* us with.

### 4. "Why Do Christians Seek to Convert People?"

"Why don't you just preach Christ and help a man to be a better man where he is?"

The answer is: We preach conversion because Christ preached it. He said: "Except ye be converted, and become as little children, ye shall not enter into the kingdom of heaven" (Matt. 18:3, KJV).

There is a difference between conversion and proselytism. Jesus condemned proselytism (see Matt. 23:15), but He commanded conversion. Proselytism is an outer change of label; it is purely *horizontal* —a shift in position along the same plane. Conversion is an inner change of *life*—wrought by God. It is primarily *vertical*—a change in position from one level to another.

A Catholic missionary in India hired a Muslim cook. Unexpectedly one day the cook said to his employer: "Sir, I want to become a Christian; please baptize me." So the missionary appointed a day and performed the rite of baptism. He poured some water on the servant's head and said, "You are no longer Abdul [a Muslim name]; from now on you are Da-ood [David]."

After the ceremony the priest said to the new convert: "There is one thing to remember. As a Christian, you must not eat mutton on Friday, but only fish."

Everything went well for a few weeks, until one Friday some special friends of the cook unexpectedly came for a visit, and he felt he must give them special treatment by preparing mutton *pillau* (meat cooked in rice). As he was cooking the meat, the aroma came to the attention of the priest who called him and said, "Da-ood, I told you, no mutton on Friday—only fish."

"Sir," replied the cook, "I'm cooking fish, not mutton."

The priest answered, "Da-ood, you can't fool me. That's mutton you're cooking."

So they argued for a while, the priest insisting it was mutton, and the cook declaring it was fish. Finally, in desperation the servant said, "Sir, you're not the only clever one. You poured some water on my head and said, 'You are no longer Abdul; from now on you are Da-ood.' Well, I poured some water on the meat and I said, 'You are no longer mutton, you are fish!'"

That's an example of proselytism—an outer change of label without an inner change of character.

But there was another Muslim, a university student, who carefully studied the New Testament, became convinced that Jesus was the Savior, put his trust in Him, and was baptized as a Christian.

Shortly thereafter, the new convert was walking along the street on his way to the university, when some of his student friends met him and asked, "Ahmed, we hear that you have changed your religion; is that so?"

Quick as a flash, he answered, "Oh, no, you've got it all wrong. I haven't simply changed my religion. My religion has changed me!"

That's conversion—an inner change of life.

Conversion is essential to all of life. All around us, 24 hours of the day, a process is taking place which scientists call "photosynthesis." It is that process by which plants take carbon dioxide from the air and convert it into carbohydrates. All food production is dependent upon this conversion process in nature.

Our bodies live by conversion. They take in meat, vegetables, and fruit, and convert them into blood, muscle, sinew, bone, and tissue. Every time we go to the table to eat, we are involved in a process of conversion.

Industry also operates by conversion. Factories take raw materials and convert them into finished products. The shirt you are wearing was once—at least in part—cotton out in the field. The table at which you sit was once part of a tree out in the forest. The glass in your spectacles was once sand on a beach. The newspaper you read was once wood pulp.

Everything around us has been converted. The big question is: Have *we* been converted? Spiritual conversion is conversion at the highest level, whereby the bad becomes good, the weak becomes strong, the impure becomes pure.

Spiritual conversion is necessary for all people—for rich and poor, educated and uneducated, high caste and low caste, European and Asian, nominal Christian and non-Christian. So we do not single out Buddhists, Muslims, Hindus, and atheists as the only candidates for conversion. Nominal church members need conversion just as well. It is not Christians who say to non-Christians, "You must be converted." Christ says to all men, regardless of race, nationality, or religion: "You must be converted; you must be born again" (see John 3:3, 7, KJV).

# 4

# The Gospel
# Versus Religion

*By grace are ye saved through faith;
and that not of yourselves:
it is the gift of God:
not of works, lest any man
should boast.*

—Eph. 2:8-9, KJV

A few years ago, one Sunday morning when I had just completed a missionary sermon, a member of the congregation came up to me and said, "I can't understand you missionaries. We hear that India is the home of many religions, that it is an exceedingly religious country. Why then do you go to introduce yet another religion and only add to the confusion? Surely, India has enough religion."

I answered, "Friend, I'm not interested in religion, but I'm deeply interested in the gospel. I wouldn't walk across the street for religion, but I'm willing to go around the world for the sake of the gospel. There is a great difference between the two."

Religion is *man-made;* the gospel is *God-given.*

Religion is *what man does* for God; the gospel is *what* God *has done* for man.

Religion is *man's search* for God; the gospel is *God's search* for man.

Religion is man trying to climb *the ladder of his own self-righteousness,* with the hope of meeting God at the topmost rung; the gospel is God coming down *the ladder of the incarnation* of Jesus Christ and meeting us as sinners at the lowest rung.

---

This chapter is from *The Supreme Task of the Church,* by John T. Seamands (Grand Rapids: Wm. B. Eerdmans Publishing Co., 1964), pp. 59-70.

Religion is good *views*, the gospel is good *news*.

Religion is good *advice*; the gospel is a glorious *announcement*.

Religion takes a man and leaves him *as he is*; the gospel takes a man as he is and makes him what he *ought to be*.

Religion ends in an outer *reformation*; the gospel ends in an inner *transformation*.

Religion *whitewashes*; the gospel *washes white*.

Religion often becomes a *farce*; the gospel is always a *force*, the power of God unto salvation to everyone who believes.

There are many religions, but only one gospel.

Notice that in the text the apostle Paul places two sets of phrases in direct opposition to each other: "not of yourselves"—that is religion: man's attempt to save himself, over against "of God"—that is the gospel: God's provision for man's plight; and "not of works"—again, that is religion: man's reliance upon his own efforts and morality, over against "through faith"—that is the gospel: man's response to God's offer of redemption and His righteousness.

This leads us to the all-important question: What are the fundamental differences between religion and the gospel? They are basically three.

## 1. Doing Versus Being

*Religion places the prime emphasis upon doing, whereas the gospel places the prime emphasis on being.*

Religion says, "Do good, keep on doing good, and eventually you will become good." The gospel says, "First of all, you must *be* good; you must become good by the grace of God; and then it shall follow as day follows night that you will do good."

Religion says, "Tell the truth, keep on telling the truth, and you will become honest." The gospel says, "First of all be honest in heart, and then you will tell the truth."

Religion says, "Think good thoughts, keep on thinking good thoughts, and you will become pure in mind." The gospel says, "Become pure in mind, and then you will think good thoughts."

Religion says, "Go out and help people, and you will learn to love them." The gospel says, "Receive the love of God into your hearts, and then you will naturally love people and want to serve them."

Thus, while religion places the primary emphasis on *outer conduct*, the gospel places the primary emphasis on *inner character*.

This does not mean that the Christian faith has no place for good works. It certainly does. Jesus was a man of action, a man of good deeds. It is written of Him that "he went about doing good" (Acts 10:38). His whole life was poured out in loving service for His fellowmen. James, in his Epistle, writes, "Faith without works is dead" (2:26, KJV).

But it is a question of priority. Which comes first? Which is the cause and which is the effect? Which is the root and which is the fruit? Is being the result of doing? Or does doing follow being? Do we become good by doing good? Or do we do good because we are good?

Paul very clearly states that good works are not the cause but the result of our salvation. In Eph. 2:9 he writes, "Not by works, lest any man should boast" (KJV). But in verse 10 he writes, "We are . . . created in Christ Jesus unto good works" (KJV). In his Epistle to Titus he drives home the same truth when he writes, "Not by works of righteousness which we have done, but according to his mercy he saved us, by the washing of regeneration, and renewing of the Holy [Spirit]." Three verses later he writes, "This is a faithful saying . . . that they which have believed in God might be careful to maintain good works" (see Titus 3:5, 8, KJV).

Jesus tells us that we cannot really do good unless we first become good. He asks the question, "How can ye, *being evil* [note this], speak good things? . . . A good man out of the good treasure of the heart bringeth forth good things: and an evil man out of the evil treasure [of his heart] bringeth forth evil things" (Matt. 12:34-35, KJV).

The Scriptures emphasize being. "*Be ye holy . . . be* filled with the Spirit . . . *be* born again . . . *be* tender-hearted and kind."

The attempt to become good by doing good is like taking a bushel of apples and tying them onto a telephone post, thereby expecting the telephone post to become an apple tree. This is impossible. The tree must *be* an apple tree; then it will produce apples.

Many years ago, in the days of the silent motion picture, a movie was being shown in a little Western town for the first time in its history. The cowboys turned out in full force to see this modern miracle. The plot of the movie centered around the usual triangle of a handsome hero, a beautiful heroine, and a villain. In the middle of the story, the villain kidnapped the beautiful girl, flung her on his horse, and made off with her. This was too much for the cowboys. They pulled out their six-shooters and fired into the screen, trying to stop the villain from carrying off the beautiful girl. They riddled the

screen with holes, but the picture went on. The villain carried off
the girl. Now, if just one of the cowboys had used his good sense, he
would have turned and fired one shot into the projector and stopped
the whole picture!

This is a spiritual parable. Many of us try to reform ourselves on
the outside; we riddle the screen with holes, but the picture of sin
and defeat goes on in our lives. We need to deal with the projector,
which is the heart. Jesus said, "Out of the heart . . . proceed evil
thoughts, adulteries, fornications, murders, thefts, covetousness, . . .
deceit, . . . pride" (Mark 7:21-22, KJV). Religion deals with the screen;
the gospel deals with the projector.

Have you ever studied the sermon of Jesus to the Pharisees, as
recorded in Matthew 23 (KJV)? It is an interesting sermon. First of
all, Jesus commends the Pharisees for their good works. He says, you
pray; you pay the tithe; you cross continents to make a single prose-
lyte; you despise swearing; you fast regularly; you build tombs for the
prophets; you keep the traditions of the elders. All well and good.

But, says Jesus, inwardly you are proud; you like to be saluted as
"Rabbi" in public. Inwardly you are selfish; you deceive the poor and
the widows. Inwardly you are ambitious; you desire the upper seats
at the feasts. Inwardly you are hypocritical; you fast and you pray
only to be seen of men. Then He says, "Ye make clean the outside of
the cup and of the platter, but within they are full of extortion and
excess" (v. 25). "Ye are like unto whited sepulchres" (v. 27). In other
words, "You have a good appearance but an evil heart."

Jesus brings His sermon to a climax when He says, "Cleanse first
that which is *within*" (v. 26).

True righteousness is not put on; it is put in. Our main trouble is
within. We need a clean heart; we need an inner transformation. We
need to be "born again." We need to become "new creatures" in
Christ Jesus.

Religion emphasizes the *outer action;* the gospel emphasizes the
*inner condition.* Religion tries to work from the circumference to
center, from the outside to the inside. The gospel goes straight to the
center and works from the inside out. Religion ends in an outer reformation; the gospel ends in an inner transformation.

## 2. Principles Versus a Person

*Religion places the emphasis on principles and precepts, on codes and creeds;
the gospel places the emphasis on a Person.*

Religion offers us a set of teachings and says, "Accept these; believe and follow these." The gospel presents a Person and says, "Accept Him; believe and follow Him."

The Christian faith, of course, does have its wonderful teachings, its lofty ethics, its systems of philosophy and theology, its ritual and its creeds. But the Christian faith is more than this. The Christian faith is Christ, and is what it is because He is what He is.

One of the great differences between the non-Christian religions and the gospel is that there is no intrinsic relationship between these religions and their founders, while in the Christian faith there *is* such relationship. You can take Buddha out of Buddhism, and Buddhism still remains with its Four Noble Truths and its Eightfold Path. You can take Mohammed out of Islam, and Islam is still intact with its Five Pillars of Action and its Six Articles of Belief. Though Hinduism has no particular founder, you can take such deities as Rama and Krishna out of Hinduism, and Hinduism, with its philosophical and religious concepts, still remains. But if we take Christ out of the gospel, we have nothing left. For the gospel is Christ and is what it is because He is what He is.

Christ said, "*I* am the way, and the truth, and the life" (John 14:6). He did not say, "I will *show* you the way; I will teach you the truth; I will give you life." He said, "I *am* the way, and the truth, and the life." Accept Christ and you are on the way; accept *Him* and you have the truth; accept *Him* and you are alive!

So to be a Christian is more than just belonging to the organization of the church; it is more than just accepting the creeds and catechism of the church; it is more than merely practicing the ritual of the church. To be a Christian is essentially to put one's trust in the person of Christ, to receive Him as Lord and Savior, to enter into fellowship with Him, to become a new creature in Him.

Thus the fundamental distinction between the gospel and the religions of the world lies not in the difference between systems of thought but in the difference between persons. Buddha never taught that men should worship him; he was himself a seeker after the truth who sought to teach others the truth which he had found. Mohammed clearly stated that he was merely the prophet of God; Muslims are quick to inform us that they do *not* worship him. Confucius is not the object of worship in Confucianism; he is merely the object of respect as a great teacher. Many of the deities of Hinduism are mere mythological figures, who partake of many of our human frailties.

But Christ claimed to be the Son of God; He claimed to be the Savior of all men; He commanded faith in His person and required that all men should worship Him.

Christ makes the difference. Just this is the great lack of the non-Christian faiths. There are fine things in their culture and thought; we admit it and thank God in real sincerity for them. But the real lack, the lack for which nothing else can atone is exactly—Christ.

Sadhu Sundar Singh, a convert from Sikhism to Christianity, was one of India's greatest Christians. One day a European professor of comparative religions—an agnostic—interviewed the sadhu, with the evident intention of showing him his mistake in renouncing another faith for Christ. He asked, "What have you found in Christianity that you did not have in your old religion?"

The sadhu answered, "I have Christ."

"Yes, I know," the professor replied somewhat impatiently, "but what particular principles or doctrine have you found that you did not have before?"

Sundar Singh replied, "The particular thing I have found is Christ." Try as the professor might, he could not budge him from the position. He went away discomfited but thoughtful. The sadhu was right. The religions of the world have fine things in them, but they lack Christ.

Furthermore, the unique fact about Christ is His resurrection. He went down into death for our sake, but then came up on the other side and said in triumph, "I am the resurrection and the life; he who believes in me . . . shall never die" (John 11:25-26).

A Muslim in Africa recently became a Christian. Some of his friends asked him, "Why have you become a Christian?"

He answered, "Well, it's like this. Suppose you were going down the road, and suddenly the road forked in two directions, and you didn't know which way to go; and there at the fork in the road were two men—one dead and one alive—which one would you ask which way to go?"

He had discovered the supreme distinction. Mohammed, Buddha, Confucius, Rama, and others lived and died and passed off the scene of human history. Jesus lived and died, but He rose again and is alive today as our Contemporary. He steps out of the 1st century into the 20th century and walks straight into our hearts. So He is not merely our Teacher and Example, He is our Redeemer and Lord. He can live within us and give us the power to follow in His footsteps.

### 3. Works Versus Grace

*Religion emphasizes works; the gospel emphasizes grace.*
Religion says, "Attain"; the gospel says, "Obtain."
Religion says, "Attempt"; the gospel says, "Accept."
Religion says, "Try"; the gospel says, "Trust."
Religion says, "Develop yourself"; the gospel says, "Deny yourself."
Religion says, "Save yourself"; the gospel says, "Surrender yourself."
Religion says, "Do—do this, and do that, and thou shalt be saved."
The gospel says, "It is done. Believe, and thou shalt be saved."

When Jesus cried on the Cross, "It is finished," He meant that God had now done all that was necessary for our salvation. There is nothing that we need do, nor indeed can do. It is not a *reward* but a *gift*. We cannot earn salvation; we cannot merit it or purchase it; we cannot work it out for ourselves. We merely have to receive what God has done for us on the Cross through His Son. We have to receive it simply as a gift from the hand of God. It is purely by grace, the unmerited favor of God.

Therefore, the important question of the gospel is simply this: What are you going to do about what God has done for you? God has acted; how will you react? Will you receive or reject, believe or deny?

It means that we must humble ourselves, come just as we are, and with grateful hearts receive God's gift. In all sincerity we say to Him: "Nothing in my hand I bring, / Simply to Thy cross I cling."

In the words of the familiar hymn we say:

> *Just as I am, without one plea,*
> *But that Thy blood was shed for me,*
> *And that Thou bidd'st me come to Thee,*
> *O Lamb of God, I come! I come!*

We don't try to fix ourselves up and then come to Christ; we come just as we are, and He will fix us up. He will *take* us over and *make* us over.

Several years ago I was making a long journey by train in India. I soon fell into conversation with a Hindu fellow passenger, the only other occupant of a first-class compartment. He told me that he was on a long religious pilgrimage to one of the sacred places of India. "In fact," he said, "I have been on religious pilgrimages the better part of my life."

"Why do you make so many pilgrimages?" I asked.

"In search of God," he replied.

"Tell me," I said, "after so many pilgrimages, have you not found Him as yet?"

He hung his head, and a look of despair settled across his face. "No," he answered, "I can't say that I have found Him, but one day I hope to."

With a smile I said, "May I tell you about my pilgrimage?"

When I mentioned the word "pilgrimage," his eyes lit up. "Oh," he said, "have you made a pilgrimage?"

"Yes," I said, "one day in my life I made a pilgrimage of 20 steps, and at the end of those steps I found God."

"Tell me about it," he pleaded.

Then I told him that I was born in a Christian home, the son of a Christian missionary. I learned to read the Bible and to pray at an early age. At the age of 15 I joined the church and became a Sunday School teacher. From all outward appearances I was a good Christian. I knew much about God and His Son, Jesus Christ. But inwardly I was empty and dissatisfied. God seemed to be so distant, so unreal. Then I told him that as a college student in America I heard an evangelist explain that to be a Christian was more than just belonging to a church, or accepting the creeds, or going through the ceremonies. To be a Christian was to repent of our sins, to receive Jesus Christ as our personal Savior, and to obey Him in all things. At the end of his sermon the evangelist invited those who wanted to receive Christ as Savior to come down to the altar and pray and believe.

"It was then," I said, "that I made my pilgrimage. I arose from my seat and walked about 20 steps to reach the altar. I fell on my knees, confessed my sins to God, and put my personal trust in Jesus Christ as my Savior. Suddenly God came very close to me; He became real to me. I felt at last that I had found Him. Since that day I have been conscious of His wonderful presence in my life."

"That's wonderful," said my Hindu companion. "I wish I could find Him like that."

Then I explained to him that he, too, could find God. It was not by our long pilgrimages, or many good works, or by our own efforts. It was "by grace through faith." I said to him, "You don't even have to take 20 steps to find God. No man is more than 1 step away from Him. Just turn around and there you are in the arms of redeeming love."

Not many days later I received a letter from the Hindu gentleman. With great joy he wrote, "I have just made my shortest and last pilgrimage. Just as you said, it took only one step. Thank God, I have found Him!"

We can now summarize the main points of the gospel thus:

*a.* The gospel emphasizes *being.* It commands, "Be ye holy, for I am holy" (1 Pet. 1:16, KJV). It starts with inner character and moves to the outer conduct.

*b.* Being is by *becoming.* So Jesus commanded, "Ye must be born again" (John 3:7, KJV). He also declared, "Except ye be converted, and *become* as little children, ye shall not enter into the kingdom of heaven" (Matt. 18:3, KJV, italics added). By nature we are sinful; we need a moral transformation by the grace of God.

*c.* Becoming is by *belonging.* When we accept Christ as Savior, we enter into fellowship with Him. He comes to live within our hearts. He takes us over and makes us over. "Therefore, if any one is in Christ, he is a new creation; the old has passed away, behold, the new has come" (2 Cor. 5:17).

*d.* Belonging is by *believing.* We enter into fellowship by putting our trust in Him. Faith is the link that joins us to Christ. "As many as *received* him, to them gave he power to *become* the sons of God, even to them that *believe* on his name" (John 1:12, KJV, italics added).

This is the message that we seek to proclaim to the people of the world: not another religion, but the gospel; not a set of teachings or a system of theology, but good news about a wonderful Person. There are many religions, but there is only one gospel. Religion cannot redeem, but Christ—and He alone—can save the world.

PART 2

# Methods and Principles of Communicating the Gospel

# 5

# Methods of Approach
# to Communication

We come now to some basic, underlying methods of approach to communicating the gospel. Though we are looking at the subject primarily from the standpoint of communicating to non-Christians, the ideas presented will also be helpful in witnessing to nominal Christians who do not have a personal relationship with Christ.

Let us first look at two methods of approach that are negative and harmful in character and which we should avoid. Then we shall discuss three positive and effective methods which we need to cultivate in presenting the Good News.

## A. UNACCEPTABLE METHODS

### 1. The Head-on Approach

This is the method of aggressive refutation and condemnation of other faiths. This attitude assumes that all other religions are the work of the devil, are false, and devoid of any value. There are, therefore, no points of contact or bridgeheads for the preaching of the gospel. Some non-Christians have called this method "a declaration of war" or "the imperialistic approach." Personally, I like to call it "the billy goat approach," for it reminds me of the story of the goat that ran out on the railway track and charged the engine of an oncoming express train. Courage, 100 percent; good sense, zero!

In his book entitled *Christian Missions*, Mahatma Gandhi tells how he became prejudiced against the Christian faith while a student in high school. He writes: "I developed a sort of dislike for it [Christianity]. And for a reason. In those days Christian missionaries used to stand in a corner near the high school and hold forth, pouring abuse on Hindus and their gods. I could not endure this. I must have stood there to hear them once only , but that was enough to dissuade me from repeating the experiment."[1]

Several years ago the state government of Madhya Pradesh in India appointed a committee to inquire into the activities of Christian missionaries within their jurisdiction. The chairman of the committee was a very orthodox Hindu, and the printed report no doubt reflects much of his personal prejudice against Christianity, but there are certain criticisms in the findings that we should note. In the section entitled "Various Methods of Propagating Christianity," the committee reports that an American missionary, in his preaching round, "attacked idol worship in various offensive terms, with the result that a complaint was made to the district magistrate against him." Another preacher "recited kirtans [lyrics] and denounced Hindu Gods." At a public fair one of the Hindu goddesses was "denounced as an adulteress." Yet another preacher "denounced Hindu Gods as stone Gods and dead Gods." "The lives of Rama and Krishna were attacked in a way offensive to the Hindus." "Other religions are referred to as false religions" and "the protection of cows is also ridiculed." The report then asks: "Can any right thinking man assert that such vile attacks on the religion of the majority community in India is part of Christian religion or is conducive to public order or morality?"[2]

A number of years ago an outstanding Bible teacher and evangelist from America, who has written many excellent books, was asked to bring the chapel message one morning in Lucknow Christian College in northern India. He stood before an audience made up, for the most part, of Hindus, Sikhs, and Muslims, and said in a booming voice: "Dear friends, I am going to share with you today what I, as a Christian, feel about the other world religions. I believe that the gods of Hinduism are all demonic spirits, and that Mohammed is another name for the devil." His remarks caused quite a stir, and several students walked out of the assembly. Fortunately, this happened during the colonial period when the British were still in power. If it had happened in the post-independence era, he probably would have been severely beaten. When asked why he took such an approach, the evangelist's defense was: "The old-fashioned way of trying to be tactful and polite, and just beating around the bush, has produced no results whatsoever. I have come to the conclusion that we need to meet the issue head-on and tell it like it is. People must know the truth."

An additional illustration of the head-on approach is found in Don Richardson's latest book, *Lords of the Earth.* The missionary who was working among the Yali tribe in Irian Jaya, Indonesia, wrote a hymn in the Yali language and then insisted that a gathering of men and boys sing it after him. In effect, the words said: *"Kembu's* words we reject, we reject, we reject; *Kembu's* words we reject—*Kembu,* he is bad!" (*Kembu* is the name given to their spirit-god.) When the Yalis heard the words of the song, their "jaws dropped open in shocked unbelief. Horror flooded every countenance." They refused to learn the song, and the missionary finally gave up. But the backlash caused by this incident hindered evangelistic work among the Yalis for a long time.[3]

Such an approach is most unwise in these days of strong nationalistic sentiment in many Eastern countries, and especially in areas where there is a decidedly anti-Western attitude. Frontal attacks on the beliefs and gods of other religions only arouse resentment in the minds of the listeners and build up prejudice against the Christian faith. Furthermore, such an approach is completely unnecessary, for we don't have to tear down another man's religion in order to build up the Christian faith. The gospel can stand on its own merits. A wise salesman never denounces the brand of gadget that the householder possesses; he merely points out all the fine qualities of his brand and then demonstrates it firsthand.

The apostle Paul gives us a good example in this regard. During his preaching mission in Ephesus, a man named Demetrius, a silversmith who made shrines for the goddess Diana, stirred up the whole populace by accusing Paul of denouncing gods made with hands and turning followers away from the worship of the mighty Diana. When it appeared that a riot would ensue, the town clerk arrived on the scene, quieted the mob, and said to the people: "You have brought these men here who are neither sacrilegious nor blasphemers of our goddess" (Acts 19:37). Then he persuaded the crowd that if they had any legitimate complaint, they should bring it before the appointed courts of the city in a peaceful manner. The official's statement concerning Paul and his helpers, however, gives us firsthand insight into the preaching method of the apostle. Though he fearlessly proclaimed Christ as the only Savior, he did not attack the gods or beliefs of his listeners.

The late Dr. E. Stanley Jones, a more recent missionary statesman, is also a good example to us. In his book *Along the Indian Road,* he
writes:

> I have made it a policy and a principle never to attack anoth-
> er man's faith in public address. I present what I have and leave
> him to come to his own conclusions. Again and again I am pressed
> by Hindus to show the difference between the faiths. I always re-
> fuse. For the moment I call attention to differences there is
> controversy. And Christianity cannot be seen in a controversy.[4]

## 2. The Shake-Hands Approach (The Method of Accommodation)

This is a watering down of the gospel in order to make it more
palatable and easier for the listener to accept. Such an approach we
must reject, for it is a tragic betrayal of our trust. We are permitted to
adjust the *form* of the Christian message, but we have no right to
change its *content*.

I trace my call to be a missionary to India to an unforgettable
experience I had as a high school student in India. At midnight I
watched a religious procession moving past the main entrance of the
school compound. It was supposed to be a "Christian" procession, but
in every way it was Hindu. Several men were pulling a *ratha* (wooden
idol-cart) through the streets with heavy ropes and chains. Others
were beating their drums and dancing in front of the cart. Hundreds
of people were gathered all around, throwing rice and bananas and
flowers on the images placed on the *ratha*. The only difference between this "Christian" procession and a typical Hindu procession was
that images of St. Patrick, St. Joseph, Christ, and Mary had been substituted for images of Krishna, Shiva, and Durga. For the devotees it
was an easy shift from Hinduism to Christianity.

Unfortunately this type of syncretism has characterized the
Christian movement in Latin America for a long time, especially
among the many Indian tribes. Early in the history of the continent
a kind of Christo-paganism developed, in which Mary, the mother of
heaven, became a substitute for the former moon goddess. Present-
day church leaders are doing their best to offset these syncretistic
tendencies with a genuine biblical faith.

Some of the theological fads of our day, such as "universalism"
and "anonymous Christianity," are falling into the trap of the accom-
modation approach. The proponents of these theologies are trying to
make Christianity more acceptable to Muslims and Hindus and Buddhists by insisting that Christ is already inherent in their own faiths;

that they are already "saved" or are "Christians" and don't know it. So it is not necessary for them to be "converted" from their religion to the Christian faith. Teachings such as these surrender the uniqueness of the gospel and make Christianity merely one religion among many. This is a position we cannot condone.

Now let us turn from these unacceptable approaches to others that are legitimate and effective in the proclamation of the gospel. We highly commend the following methods.

## B. ACCEPTABLE METHODS

### 1. The Heart-to-Heart Approach

Although the religious background of our listeners is very important, in our communication of the gospel we are primarily concerned with people, not with the religious systems they represent. People are first of all human beings, then Muslims or Hindus or Buddhists. There is a universal point of contact to be found in the common denominator of human nature and the human predicament. Fundamentally, down underneath, people are all alike. They have the same religious consciousness, the same aspirations, longings, and needs. All have the same physiological needs; all have the need for security and freedom from anxiety, all have the need to love and be loved; all have the desire to belong and be accepted; all have the longing for self-fulfillment. People everywhere have the same temptations. Everyone has to face the reality of death. There is the universal need for forgiveness, the universal hunger for fellowship with God.

The gospel as a universal faith has universal application to the fundamental needs of people. It offers meaning in life, power for living, forgiveness of sins, reconciliation with God, unconditional love, victory over death, and eternal life. Preaching, therefore, is the process of getting a message from the heart and mind of God, and then allowing it to flow through our hearts and minds into the hearts and minds of others. We put ourselves alongside men and women everywhere, as having the same needs and aspirations, and receiving the same promises and gifts from God. It is not the I-You relationship, but the God-Us relationship; not "I have something for you," but "God has something for all of us."

The heart-to-heart approach is a general approach which should underlie all our witnessing and preaching. It is especially effective with those who are in a spiritual vacuum, and with audiences of mixed religious backgrounds.

Illustrations of the effectiveness of the gospel in meeting universal human needs are found on every hand.

A missionary couple labored and preached in an African village for a long time without any response from the people. Finally, one family accepted Christ and publicly witnessed to their faith by baptism. Shortly afterward the young son in this family became seriously ill and seemed to be on the verge of death. Soon the news went about the village: "See, the evil spirits are angry with this family and are punishing them for leaving their old religion and accepting the missionary's religion. The boy will surely die."

When the missionary couple heard the rumor, they were greatly disturbed. They fasted and prayed and begged the Lord to spare the boy's life. They feared the death of the boy would only confirm the superstitious belief of the people, and completely close the door to future evangelism in that area.

A few days later, however, the young lad died. The missionary conducted a Christian funeral with the family, while the rest of the village looked on with curiosity. Shortly afterward, the village elders came to the missionary and said, "Bwana, we have decided to become Christians. Please baptize us."

The missionary was dumbfounded. "Why," he asked, "have you come to this decision?"

The leader of the group replied: "You know how we people act in the face of death; how we wail and scream and beat our breasts. But when the boy of this Christian family died, you all sang hymns and prayed and thanked God for his life. If this Jesus you have been telling us about can take the fear out of death, then we are ready to follow Him!"

On the morning of July 6, 1962, my heart literally burned within me as I read the following item in the daily newspaper:

### "Monk Hanged as Assassin"

Colombo, Ceylon (AP)—Talduwa Somarama, a Buddhist monk, was hanged today for the assassination of Prime Minister Solomon Bandaranaike in 1959.

Prison officials said Somarama was baptized as a Christian 24 hours before the hanging so that *he could ask for the forgiveness that the Buddhist religion does not grant.* [Italics mine.]

Here was a Buddhist who felt the weight of his crime and the guilt of his sin upon his heart, but could find no solace in his own religion. Only when he turned to the One who died in his place on the Cross, could he find the deliverance for which he longed.

What a privilege is ours to speak heart-to-heart and apply the gospel to the universal needs and problems of people everywhere!

We must, however, give one word of caution about the heart-to-heart approach. Though it contains much basic truth, and should, in a general sense, be our guide, we must also keep in mind that one cannot really understand a person without a thorough knowledge of the religious system that has molded his life. So though there is a general approach suitable to all men, simply because they are men, there is also the specific approach to the person who is a Hindu by religion, to the person who is a Muslim, etc. In their respective beliefs we find certain ideas that are hindrances and helps to their understanding and receiving the gospel. It is our duty to discover this particular approach in order to reach all men most effectively.

## 2. The Point-of-Contact Approach

In this approach we seek to find something in common between ourselves and the listener to use as a starting point in presenting the gospel. We proceed from the known to the unknown, from areas of agreement to areas of disagreement. This is both tactful and effective.

Points of contact can be found in three different areas:

*a In common interests.* Jesus was a master at this approach. To the disciples, many of whom were fishermen, He talked about becoming "fishers of men" (Matt. 4:19). To the farmer He spoke about the seed and soil, about sowing and reaping. To the Samaritan woman who had come to draw water from the well of Sychar, He spoke about the "living water" and the "spring . . . to eternal life" (John 4:10, 14).

Harry Emerson Fosdick, famous pastor in New York City, used to say, "Every man is like an island. You row around him until you find a place to land. It may take minutes; it may take years." This means we need to listen carefully to what the other person is saying in order to discover what interests him. We need to find the door that opens into his heart and mind.

During my first year as a missionary in India, I was traveling on the train from Bangalore to Madras one day. I noticed a black gentleman in the compartment and soon struck up a conversation with him. When I asked his name, he told me he was commonly known as Gunboat Jack. Then I asked what he did for a living.

"I'm a fighter," he replied. "I'm the champion in the middleweight division. What do you do?"

I smiled and said, "I'm a fighter too, but of a different sort. I'm a preacher and I'm fighting the devil."

Quick as a flash, he said, "Mighty tough opponent you got there!"

This afforded the opening I needed. From then on I talked about the ring of life, the fight in which we are engaged, and the crown for which we strive. I asked him, "Gunboat Jack, how are you getting along in the ring of life?"

"Not so good," he answered. "I've been knocked out again and again by the devil." And he went on to describe his battle with drink, sex, and gambling.

"Gunboat Jack," I said, "may I introduce you to the best Manager a person can have? His name is Jesus Christ. If you follow His instructions, you can land a knockout blow to the devil every time."

We went on talking in these terms until we reached our destination. Not until 17 years later did I see Gunboat Jack again. He was old now, and sitting on a stool on a busy sidewalk in Bangalore, with a New Testament in his hand, witnessing to people as they passed by. I went up to him, put out my hand, and said, "Gunboat Jack, how are you?"

He looked up at me somewhat quizzically and said, "Your face sho' look familiar. I think I've met you before."

I smiled and said, "Mighty tough opponent you got there!"

Suddenly he made the connection. "Oh!" he exclaimed, "are you the one I met on the train a long time ago and you talked to me about the ring of life?"

"Yes, I'm the one," I replied. "I've never forgotten our conversation."

"Well," he answered slowly, "I want to tell you something. At the time I didn't pay too much attention to what you said. But a few years later, after I had wasted all my fortune, I hit rock bottom. I was desperate. Then I suddenly remembered what you had said about Jesus being the greatest Manager in the ring of life. So I knelt then and there and surrendered my life to Him. Now the greatest joy I have is telling others about Him."

Some years later I was traveling by plane from Dallas to Atlanta, when I started a conversation with the very attractive young girl seated by my side. She had long, blonde hair and was wearing a miniskirt.

I asked her, "Where are you going?"

"To Atlanta," she replied. "Where are you going?"

"To Lexington via Atlanta," I answered.

Then I asked her what kind of work she was doing. I noticed that she was reluctant to tell me, so I prompted her a few times. "Are you a student in college? . . . Are you a secretary in an office?"

Each time she answered in the negative. Finally, somewhat embarrassed, she said, "I'm a go-go girl in a nightclub in Atlanta."

I put out my hand and said, "Shake! I'm a go-go boy."

She looked surprised. "Go-go boy? That's something new. Which nightclub do you work in?"

"Oh," I said, "our operation has branches all over the world." I kept her guessing for a while, and finally I said, "Let me explain what kind of a go-go boy I am. I am a follower of Jesus Christ; He's my Boss. And He has commanded all His disciples to 'go into all the world, and preach the gospel to every creature.' He has commanded us to go and disciple all nations. This means every follower of Christ is a go-go boy or a go-go girl. We're all on the 'go' for Christ." Then I went on to tell her about Christ and His claims. I've never seen the girl since then, but I hope that simple witness, along the line of her interest, found a way into her heart.

As witnesses for Christ we need to cultivate the art of sharing the Good News through the avenue of people's interests and vocabulary.

*b. Common needs and problems.* As has already been pointed out in the heart-to-heart approach, one of the major points of contact for the presentation of the gospel is to be found in needs and problems that are common to all men.

A seminary professor had just boarded a plane and was fastening his seat belt for takeoff, when he noticed the passenger by his side reach down, open up his briefcase, take out a small bottle of whiskey, and take a few sips from it. The man realized that his fellow traveler was watching, so he explained with some embarrassment: "When we get up in the air and the plane begins to bounce around, a few sips of this stuff helps me to stay calm."

Immediately the professor reached down, opened up his briefcase, took out a copy of the New Testament, and said to the man: "When we get up in the air and the plane starts to bounce around, I open up this book and read, 'Fear not, I am with you . . . my peace I give unto you.'"

The man's response was quite unexpected. He said rather sheepishly, "Quite a big difference, isn't it?"

This provided a good opening for the seminary professor to give witness to the comforting and sustaining presence of Christ in his life.

Another illustration comes from a conversation which took place in a coffee shop in a Chicago hotel. A minister was finishing his breakfast when a man slid onto the stool beside him and nervously ordered "some rolls and a cup of coffee." Then, "Did you see that headline?" the stranger asked, pointing to a bold streamer across the morning paper: "Air Crash Kills 52." "I'm supposed to catch a plane for Los Angeles this noon, and frankly, I'm scared stiff. If I didn't have to be there for a meeting in the morning, I'd cancel my ticket and take the 'Chief.'"

As they sipped their coffee, they exchanged a few words on the relative safety of travel by air and by train. The minister also had a plane reservation for Buffalo, and he intended to use it.

"Well, I guess it's all in the way you look at it," mused the stranger. "When your number's up, it's up."

The minister looked at the frightened man a moment and then replied, "Yes, I suppose so. But I happen to know the Man who puts the numbers up."

The stranger put his cup down as though he were afraid he might drop it. Could this man be joking? But before he could bring himself to ask, the minister continued: "You see, the Man who puts the numbers up happens to be my Father." Then he went on to tell the stranger of the loving care of the Heavenly Father, who has promised to keep him in all his ways. Both he and his "number" are in the Father's hand—and his number will not be "up" until his Father puts it there.

With the help of the Holy Spirit we must discover the fears, the hurts, and the longings of people whom we meet, and try to speak to their particular needs out of the Word of God.

*c. Common religious ideas.* This is where we look for ideas and practices in the other religions that are similar to those in the Christian faith, to use as bridgeheads for the presentation of the gospel.

Some years ago an Indian lay evangelist, who was a good friend of mine, and I were traveling on the train together. The third passenger in the small compartment happened to be a Muslim merchant. During the day I noticed that whenever the regular time for prayer arrived—five times a day for a Muslim—the man got out his prayer rug, spread it on the floor of the train, and went through his prayer ritual from the Koran. Meanwhile my evangelist friend and I had completed our morning devotions with a reading from the Bible and silent prayer. When the Muslim passenger had finished his third prayer time for the day, I said to him:

"Friend, I see you are a very religious man. You believe in prayer and keep the prayer time very faithfully. We Christians also believe in the importance of prayer. Can you please share with my friend and me what prayer means to you?"

Without hesitation he replied: "I must honestly say that all this praying doesn't mean much to me. It is just a routine that I do out of a sense of duty."

Then I said, "May I share with you what prayer means to me?" On receiving his consent, I proceeded to explain how there was a time in my life when prayer was just a dry ritual. "I, too, prayed as a matter of duty. But then I came to know God as my personal Savior and Lord, and since then prayer has taken on new meaning. It is like a son talking to his father. When I pray, I feel His presence very near." I even gave one or two illustrations how God had answered prayer in a definite way. My evangelist friend also gave a similar witness. The Muslim passenger listened with keen interest as the two of us went on from the subject of prayer to that of a personal experience with God through Christ.

In this case the common practice of prayer became our point of contact for the gospel.

Rev. Dr. Marshall Murphree, veteran missionary to Rhodesia, has pointed out some of the valuable points of contact in the beliefs of the Shona tribe, who are animists by religion. In the first place, these people are monotheists and believe in a supreme God, the Creator, whom they call *Mwari*. The Christian messenger needs only to put a full biblical content into their concept of God, and to emphasize His redemptive love for sinners and His involvement in the daily affairs of men. In addition, the Shona people have a legend that at one time God walked and talked with man, but man became so evil that one evening God crossed the river, walked off, and left him stranded. The good news of the gospel at this point is that God came back across the river in the person of Jesus Christ and seeks to reconcile man to himself.

Then again, the Shona concept of mediatorship is a helpful point. They believe that the spirits of the first men who died became the mediators between God and man. They need to be told that a mediator indeed is necessary, but "there is one mediator between

God and men, the man Christ Jesus, who gave himself as a ransom for all" (1 Tim. 2:5-6).

Finally, in the Shona idea of spirit possession there is a splendid basis for the teaching of the infilling of the Holy Spirit. For people who believe that it is possible for an outside, evil spirit to possess them and bring .harm to them, causing them to do things they ordinarily would not do, it is relatively easy for them to understand how the benign Spirit of God can live within them, bring only good to them, and cause them to walk in ways of righteousness. In fact, this may be easier for the Shona in Rhodesia to accept than the agnostic in some Western country.

There is just one word of caution that needs to be given in regard to the point-of-contact approach. Be sure that the similarity is genuine. Often what seems like a real counterpart may, on closer examination, turn out to be superficial. For example, it is true that the Hindus believe in the idea of incarnation—in fact they talk about 10 incarnations—but the nature and purpose of incarnation may be entirely different from that of Christ's incarnation. In the various incarnations of Hinduism, one is in the form of a fish, another a tortoise, another a wild boar, and still another half animal and half human (the lion-man). Furthermore, the *purpose* of incarnation is to destroy the wicked and preserve the righteous. All this is far removed from the biblical incarnation.

Aside from this, however, the point-of-contact approach, when used selectively and wisely, can be a very effective method of communicating the Christian message.

### 3. The Antithesis Approach

This is directly opposite to the point-of-contact approach, for it seeks to find the contrasts, rather than the similarities, in Christianity and the other religions. Such an approach is logical, for if the Christian faith is a unique revelation, in a class by itself, then we would expect to find many points of antithesis between the gospel and the world religions.

As illustrations of such points of contrast we may cite the following:

*a.* In contrast to gods who punish arbitrarily and evil spirits that molest and destroy, there is the revelation of the Heavenly Father who cares deeply, loves unconditionally, and desires only our good.

*b.* In contrast to the desperate, continuous seeking for God which we find among many religious devotees, there is the biblical revelation that God is seeking *us* so beautifully portrayed in the parables of the lost sheep and the lost coin.

*c.* According to the Hindu concept of Karma every man "must eat the fruit of his deeds." Technically there is no possibility of forgiveness. According to the Scriptures, "If we confess our sins, [God] is faithful and just, and will forgive our sins and cleanse us from all unrighteousness" (1 John 1:9).

*d.* In contrast to Krishna, the playboy of Hindu mythology, who sported with the milkmaids and stole butter from a housewife, there stands the spotless, holy Son of God, "who in every respect has been tempted as we are, yet without sin" (Heb. 4:15).

*e.* According to Hindu scriptures, the purpose of any incarnation is "the destruction of the wicked and the protection of the good" (Bhagavad Gita 4:7-8). As to the purpose of His coming into the world, Jesus said very clearly: "The Son of man came to seek and to save the lost . . . I came not to call the righteous, but sinners" (Luke 19:10; Matt. 9:13).

The antithesis approach has the advantage of forcefulness, for such marked, striking contrasts reveal the uniqueness of the gospel and grip the minds of the listeners. One can almost feel the impact upon those who hear these truths for the first time.

However, here again we must sound a note of caution. In using this method, it is wise for the Christian messenger not to verbally point out the contrast, but merely to present the distinctive truth of the gospel in a positive manner and allow the listeners to make the contrast in their own minds. For example, we don't need to say, "Krishna was immoral, but Jesus was perfectly holy." It is enough to present the holiness of Christ, and people will readily see that He is utterly different. We don't need to come right out and say: "Your gods punish you with disease and are to be feared, but our God is a God of love and desires only your good." Simply present the compassion, the concern, the love of God, and that will speak for itself. We don't need to say: "In your religion there is no place for forgiveness; in Christianity there is." It is sufficient to describe how Jesus forgave the prostitute, the paralytic, the thief on the cross, and boldly announce God's offer of forgiveness by quoting many of His promises. In other words, the contrasts have to be presented in such a way as not to belittle the beliefs of the listeners and thus arouse their ill feelings. They must be presented in a tactful, positive manner.

*     *     *

The three methods that we have discussed are not mutually exclusive but are complementary to each other. All three may be used in any given sermon. Throughout the message there will be the underlying heart-to-heart approach, talking to people as people, relating the gospel to basic human needs and problems. In the beginning we can use the point-of-contact approach, meeting the listeners on common ground, using concepts that are familiar to them. Then we can employ the antithesis approach, carefully pointing out the unique truths of the gospel in a positive manner, and confronting the listeners with the radical claims of the Savior. The three approaches will blend into each other, reinforce each other, and provide variety and forcefulness in our communication of the truth.

# 6

# Preparation for Communication

Effective communication of the gospel requires adequate preparation. Communication is not a separate and isolated entity, but is dependent upon certain antecedents. There are four areas in particular to which the Christian messenger needs to give attention.

## 1. Study the Religion(s) of Your Field

A missionary serving in India will certainly want to be conversant with Hinduism and Islam. Someone serving in Africa should be familiar with traditional religion (animism) and Islam. Those ministering in Southeast Asia and the Orient will be confronted with the Buddhist religion. This study can begin before going to the field and should continue for years to come.

Read a good biography of the founder of the religion (if any), for in the various experiences of the person you may find a clue to the development of his basic concepts. Siddhartha Gautama's obsession with the universal questions of pain and suffering led eventually to the Four Noble Truths of Buddhism. Mohammed's early contacts with Jews and Christians led him to accept certain concepts from the Judeo-Christian system, while the fact that he was illiterate resulted in a distortion of some of the biblical events referred to in the Koran.

Read also the scriptures of the religion, for therein are to be found the basic beliefs and practices. How can one know about Christ and the Christian faith without reading the New Testament? Likewise, how can one really understand Islam unless he reads the Koran; or Hinduism unless he reads the Vedas, Upanishads, and Bhagavad Gita?

Be sure to read a commentary on the religion written by a *follower* of that religion. He speaks from the inside, from personal conviction. Too often we are satisfied with a book on some world religion that is written by a Christian. Though the writer may try to be very objective in his discussion, it is still difficult for him to get to the heart of the other religion.

Learn about the deities, the feasts and festivals, rituals, and modes of worship. Non-Christians are usually quite willing to answer questions about such matters, when they realize we are sincerely seeking information about their beliefs and practices.

Also try to discern the "spirit" of the religion and the goal it seeks. Is there an underlying spirit of fatalism, fear, or humanism? What is meant by Nirvana, Moksha, or Paradise?

Discover the common ground, the points of contact, differences and contrasts between the religion in question and the Christian faith. What are the elements of truth that can be used as bridgeheads in presenting the gospel? What are the intellectual hang-ups that make it difficult for the adherents of the religion to understand and accept the basic truths of Christianity?

All this is a tough assignment. It will take time and energy and serious study on our part. But for effective communication of the gospel it is very essential.

Perhaps we can benefit from a crucial experience in the career of Dr. Frank Laubach, one of the great missionary statesmen of the 20th century. His first assignment under the Congregational Mission Board was to the island of Mindanao in the Philippines. For 15 years he labored among the fierce Moro people (who are staunch Muslims) with little or no outward results. The people seemed to be indifferent, unfriendly. Tired and discouraged, one evening he climbed up Signal Hill behind the little mission station, and there spent a long time in contemplation and prayer. Suddenly an inner voice seemed to be speaking: "My son, you have failed with these people because you do not really love them. You feel superior to them." In anguish Frank Laubach cried out, "Lord, it's true. I *do* feel superior to these people; I *don't* really love them. Lord, come and change me; make me over." Suddenly he felt as if God were stripping away his prejudice and unloving attitude, and filling him with love for the Moros. He felt he could put his arm around the first Moro that came along and say to him, "God loves you; I love you."

Again the inner voice spoke: "If you want the Moros to be fair to your religion, be fair to theirs. Study the Koran with them."

Frank Laubach walked down the hill with a whole new attitude toward the Moros and his work. On the way he passed some
Moro priests and saw the usual hatred in their eyes. Following an
inner impulse, he called out to them, "I want to study your Koran.
Will you teach me?" The priests looked at him in amazement.

One said, "I think he wants to become a Muslim." The next day
a group of priests from all around Lake Lanao called at Rev. Laubach's home, each armed with a Koran. As they filled the room and
began to talk freely, he realized that at last the barrier had been
broken.

This experience was the turning point in Frank Laubach's ministry. He began to look around for ways and means to help the Moros.
He reduced their Maranaw language to writing and within a short
while developed an excellent method for teaching the people how
to read. He trained and employed 20 teachers to conduct adult liter-
acy classes, and soon the Moros were learning to read by the hundreds. Suddenly the missionary discovered that the attitude of the
Moros had changed completely. Their previous animosity and prejudice had melted away. Within a year most of the people in the
province had become his friends. The Moros, including the chiefs,
now started coming to the religious services. When young people
declared their faith in Christ and joined the church, there was no
open opposition even from the priests. And it all started when Frank
Laubach asked the Moros to teach him the Koran. When he showed
an interest in their faith, and in them as people, they took an interest
in his faith—and in him.[1]

## 2. Seek to Master the Language of the People

For those who are engaged in cross-cultural communication,
command of the language has top priority. Mastery of the language
can spell the difference between effectiveness and ineffectiveness in
the life and work of the missionary. Language is one of his major
tools.

Dr. Eugene Nida of the American Bible Society tells about an
area of South America where missionary work had gone on for more
than 30 years, with more than 20 different missionaries serving at
different times. In all these years not one of the missionaries had
learned to speak the Indian language with any degree of intelligi-
bility. In fact, only 1 missionary made any marked effort to do so.
The result was that not more than 16 Indians were said to be converted, and more than half of these reverted to their old beliefs.

Dr. Nida comments: "If a culture cannot and does not transmit its own concepts except by language, how can missionaries expect to inculcate wholly foreign concepts without using the only language which the people really understand?"[2]

Command of the language is necessary in order to understand people, for language is the key to their *mind*. It reveals the way they think, reason, and feel. Language is also necessary to get close to people; it is the key to their *heart*. One of the best ways to feel at home with people and to love them is to learn their mother tongue. Finally, language is essential to effectively communicate the gospel; it is the key to the *soul* of a people. A missionary is essentially a man with a message to proclaim. This gospel, while it seems so simple to most of us, contains many ideas which are absolutely foreign and strange to those who have never heard it. These ideas are revolutionary in their nature and also in the results which they effect in the lives of those who accept them. It is of utmost importance, therefore, that a missionary become thoroughly familiar with the language of a people in order that he may put before them, as simply and as clearly as possible, those great truths of divine love and grace. The message of the Cross is best communicated in the thought forms of the people, in their idioms, and their proverbs. We have to find those words that convey best the Christian concepts we want to declare.

Robert Moffatt (1795-1883), pioneer missionary in southern Africa, discovered this fact early in his ministry among the Bechuana people at Kuruman. At first it was slow work to find the way into their minds and consciences. A revolution took place when Moffatt was led to realize that the only key was the language of the people. For some years he had made use of Cape Dutch, which was understood by some of the men but none of the women. Mastering the Tswana language was a formidable task for Moffatt. It was an unwritten language, and he was without training in linguistics. He first had to catch the sounds, then reduce them to writing, then master a wholly unknown grammar, and finally discover the proper vocabulary for Bible translation. But he persisted, and by 1857 the Bible translation had been completed and seen through his own press. "More important still, once the language had been learned, the attitude of the people toward him seemed completely to change; the Gospel began to take hold, something like a religious revival broke out, and the first baptisms took place in 1859."[3]

Recently I conducted a study tour in India for seminary students, and one day we visited a typical village to observe rural life in the country. For the noon meal we were guests in the home of a well-to-do Christian farmer. After a sumptuous meal we were resting in the shade of some mango trees in the backyard. Alongside the home was a path which led to a nearby village, and people were coming and going. After some time I noticed that a good number of people had gathered along the path, sitting on their haunches, gazing down at us. At first I thought: "These village people have never seen so many white Americans at one time, so they are watching us out of curiosity."

But then our host said to me, "Do you know why these people are watching us? They have heard you speaking to me fluently in the Kanarese language, and they are simply fascinated. Why don't you go up to them and say a few words to them in Kanarese. It will please them greatly."

So I went over to them and said, "I understand you speak the same language I do." They nodded with a smile. "It's a beautiful language, isn't it?" They smiled even more. Then I joked with them briefly and they responded with laughter. Finally I said to them, "You know, I am a religious preacher and I love to talk about my faith. If you agree, I will be glad to share something about the Person I worship." On receiving their assent, I proceeded to preach Christ to them for about half an hour. No one moved. They listened with keen interest, and when I finished they heartily thanked me. Now that never would have been possible if I had not known their language. But when they heard me speaking in Kanarese, they listened gladly. This was the key to their heart.

## 3. Seek to Identify with the People

Identification is absolutely essential for effective communication. Our Lord himself is the supreme example in this regard. "Though he was in the form of God, [He] did not count equality with God a thing to be grasped, but emptied himself, taking the form of a servant, being born in the likeness of men. And being found in human form he humbled himself and became obedient unto death, even death on a cross" (Phil. 2:6-8).

Jesus identified completely with our humanity. He identified with our poverty: He was born in a stable and had no place to lay His head. He identified with our toil: He worked at a carpenter's bench. He identified with our physical needs: He was often hungry and thirsty. He identified with our temptations: He "was in all points tempted like as we are" (Heb. 4:15, KJV). He identified with our trials: He was misunderstood, rejected, and ill-treated. Jesus identified himself with the suffering and sin of humanity. He was called "a man of sorrows, and acquainted with grief" (Isa. 53:3). He was baptized by John the Baptist along with sinners. He became sin on our behalf and died on the Cross between two thieves.

Jesus also identified himself with the culture of His own people. Though He was fully a Jew, He did not share their bigotry and narrow-mindedness. In view of all this, it is no wonder that when Jesus spoke, the people said of Him, "No man ever spoke like this man!" (John 7:46).

The apostle Paul was a very effective communicator of the gospel because he also identified himself so closely with the people whom he served. He describes in detail the extent of his identification in writing to the church at Corinth:

> For though I am free from all men, I have made myself a slave to all, that I might win the more. To the Jews I became as a Jew, in order to win Jews; to those under the law I became as one under the law—though not being myself under the law—that I might win those under the law. To those outside the law I became as one outside the law—not being without law toward God but under the law of Christ—that I might win those outside the law. To the weak I became weak, that I might win the weak. I have become all things to all men, that I might by all means save some (1 Cor. 9:19-22).

In the same way, the effective communicator of the gospel must identify himself with the people to whom he ministers. He must become one of them, so that he might be aware of their ideas, understand their viewpoints, and be genuinely sympathetic with their struggles for self-expression, even though he may not condone its forms. He must identify himself with the people's trials and sufferings, with their longings and needs. He should adapt to the culture of the people, not necessarily in all externals, but certainly in inner mind and spirit. The receptor must be convinced that the messenger understands his—the receptor's—background and has respect for his views even though he may not agree with them.

In striving to identify ourselves with people, our aim is to achieve a feeling of togetherness or oneness. This is not simply a meeting of ideas but a meeting of persons. It is more than contact; it is communion. It is a feeling of at-homeness, so that we feel we belong to the country and the people. Then we are no longer outsiders or spectators; instead we become insiders or participants, so that mutual insight and sharing of mental states become possible.

Identification is more than mere sympathy. This can be just an expression of a kind of paternalistic superiority. True identification goes beyond sympathy to empathy, where we put ourselves in the place of the other person and try to discover his thoughts and feelings. Empathy is the capacity to enter understandingly and sympathetically into the lives of people, so that they cease to be mere audiences or classes to be helped, and we begin to value them as individuals.

Identification is essential to communication, for the Good News is not an intangible something, but is wrapped up in a person. Effective communication involves the proper relationship between messenger and hearer. Unless the listener accepts the messenger as a person, it is unlikely he will accept his message.

Identification does not come all at once. It must be developed and cultivated through actual participation in shared experiences. By mingling with people, visiting in their homes, making their friendship, learning their language, and being "one with them" in heart and mind, the missionary may achieve identification to a large degree.

A missionary in India was invited by a small group of low-caste people to share with them the message of the Christian faith. They were very poor people who lived in simple mud huts. On the appointed day the missionary gathered with about 12 adults in one of their homes. A water buffalo and some chickens were in one corner of the room; there was little or no ventilation, and only a small oil lamp which provided faint light. The floor of the hut was dried cow manure. The missionary sat on a mat on the floor with the group and patiently shared with them the story of Christ and the meaning of the gospel. After several visits and much prayer, the little group trusted in Christ as their Savior and received Christian baptism. A church was born!

Some time later, on one occasion when the missionary was visiting these new converts, one of the men said to him, "Missionary, do you know why we listened so attentively to your words when you first came to us? It was not just what you told us that caught our attention, though the story of Christ was very wonderful and touched our hearts. It was the fact that you as a rich American [rich in their eyes] were willing to come into our humble homes, sit on the dirt floor, eat our meager food, and make yourself at home with us, that really convinced us that what you were saying was true and caused us to listen with a whole heart."

Only then did the missionary realize how important it is to "become all things to all men" in order that he might win some.

### 4. Try to Be a Good Listener

It is important to listen as well as to communicate. Both in the ministry and in missionary work it is usual for the religious professional to do most of the talking. Too often the preacher regards himself as solely the intermediary of a superior message from God. He has gone forth to tell the people the truth, not to listen to other people's ideas about the truth. He says to himself, "I have the truth; let them listen to me." If this attitude is pushed to the extreme, the message will inevitably be irrelevant. Even though it may be true, it does not reach its receptor.

As messengers of God, do we have any right to expect others to listen to us when we are not willing to listen to them? We must first win the right to speak.

A missionary in China was once asked to visit a leading man in a village who was notoriously anti-Christian. He was a confirmed Confucianist and a notable scholar of the Chinese classics, but bitter in his opposition to the newly established Christian congregation in his village. The missionary did his best to get in a few words of testimony; but, to his dismay, his host monopolized the whole conversation, all the time criticizing Westerners and Western customs. After about one and one-half hours, the missionary politely bade his host farewell and returned to his room with a sense of utter failure. Nothing, he felt, had been accomplished, nor had the Lord been glorified. The following morning, to his amazement, the friend who had so earnestly requested him to make the call came to see him and jubilantly exclaimed: "That was the best day's preaching that you ever did!" He then went on to say, "Last night the scholar was going all around the village singing your praises to everyone, as a truly great man, because you were so humble and patiently listened to all that he said. He is coming to church tonight to show his appreciation of you publicly."[4]

Then again, how can we as communicators of the gospel fit the message to the specific needs of the listeners, unless we first listen to their beliefs, their aspirations, and their hurts?

During my career as a missionary-evangelist in India, I quickly learned that I should first listen and then preach. If I went to a new village and started preaching straightway, I found all sorts of problems. The people were usually indifferent and stood around with questioning glances as if to say: "Who is this stranger? What is he up to anyway? What's his line of propaganda?" Furthermore, I found that what I said didn't seem to make much impact. I appeared to be off target. But things were different if I first took time to visit the people in their homes and get acquainted with them. So in the morning I would visit the headman of the village, some members of the *panchayat* (the village council), the teachers and students in the local school, and any others who showed signs of friendship. A lot of questions were asked back and forth, and in this way much prejudice and suspicion were dispelled in the minds of the village people.

By afternoon I felt I had a good degree of rapport with them. I was no longer a stranger; I was a guest in their midst. But more than this, by carefully listening to what the people talked about, I was able to discover their hurts, their sorrows, their longings, and their problems. Then when I stood before the group to preach in the evening, I was able to emphasize those facets of the gospel which spoke most clearly to their situation and needs. By the look on people's faces, I could see that the message was hitting home.

Not only is it necessary for the messenger to listen *before* he preaches, but also *after* he preaches, in order to make sure that his listeners have correctly understood the message. Effective communication is not just in one direction, from speaker to receptor. There must be what is commonly known as "social feedback," from hearer to speaker, or the results may be disastrous. In war, for example, the general must know not only how to give orders to his men; he must also know how the troops are faring, or his orders are likely to result in bungling tragedies. Orders must go out, but information must be fed back continuously. In like manner, the Christian communicator must be aware of how the message is faring in order to make any necessary corrections or adjustments.

A friend of mine, who is serving with Wycliffe Bible Translators in Mexico, has been translating the New Testament into one of the Aztec Indian dialects. When he completed the Third Epistle of John, he read the verses back to the informant to check the accuracy of his translation. When the missionary read the first verse—"John writes to the beloved Gayo . . ."—there was a puzzled look on the face of the Indian. "Why," he asked, "was John writing to a chicken?" Only then did the missionary discover that "gayo" means "chicken" in that particular dialect. So he had to change the translation to "John writes to a man called Gayo," which was perfectly all right, for the Aztecs often give animal names to people.

By studying the religion of the area, learning the language, identifying with the people in their particular situation, and by practicing the art of listening, the Christian messenger can more adequately prepare himself as an effective communicator of truth.

# 7

# Basic Principles of Communicating the Gospel

Having discussed several practical suggestions to guide us in preparation for communication, we now come to certain basic principles in the actual presentation of the gospel. Though we are relating the discussion to ministry among non-Christians, these principles indeed have universal value and can be followed in ministering to nominal Christians as well. What, then, are these basic principles?

## 1. Be Simple In the Presentation

The necessity for clear communication is especially true when we are preaching or witnessing to simple, rural people. To the educated philosopher, a more sophisticated approach may be justified. But in general, when dealing with those who have little or no background in Christian teaching, we should begin by presenting the simple, basic facts of the gospel. We should avoid heavy theology and profound exposition. All this might be very helpful for mature Christians who are in the Way, but most inappropriate for those who have not yet entered the Way. If we study carefully the preaching method of Jesus, we note that He used primarily the storytelling method, and He took His illustrations from common, everyday life. He talked about the shepherd and his sheep, the flowers and the grass, doors and roads, rivers and wells, water and food, trees and fruit, buildings and foundations.

Several years ago an article appeared in *World Vision* magazine, entitled "Lessons to Be Learned from the New Religions of Japan." At the top of the list of five lessons was this: we need a more simple message for the people—less theology. And third on the list was the need to relate the Christian message to practical living. The writer suggested that one of the reasons the new religions are growing rapidly was the fact that their teachings are simple, easy to understand, and easy to follow. At the same time he suggested that one of the reasons for the slow growth of the Church in Japan is that much of the preaching in the congregations is centered on doctrinal matters and above the heads of the people. Thus the exhortation for a simple message, related to the needs of the listeners![1]

It was my privilege many times to hear Dr. E. Stanley Jones proclaim the gospel to a group of educated, high-caste Hindus in India. He usually employed philosophical and psychological concepts in his approach to such an elite audience. But when I heard him preach to a group of common people on one occasion, his approach was entirely different. I shall never forget his simple, yet effective outline. Each major point spoke directly to the religious and social background of the hearers. Speaking on the subject "Who Is a Christian?" these were the points he emphasized:

A Christian is one who:
(1) Believes in one God—not many gods
(2) Believes in one brotherhood—worldwide
(3) Believes in one Savior—Jesus Christ
(4) Has one object in life—to glorify Christ
(5) Believes in one chance—here and now in this life

Those people understood what Brother Stanley was talking about and felt the impact of his message.

We need to return to the simplicity and clarity of the New Testament gospel which the early disciples proclaimed. Dr. John R. W. Stott, one of England's leading Bible teachers, suggests that the disciples' Good News contained at least five basic elements.[2]

(1) The Gospel Events: the death and resurrection of Jesus (Luke 1:1; 24:14, 18; 1 Cor. 15:3-5). These were historical events, but more, they were saving events. "Christ died for our sins" (the divine purpose), and He "was raised again for our justification" (the divine vindication; see Rom. 4:25).

(2) The Gospel Witnesses: the evidence to which the apostles appealed for the authentication of their message. This consisted of the Old Testament Scriptures, whose prophecies were fulfilled in

Christ, and in the personal firsthand testimony of the apostles, which later came to be recorded in the New Testament (Acts 1:8; 2:32; 3:15; 5:32; 10:39-42).

(3) The Gospel Affirmations: that Jesus is Savior with authority to forgive sin and bestow salvation. And He is Lord with authority to demand submission (Acts 5:31; Phil. 2:9-11). The early Christians emphasized not simply what Christ *did* back there, but what He *is* today. The historical Christ is the contemporary Christ.

(4) The Gospel Promises: note Peter's sermon on the Day of Pentecost. In the name of Christ he offered remission of sins and the gift of the Holy Spirit—forgiveness of the past and a new life in the present through the indwelling presence of the Spirit (Acts 2:38).

(5) The Gospel Demands: repentance and faith. The disciples called upon men to turn away from their sins and to commit their lives totally to Christ (Acts 3:19; 16:31). And in all this there was a note of urgency—"now!" (Acts 17:30).

## 2. Be Positive in the Preaching

It is so easy for the Christian messenger, both at home and abroad, to fall into the trap of emphasizing the prohibitions of the gospel—"Thou shalt not kill. Thou shalt not commit adultery. Thou shalt not steal," and so on (Exod. 20:13-15). Often he is prone to add to these biblical prohibitions his own cultural taboos—Thou shalt not dance, Thou shalt not play pool, Thou shalt not go to the movies, etc. And so the gospel is interpreted primarily as a series of negations.

In his book *The Dynamics of Church Growth*, Bishop J. Waskom Pickett describes how, early in his missionary career in India, he learned the hard way the danger of presenting the Christian faith in negative terms.

A group of low-caste leather-workers asked him to visit their village and explain Christianity to them. Some of their Hindu relatives had recently become Christians and were urging them to do likewise. When Rev. Pickett arrived at the appointed place, he found some 50 men and women gathered to hear him. He spoke for more than an hour, entirely in negative terms. Disciples of Jesus should not worship idols, should not drink liquor, should not gamble, should not eat the flesh of animals that had died of old age or disease. The speech dealt with all the harmful practices of the leather-workers of that area. The writer comments, "It gave good advice, but it was not the gospel."

When the speech was finished, a Hindu priest, who was serving as a spiritual advisor to the community, asked if he might say a few words. On obtaining permission, he said to the group: "All along I have told you you should not do the things that the missionary has mentioned. But I go even further than he does. I tell you not to eat the flesh of any animal. I tell you also not to eat tomatoes or beets because they are red like blood. I tell you not to eat eggs or eggplants." In this way the Hindu priest greatly added to the missionary's list of prohibitions.

Bishop Pickett confesses he had made a terrible blunder. He had failed completely to present Christ and the gospel to those inquiring, needy people. How disappointed they must have been! Finally he comments: "Christians dare not reduce the Gospel to a body of denials. The Church of Christ cannot compete with Hinduism, Buddhism, or even many animistic religions in denials and prohibitions; but no man-made religions can compete with the Gospel of Christ in the richness and power and the glory of its affirmations about God and man and life."[3] It was two years later, after many visits and much hard work, that Rev. Pickett was granted the privilege of baptizing nearly the entire company of those leather-workers and of receiving them into the fellowship of the church.

There is a tale told of a missionary in a dark corner of Africa, where the men had a habit of filing their teeth to sharp points. The missionary was hard at work trying to convert a tribal chief. Now the chief was very old, and the missionary was very Old Testament. His version of Christianity leaned heavily on "thou shalt nots." The African listened patiently.

"I do not understand," he said at last. "You tell me that I must not take my neighbor's wife."

"That's right," said the missionary.

"Or his ivory, or his oxen."

"Quite right."

"And I must not dance the war dance and then ambush him on the trail and kill him."

"Absolutely right."

"But I cannot do any of these things," said the chief regretfully. "I am too old. To be old and to be a Christian—they are one and the same thing!"

As Christian messengers we should carefully avoid such a negative presentation of the gospel. Instead, we should emphasize the magnificent affirmations and promises of our Lord. This is the "good news" we must proclaim.

A further piece of good advice to the Christian preacher is this: Don't argue—witness! You may win the argument but lose the man. Remember, your objective is to win people, not arguments. You are not primarily a lawyer advocating a case for Christianity; you are a witness testifying to the great truths of the gospel.

I shall never forget how Dr. Frank Stanger, president of Asbury Theological Seminary, introduced Dr. Robert Mayfield to a large congregation at a ministers' conference several years ago. Dr. Mayfield previously had been a lawyer by profession but at that time was serving as general secretary of the Board of Lay Activities of the United Methodist church. In introducing the speaker, Dr. Stanger said: "Perhaps the effectiveness of Dr. Mayfield lies in the fact that he was once lawyer but has now turned witness. And perhaps the ineffectiveness of many of us preachers lies in the fact that we are supposed to be witnesses but have become lawyers."

How true! Too often we are engaged in pleading the case rather than proclaiming the Christ.

On several occasions I heard Dr. E. Stanley Jones describe his first experience in preaching. He had recently been converted when he was asked to preach in his home church in Baltimore at the Wednesday evening prayer service. He worked many hours in preparation. With the use of concordance and commentary he wrote out his sermon and then proceeded to memorize it. When he got up, in fear and trembling, to present his sermon, everything went smoothly for the first few sentences. Then he stumbled over the word *indifferentism*, and a couple of girls in the audience started giggling. This upset Brother Stanley, and suddenly his mind went blank. He stood there for two or three minutes, trying to recall his sermon, but to no avail. So he said to the congregation rather dejectedly: "Well, friends, I am sorry to tell you, but I've forgotten my sermon." Then he proceeded to walk down from the pulpit and take his place in the congregation.

But as he walked, the inner Voice said to him: "Stanley, haven't I done anything for you?"

He replied, "Yes, of course You have."

"Then couldn't you tell that?"

"Perhaps I could." So instead of taking his seat, he came around in front of the altar and said: "Friends, as you see, I can't preach, but the Lord has done something for me and I want to tell you about that." As a result of his personal witness a young man was converted that evening. He became a minister, and later his daughter became a missionary to Africa.

In describing the incident, Brother Stanley would say: "That was a dramatic turn for me. As a lawyer for God, putting up His case, I was a failure. As a witness for God, telling what He had done for me, I was a success. As in a flash I saw my calling: I was to be a witness."[4] In due time, Brother Stanley turned out to be one of the greatest preachers of his day, but first and always he was a witness to God's redeeming grace. And so are we!

When giving our witness, we must make sure that our witness is relevant to the religious and cultural background of the hearers. To get up in a midweek prayer service and say: "Dear friends, I want to testify to the fact that Christ has saved and sanctified me," might be meaningful in some quarters—enough to evoke a few hearty "Amens"; but in other settings it might be absolutely meaningless. Perhaps putting it this way: "Christ has changed my habits and cleaned me up on the inside," might be more effective among people who have little or no theological background or are biblically illiterate.

Now if this principle is valid when witnessing to people who live in a nominally Christian country and yet are different in their environmental background, how much more valid it is when we are seeking to minister to people of a totally different religious and cultural background.

In witnessing to Hindu audiences in India, I have discovered that one of the most effective ways of telling what Christ has done for me is to testify to the fact that He has given me His *shanti* or peace. Everyone in India is seeking *shanti,* and to point to Christ as the *shanti-dayaka* or Giver of peace, is a most meaningful and attractive concept to the Hindu. Jesus stated very clearly: "Peace I leave with you; my peace I give to you: not as the world gives do I give to you" (John 14:27).

To those of an animistic background, who live in dread fear of all the evil spirits around them, pointing to Christ as the Conqueror of all evil spirits and as the One who can deliver us from fear, is indeed the essence of the "good news." In the Gospel narratives Jesus said, "Fear not," more often than He said, "Sin not."

Another effective approach to the people of India is to present Christ as the great Burden-bearer. It is a common sight to see people carrying heavy burdens on their heads: everything from a single *coolie* (porter) carrying two or three suitcases along the railway station platform, to a group of four men or women carrying an upright piano down the street.

As a result you see many tired people, sleeping on the hard stone pavement or under trees, or on the station platform. They are so exhausted that they are oblivious of the hardness of the pavement or the noise all around them. To such people we can talk about the heavy burden of sin and how Jesus promises to all: "Come to me, all who labor and are heavy laden, and I will give you rest" (Matt. 11:28).

In India people send their dirty clothes to the *dhobi*, the washerman, who dips an article of clothing into a stream, rubs it with soap (when he has soap!) then beats the clothes on a stone slab. I shall never forget how a Canadian missionary, preaching in a jungle camp meeting, took his wool scarf and beat it on the ground over and over again as he described how his sins had been washed away at the stream of Calvary. He went down the list—jealousy, anger, resentment, hypocrisy, deceit, lust, etc. You could almost see the sins floating downstream as he beat the ground with his scarf. Nobody went to sleep during that illustration!

### 3. Be Christ-centered in the Proclamation

It's not the what-emphasis, but the who-emphasis that is basic; not precepts, but a person; not what we believe, but whom we trust.

A careful study of the New Testament reveals that Christ was central in the evangelistic message of the Early Church. Note the following verses:

> And with great power the apostles gave their testimony to the resurrection of the Lord Jesus *(Acts 4:33)*.
>
> And every day in the temple and at home they did not cease teaching and preaching Jesus as the Christ *(5:42)*.
>
> Then Philip opened his mouth, and beginning with [the] scripture he told him the good news of Jesus *(8:35)*.
>
> And in the synagogues immediately he [Saul] proclaimed Jesus, saying, "He is the Son of God" *(9:20)*.
>
> We preach Christ crucified . . . I decided to know nothing among you except Jesus Christ and him crucified *(1 Cor. 1:23; 2:2)*.

Christianity must be defined as Christ, not the Old Testament, nor Western civilization, not even the system built around him in the

West, but Christ himself; and to be a Christian is to follow Him. Dr. E. Stanley Jones discovered this secret very early in his missionary career. He testified:

> When I first went to India I was trying to hold a very long line—a line that stretched from Genesis to Revelation, on to Western civilization and to the Western Christian Church. I found myself bobbing up and down that line, fighting behind Moses and David and Jesus and Paul and Western civilization and the Christian Church. I was worried. There was no well-defined issue. I found the battle almost invariably being pitched at one of these three places: the Old Testament, or Western civilization, or the Christian Church. I had the ill-defined but instinctive feeling that the heart of the matter was being left out. Then I saw that I could, and should shorten my line, that I could take my stand at Christ and before that non-Christian world refuse to know anything save Jesus Christ and Him crucified. The sheer storm and stress of things had driven me to a place that I could hold. Then I saw that there is where I should have been all the time. I saw that the gospel lies in the person of Jesus, that He Himself is the Good News, that my one task was to live and present Him. My task was simplified—it was vitalized. I found that when I was at the place of Jesus, I was every moment on the vital.[5]

In one of Dr. Jones's meetings, a Jain lawyer, a brilliant writer against Christianity, arose and asked him a long list of questions regarding things in the Old Testament. Dr. Jones replied, "My brother, I think I can answer your questions, but I do not feel called on to do so. I defined Christianity as Christ. If you have any objections to make against Him, I am ready to hear and answer them if I can." The lawyer replied, "Who gave you this authority to make this distinction? What church council gave you this authority?"

Dr. Jones replied that it was no church council but Christ himself who gave it to him, for He himself had said: "Ye have heard it said of old time . . . but I say unto you." So he was simply following his Master's lead, for He made His own word final even in Scripture. He was bringing the battle up from that incomplete stage of revelation to the final—to Jesus. Revelation was progressive, culminating in Him. "Why then should I," asked Dr. Jones, "pitch the battle at an imperfect stage when the perfect was here in Him?" The lawyer saw with dismay that his question was beside the point.[6]

It is Christ that makes the big difference. Just here is the great lack of the non-Christian faiths. There are many fine things in their culture and thought—we readily admit it and thank God in sincerity for them—but the real lack, the lack for which nothing else can atone is just—Christ.

One of the outstanding converts from Hinduism to Christianity in India was a high-caste Brahman named A. C. Chakravarti. Early in life he developed a great desire to find peace. So he carefully studied the Hindu scriptures and even the Koran but was dissatisfied in his heart. Then he turned to asceticism for a period; but finding no peace, he decided to take up business, make as much money as he could, and immerse himself in the comforts and pleasures of the world. Still no peace. Finally, he became a priest in a temple in Vrindaban, one of the sacred cities of the Hindus.

One day Chakravarti heard that a new Christian convert had come to town. Like him, the convert had come out of a high-caste Hindu family. So Chakravarti thought it was his duty to seek out the new Christian and win him back into Hinduism. But every time he brought up an argument, the Christian quoted a verse from the Bible. This frustrated Chakravarti, so he decided to buy a copy of the New Testament and read it, with a view to find its faults and failures. Then alone, he felt, could he meet the Christian on his own ground. But as he read the New Testament, he began to see his sin and need for a Savior. Finally, when he came to John 14:6—"I am the way, and the truth, and the life"—he said to himself, My search is at an end. I have found truth and peace in Jesus Christ. As a result he accepted Christ and was baptized. Then he decided to start an evangelistic center in the same city.

One day Chakravarti walked into the courtyard of the Hindu temple and was soon surrounded by some of his priest-friends. They began to fire questions at him: "Tell us, Chakravarti, why have you become a Christian? What is there in Christianity that we as Hindus do not have? We have our sacred books, our great temples, our famous *gurus*, our great system of philosophy and ethics. What is there new in Christianity?"

Chakravarti answered, "My brothers, just one thing. I have found Christ. *He* has made the difference!"

That's it! The difference is Christ. But that makes a world of difference.

A couple of illustrations from the history of Christian missions will suffice to show us the folly of getting off-center in our preaching. When Moravian missionaries first landed in Greenland in 1740 and started preaching to the inhabitants, they felt their first task was to convince them of the existence, the attributes, and the perfection of God, and enforce obedience to the divine law, hoping by this means gradually to prepare their minds for the reception of the sublimer and more mysterious truths of the gospel. Abstractly considered, this approach may appear to be the most rational; but when reduced to practice, it was found wholly ineffectual. For five years the missionaries labored along this line but could scarce obtain a patient hearing from the people. Then they decided in the literal sense of the word to preach "Christ and Him crucified." No sooner did they declare unto the Greenlanders the word of reconciliation in its original simplicity than they began to witness its convicting and converting power. This reached the hearts of the people and produced the most astonishing results. Within a short period, many of the islanders had come to genuine faith in Jesus Christ as Savior, and their lives were changed.[7]

The second illustration comes from the story of the conversion of the Batak people living in the northern part of Sumatra, Indonesia. After a two-year period of explaining the Christian religion by the pioneer Norwegian missionary, Ludwig Nommensen, the old Batak chief told the missionary that the *Adat* or common law of the Batak nation was very similar to the teachings of the Mosaic Ten Commandments and the Sermon on the Mount. "We are in full agreement with what you have told us," he declared. Nommensen then realized that he had failed to make clear the uniqueness of the gospel. Like Paul, he too began to preach Christ and Him crucified. Later the old chief again came to the missionary and said, "Our *Adat* tells us not to steal, lie, commit adultery, and bear false witness, and to treat our neighbors justly; but we do not obey it. We are bad Bataks for we break our own laws. You have for the first time told us of a way by which we can find strength to obey our *Adat*. If Jesus can give us the power to be good Bataks, we want Him as our Master."[8]

Today over a million-and-a-half of the Batak people are disciples of the Lord Jesus, and the Batak church is one of the largest and most indigenous churches in all of Southeast Asia.

The uniqueness of the gospel lies in the person of Jesus Christ and His transforming power. We are effective communicators only when we center our message around Him.

## 4. Be Christlike in Demonstrating the Gospel

The missionary himself is part of the message. Effective communication is more than mere verbal enunciation of the truth with good words; it is always a vital demonstration of the truth with good works.

Professor Radhakrishnan, the brilliant Hindu exponent, once said, "It seems to me you Christians are an *ordinary* group of people, making *extraordinary* claims." In one sense he was absolutely right, for we Christians are just an ordinary group of people—at best, sinners saved by grace—pointing to a unique Savior. But what he really meant was that the lives of most people who call themselves Christians are not much better than those of other religious adherents, and yet we make such fantastic claims about the saving power of Jesus Christ. There is enough truth in this indictment to make us wince.

Dr. E. Stanley Jones said that India's attack on the gospel has gone through three stages. First the people said, "It isn't *true.*" Then they began to say, "It isn't *new.* What you have in Christianity we also have in essence in our religion." Today they say, "It isn't *you.*" That is, "You Christians profess one thing but practice another." And this, we must confess, is the most serious attack of all.

Dr. Eugene Nida, expert translator of the Bible, has put it very succinctly:

> All divine communication is essentially incarnational, for it comes not only in words, but in life. Even if a truth is given only in words, it has no real validity until it has been translated into life. Only then does the Word of life become life to the receptor. The words are in a sense nothing in and of themselves. Even as wisdom is emptiness unless lived out in behavior, so the Word is void unless related to experience. In the incarnation of God in Jesus Christ, the Word (expression and revelation of the wisdom of God) became flesh. This same fundamental principle has been followed throughout the history of the church, for God has constantly chosen to use not only words but human beings as well to witness to His grace; not only the message, but the messenger; not only the Bible, but the church.[9] *pg 226*

The message of the Old Testament is presented more by demonstration than by definition. When speaking of faith, it does not seek to define faith in so many words, but causes a man of faith, Abraham, to pass before our eyes as an illustration of the nature and power of faith. The Old Testament doesn't define courage and obedience but tells us about the three Hebrew men in the fiery furnace and about Daniel in the lions' den. It doesn't define purity but paints a life picture of purity in the conduct of Joseph toward Potiphar's wife. And so on down the line.

In the New Testament Christ is presented as the center of our faith, and the central fact about Christ is that He is the Word become flesh. He is the demonstration, the personification of the Christian message. The Gospel writers don't give us a treatise on compassion but describe Jesus ministering to the blind, the lame, the hungry, and the forlorn. Thus we see compassion in action. We find no definition of love, but we hear Jesus crying from the Cross, "Father, forgive them; for they know not what they do" (Luke 23:34). Again we find no essay on purity, but we see Jesus, tempted in all points like we are, yet living a sinless, holy life. We find no definition of power, but we see Jesus standing before an empty tomb, saying, "I am the resurrection and the life; he who believes in me . . . shall never die" (John 11:25-26).

The same is true today. All effective communication is incarnational; it comes not just from the lips but through the life of the preacher. We cannot divorce the message from the messenger. The analogy of the sower and the seed, representing the preacher and the Word, is a good illustration; but it breaks down at one point. The quality of the seed is not affected by the character of the sower. If it is good seed, it will grow, regardless of how the farmer lives. But in the spiritual realm, the quality of the seed depends much on the attitude, the personality, and the character of the sower. Fertility of the soil depends much on the credibility of the sower. The missionary must not only *give* the message, but also *live* the message.

A lady missionary was once preaching to a group of Hindus in an Indian village. The audience listened very attentively, but in the middle of the discourse one of the villagers got up and walked over to the missionary's chauffeur who was standing near her jeep. He spoke briefly with the chauffeur, then came back and took his seat again. He appeared to be even more attentive to the speaker's words than before. The missionary was curious about the whole affair, so asked her chauffeur later what the villager had said to him. The chauffeur replied, "Madam, he told me he was very impressed with the fine things you were saying, but he wanted to know how you treated me as your servant and how you lived at home. I assured him that you are kind and thoughtful and that you live like you preach. That seemed to satisfy him!"

A missionary in Africa was traveling over a rough highway with a Muslim mechanic-helper by his side, when suddenly the car sputtered and came to a stop. The two men were having difficulty trying to start the engine again, when they saw a lorry (truck) coming down the road. They signalled the driver for help, but he waved and shouted tauntingly and sped on down the highway. The missionary's Muslim companion was furious. He shouted curses at the truck driver as he disappeared down the road. Finally the two men were able to repair the car and continued their journey. They had gone only a few miles when they spied the lorry beside the road, stuck in a ditch; the driver and his helper were trying desperately to pull it out.

The Muslim laughed with glee. He said to the missionary, "Now we'll pay them back. We'll wave at them and pass them up. Let's see how they enjoy that!"

The missionary said, "No, we can't do that. Those men are in trouble and we must help them!"

The mechanic was astounded. "What," he exclaimed, "are you going to help those rascals? They don't deserve it."

But the missionary insisted they stop and help. With much hard work they were able to get the lorry out of the ditch. When they continued on their way, the Muslim said to the missionary, "Now I think I understand what you have been trying to tell me all along about your faith. Please tell me more."

There are many people around the world who will never seriously give attention to the Christian message until they witness a demonstration of it in everyday living. They must not only hear the message but see it as well.

### 5. Be Sure to Make the Message Relevant

Effective communication must be geared to the particular needs and conditions of the listener. As Donald Soper of England puts it: "We must begin where people are, rather than where we would like them to be." This of course means that we must take time to understand the needs, hopes, yearnings, fears, longings, and deepest motives of the people to whom we are ministering. We will have to identify with these people, get on their level, listen to their hurts and hopes, and be willing to dialogue with them. Otherwise, to use an appropriate analogy, we may have a strong arrow but be completely off target.

*a.* First, we must relate our message to the specific *needs* of the listener. The emphasis here is *needs,* not *wants.* It is quite evident that most people know what they want, but they may not know what they need. The conscious wants that people express are often merely symptomatic of the unconscious, underlying needs that they possess. So the Christian communicator must probe beyond the outer want to the deeper, inner need.

It is at this point that we are indebted to psychologist Abraham Maslow for providing us with his excellent Hierarchy of Human Motives,[10] in which he has listed, in increasing order of importance, the basic needs of the human family. Though at times he speaks of additional needs, usually they fall into five categories as follows:

(1) Physiological needs
(2) Need for safety
(3) Need for belonging and for love
(4) Need for self-esteem
(5) Need for self-actualization

The basic point in Maslow's theory is that all five of these needs are intrinsic to human personality, but not all of them are dominant at one time, motivating a person's life. It is usually the need that is basically unfilled at the time, that is in the center of consciousness and is currently motivating the individual. No higher-order need will serve as a motivator until the levels below it are satisfied. For example, the hungry man will not be interested in ideological discussions until he has had a good meal. So in seeking to understand people and to communicate to them effectively, we must discover their level of need at the time.

First are the **physiological needs**, the basic bodily desires, such as hunger, thirst, and sleep. If these needs are not met, a person will spend all his energy in seeking to satisfy them; and until these needs are satisfied, he will push into the background other needs that are present in his personality. Our Lord, who was the Master Communicator, was very conscious of these basic needs in the lives of those whom He contacted. He healed the sick and He fed the hungry. Likewise, Christian missions, through its hospitals, orphanages, relief work, and other humanitarian services, has sought to minister to the basic physical needs of people. And often, giving bread has paved the way for offering the Bread of Life.

Next is the **need for safety**—concern about security, and emotional assurance. People desire stability, freedom from fear, anxiety, and chaos. In a world of constant change, and threats of food shortages, unemployment, crime, and war, these needs are very strong. Into this chaotic situation comes the gospel message of the unchanging Christ and the unshakable Kingdom, with its glorious promise of freedom from anxiety and turmoil for those who are "in Christ."

Next in the list of human motivation we find the all-important **need for belonging and love**. Psychologists seem to agree that one of the basic needs of man is to love and be loved. Coupled with this is the desire for meaningful relationships, the desire to relate to some group that will provide identity and fellowship. The common adage,

"Love makes the world go 'round," has more truth in it than we ordinarily recognize. And its counterpart is also true, "The lack of love makes the world go wrong."

A few years ago a woman in Chicago, by a clever ruse, kidnapped the baby of a young couple. When she was arrested a few days later and questioned by the police, she sobbed, "I just wanted something to love." It turned out that she had recently lost her father, her husband, and a baby through miscarriage.

There are hundreds of hippies from affluent homes all across Europe and the United States, who have fled to the beaches of Goa (India) and to the hillsides of Kabul (Afghanistan) and Katmandu (Nepal), primarily because they failed to find love and affection in their home relationships.

The message that "God cares for you; He loves you," when properly communicated by word and life, finds receptive hearts wherever this area of need is keenly felt. When people realize that they are loved unconditionally by One who gave His life for them; and when, out of pure gratitude, they begin to love Him in return, then they find their need to love and be loved gloriously satisfied. When they enter the fellowship of a caring-sharing congregation, and become members of an intimate study-prayer group, they feel they are a part of a movement that is significant and permanent. Thus their need for belonging is fulfilled.

The fourth basic need is the **need for self-esteem**—a sense of self-worth and self-respect. Many are suffering from an inferiority complex or poor self-image. They are frustrated because they feel they can never measure up to expectations. They desire prestige or status, or at the very least, attention and appreciation. The good news for such people is that God bases His acceptance on unconditional love and not on one's performance. He accepts a person as he is. It is a great liberating experience for a person to know that, in spite of his sin, weakness, and failure, he has been accepted by Christ and is now a child of God. It does something for his self-respect.

I can well remember when a group of very poor, socially despised "untouchables" in India first accepted Christ as Savior and received the inner assurance from the Spirit that they were the children of God. With confidence they said, "We may be untouchables but God has touched us. We may be outcastes but God has taken us into His kingdom. Now we can be somebody in society!"

At the highest level is the **need for self-actualization**. This is the desire to realize one's inner potential, to realize the purpose for his existence, to fulfill his destiny, and to express his individuality. According to Maslow, few people reach this stage. What a revelation it is for one to discover that there is, after all, meaning in life, that God has a special plan and place for him, and that God calls him to be a partner with himself in a worldwide ministry. By unselfishly giving himself to creative activities, the person can find ultimate, individual fulfillment.

The Maslow hierarchy may not be perfect; and though one category of need probably blends into another, yet it provides us with a useful tool to pinpoint the basic motivations of people. Furthermore, it is not only useful for approaching the individual, but the group as well, for it is evident that entire segments of a population jointly experience common needs. For example, for the poverty-stricken masses the basic physiological needs are probably the most urgent. The low-caste masses of Hindu society in India are reaching out for self-respect. Members of the affluent 400 Club, in spite of their prestige and power, are probably seeking for individual self-actualization. Young people from broken homes are, without doubt, looking for love and a sense of belonging. All of this, therefore, has significance for the Christian communicator, helping him to match the need with the particular facet of the gospel that meets that need.

*b.* Not only must the communicator make his message relevant to the needs of the listeners but also to their particular spiritual conditions.

In this regard, the hierarchy of awareness presented by James Engel and H. Wilbert Norton in their book, *What's Gone Wrong with the Harvest?* is probably the most helpful.[11]

(1) Awareness of Supreme Being but not effective knowledge of the gospel
(2) Initial awareness of the gospel
(3) Awareness of the fundamentals of the gospel
(4) Grasp of implications of the gospel
(5) Positive attitude toward the gospel
(6) Personal problem recognition
(7) Decision to act
(8) Repentance and faith in Christ

This model seeks to coordinate the interactive role of God (the divine Evangelist), the human communicator, and the receptor. God proceeds from general to special revelation and from·conviction to regeneration. The messenger proceeds from proclamation to persuasion. The listener's response advances from general awareness to specific decision.

Everyone will fall somewhere on the continuum represented in this hierarchy. According to Engel and Norton:

> Some will have awareness of the Supreme Being through God's ministry of general revelation (conscience and nature) but no effective awareness of the gospel. Others will have the necessary awareness and grasp of its implications. When this is accompanied by strong felt need for change (designated as personal-problem recognition), the individual is open to challenge to turn his life over to Christ. Prior to that time, there is neither sufficient understanding nor felt need to permit a valid response to such a challenge. Those who have made such a commitment, then, are in various stages of spiritual growth as they are being conformed to the image of Christ through the ministry of the Holy Spirit.[12]

God and man uniquely interact to bring the listener from the initial stage of awareness to the place of decision. God begins the process by bringing about an awareness of himself through general revelation—through the witness of creation and conscience. Then the preacher assumes a critical responsibility by explaining the claims of the gospel. God, through the ministry of the Holy Spirit, convicts the hearer of his sin. Once the person becomes aware of his spiritual problems, the messenger is able to *persuade* him to make a life commitment to Jesus Christ. When the individual takes this step, God imparts new life through regeneration.

The basic thesis of Engel and Norton is that "the responsibility of the Christian communicator is to approach people where they are in terms of their spiritual position and, through an appropriate combination of message and media, to cause them to progress in their decision process toward initial commitment and subsequent growth."[13]

In non-Western countries, the vast majority of people will probably be at the lowest position of awareness, while many in nominal Christian lands will probably be somewhere between positions two and four. It is our task as Christian communicators to discover where people stand and then, by the grace of God, seek to lead them on the rest of the way.

Once the recipient of the gospel has entered into the experience of the new birth and become a new person in Christ, then the role of evangelist-missionary changes from that of proclaimer to that of teacher. He seeks to lead the new believer on into the experience of the fullness of the Holy Spirit and sanctification, and on through Christian maturity into the fullness of the stature of Jesus Christ.

## 6. Have Faith in, and Depend upon, the Holy Spirit

We dare not allow ourselves to think and act as if evangelism were purely a human enterprise, depending on our own skills and efforts. Evangelism is a divine enterprise, drawing on the unlimited resources of God.

God is the first and the greatest Evangelist. Evangelism began in His heart and mind; it originated in His all-consuming concern and compassion for fallen man. The moment man sinned, God became an Evangelist. His plan of redemption was not an afterthought, dreamed up in a moment of desperation. It goes back to the beginning of time, for the Scriptures tell us that Jesus was "the Lamb slain from the foundation of the world" (Rev. 13:8, KJV).

God is a God of activity. He is at work constantly. This is in contrast to the Hindu idea of God, as the actionless one without attributes. Even among Buddhists, the image of Buddha is often portrayed as the reclining one. But Jehovah is revealed as One who works. He is constantly creating and recreating, redeeming and renewing, and bringing His plan to fruition. The Bible is primarily a record of God's redemptive activity, His great works among men in history. It is not just a collection of ideas but a narration of acts.

Now God, who is at work, calls us to work. He alone can save the world, but He does not choose to save the world alone. He calls out: "Whom shall I send, who will go for us?" (Isa. 6:8). When God wanted to make His redemption *available* to man, He had to take on human form and become a man among men. In order to make His redemption *actual* to men, He has to use men to reach men. That's why God chose Abraham, and the prophets, and Israel. That's why Jesus chose 12 disciples, sent out the 70, and created His Church. What Jesus began He now continues to do through His chosen people.

So evangelism becomes a divine-human cooperation or partnership. God is at work; He calls us to work; we now work together. Jesus said to His disciples: "Go . . . and make disciples of all nations . . . lo, I am with you" (Matt. 28:19-20). Mark's Gospel ends thus: "They went forth and preached everywhere, while the Lord worked with them and confirmed the message by the signs that attended it" (16:20). Peter said to the council members in Jerusalem: "We are witnesses to these things, and so is the Holy Spirit . . ." (Acts 5:32).

Paul wrote to the Christians at Corinth: "We are God's fellow workers" (1 Cor. 3:9). How wonderful to be partners together with God! And let us always remember, primarily we are working with God, *not* He with us. We don't use God—make our own plans and then call Him in to help. He has His master plan, and He calls us to work with Him.

A good illustration of this divine-human partnership is found in the story of Philip and the Ethiopian official, as recorded in Acts 8:26-35. Notice, the Holy Spirit took the initiative. He ordered Philip to go down to Gaza. He required a man to minister to a man in need. Philip heard and obeyed the voice of the Spirit. He left a successful preaching mission in Samaria and went down to the desert. It all seemed unreasonable, but he obeyed the Spirit's call. And when Philip contacted the Ethiopian official, he found that the Spirit had already been at work, preparing the way for his teaching ministry. For he found the Ethiopian reading from the prophet Isaiah. Philip would have had a hard time finding an appropriate text if the man had been reading from the Book of Numbers. But he was reading Isaiah, and the 53rd chapter of Isaiah in particular. What better book? What finer chapter? It was an easy matter for Philip to lead the Ethiopian from the Suffering Servant of the Old Testament to the crucified Savior of the gospel. "Beginning with this scripture he told him the good news of Jesus." As a result the Ethiopian official believed and was baptized.

God's Holy Spirit is working in the hearts and minds of people all over the world. He is even working among people who have never heard the name of Jesus. He is working in the hearts of Muslims, Hindus, Buddhists, animists, Communists, atheists, and nominal Christians. He is preparing individuals and even ethnic groups for the coming of the Christian messenger. John Wesley called this "prevenient grace." So in a sense we don't take Christ to people; Christ takes us to people, people prepared in some measure—sometimes more, sometimes less—by the mysterious working of the Holy Spirit.

Even as we proclaim the good news of Christ, the Holy Spirit is working in the hearts and minds of listeners. Jesus promised that the Holy Spirit "will convince the world concerning sin and righteousness and judgment. . . . He will glorify me, for he will take what is mine and declare it to you" (John 16:8, 14). This means that while we are preaching the Word, the Holy Spirit uses the truth to illuminate the minds of men, to show them their sin, and point them to the

Savior. Without this inner ministry of the Spirit, all our words and efforts would be of no avail whatsoever. We could have the most perfect outline, the choicest words, and the most powerful delivery; but if the Holy Spirit didn't do His work, our message would fall flat. But knowing His faithfulness and trusting in His mighty power, we are assured that God's Word will not return empty but shall accomplish His purpose (Isa. 55:11).

Several years ago I was conducting a mission to university students in the city of Trivandrum in south India. One morning a young medical student came to see me. In all sincerity he said, "I find difficulty in believing there is a God. Can you prove to me that God exists?"

So for the next hour or two I gave him all the rational arguments for the existence of God—the cosmological argument, the teleological argument, the moral argument, and the anthropological argument. But at the end of a long discussion he was still unconvinced. However, he did promise to attend the evening service and listen to the Word of God.

About two days later, just before I entered the church, the pastor handed me a note written by this young medical student. On it he had scribbled: "I think there is some truth in what you are saying. Please pray for me." The following evening when I finished my message and the congregation had dispersed, I noticed this young man was still seated in the church, his face buried in his hands. He seemed to be weeping. I went down and sat by his side. "What's the trouble?" I asked.

"Sir," he replied, "I'm a terrible sinner; please pray for me."

I prayed for him as best I knew how, and counseled him out of the Scriptures. Finally he prayed his own simple prayer, and I sensed very clearly the presence of God in our midst. Suddenly he looked up at me with a smile on his face, gripped me by the hand, and said, "Now I know there is a God. He's in my heart!"

I realized immediately that I had witnessed the gracious work of the Holy Spirit. What reason and argument could not do, He accomplished through His Word. He convicted this young man of his sin, converted him, and took him from spiritual death to spiritual life. Only the Spirit can perform these functions.

Then again, not only must we believe in and depend upon the Holy Spirit, as effective communicators of the gospel we must also be filled with the Spirit. Jesus said to His disciples: "You shall receive power when the Holy Spirit has come upon you; and you shall be my witnesses" (Acts 1:8). He also clearly commanded them: "Stay in the city, until you are clothed with power from on high" (Luke 24:49).

There is a line drawn through the New Testament, and it is drawn at Pentecost. On one side of that line we find spiritual inadequacy, moral fumbling, denial, and defeat. It is all very sub-Christian. Picture that little group of disciples huddled together in an Upper Room in Jerusalem. If they looked back, there was the Crucifixion with all its horror and tragedy. The shame of it revived within them. If they looked forward, there was the incredible assignment to go into all the world and preach the gospel to every creature. They had the message, but they didn't have the boldness to proclaim it. If they looked within, there were discouragement and defeat. Fears lurked, jealousies festered, doubts assailed, and cowardice hung like a millstone around their necks.

But in the midst of all this, two things held them steady. One was an event; the other was a promise. First, there was the fact of the Resurrection. Slow to believe it at first, they were now convinced of its reality. Their Master was alive! Then, there was the promise, "Before many days you shall be baptized with the Holy Spirit" (Acts 1:5). The Master had given His word; He would never fail them.

On the Day of Pentecost that promise passed into fulfillment, and the record tells us that "they were all filled with the Holy Spirit" (2:4). Now what do we find? On this side of the line there is spiritual adequacy, moral certainty, the power of a redemptive offense, spiritual contagion—a plus sign. The cringing become conquering; the cowardly become courageous; the vacillating become dynamic; the weak become strong. It is all so truly Christian.

The Book of Acts often describes how the power of the Holy Spirit enabled the early disciples to become effective communicators of the Word. Note these verses:

> They were all filled with the Holy Spirit and began to speak in other tongues, as the Spirit gave them utterance *(2:4)*.

> Then Peter, filled with the Holy Spirit, said to them . . . *(4:8)*.

> And they were all filled with the Holy Spirit and spoke the word of God with boldness. . . . And with great power the apostles gave their testimony to the resurrection of the Lord Jesus *(vv. 31, 33)*.

> But Saul, who is also called Paul, filled with the Holy Spirit, looked intently at him and said . . . *(13:9-10)*.

As modern communicators of the Word, how we need the fullness and power of the Holy Spirit in our lives! Pentecost is not a spiritual luxury; it is an utter necessity for Christian service. It is not an adornment, but essential equipment; not something we can take or leave as we like, but a must. We are shut up to the alternative: Pentecost or failure. For the human spirit fails unless the Holy Spirit fills.

# 8

# Overcoming Barriers
# to Communication

Some years ago I was a member of a college quartet on a world-wide evangelistic tour. We had just landed in Cape Town, South Africa, for a four-month campaign. The church official who introduced us at the welcoming ceremony said, "Dear friends, I met these young men only a few hours ago when they stepped off the ship from Southampton, England, so I don't know them very well. But one thing I can say about them for sure; they are the most *homely* bunch of fellows I have ever met."

The four of us looked at each other in amazement. We knew we were not handsome, but we didn't appreciate someone announcing this in public! However, later we discovered that the introducer was paying us a high compliment. The word *homely* among the whites of South Africa means "friendly, homelike, easy to get acquainted with." The problem was, the speaker said one thing and we "heard" another. So what was meant to be a compliment turned out to be an insult.

In this particular incident the result was humorous. But the consequence may be very serious when misunderstanding takes place in the process of communicating eternal, spiritual truths. More often than we realize, the message that we are trying to put across turns out to be a pitiful caricature of the original message, or completely meaningless to the listener.

On the surface, communication appears to be a fairly simple process. It involves only three essential factors:

(1) the source (the speaker)
(2) the message (the actual form of what is communicated)
(3) the receptor (listener)

All three components are essential, for there can be no message unless there is some source of communication, and there is no communication unless someone receives the message.

In actual practice, however, communication can be very complex in nature, for it presupposes two conditions:

(1) that the source has an intent (the speaker has something important in mind that he is seeking to convey)

(2) that there is a response from the receptor (either practical or conceptual, or both)

The problem arises when there is a discrepancy between the *encoding* (the meaning intended by the speaker) and the *decoding* (the interpretation given by the listener, as illustrated above).

It is therefore essential for us to understand the main barriers to effective gospel communication, and to find ways to overcome them. These barriers may be linguistic, cultural, or religious in nature.

## 1. Overcoming Language Barriers

*a. Verbal communication.* Differences in language construction, thought forms, vocabulary, idioms, connotations, and meanings of words make for problems in getting the message across. Anyone who has attempted to preach in another country through interpretation has no doubt discovered the potential difficulties. An American evangelist speaking in Japan said to the audience, "Friends, today I want to speak to you on the little word *I.*" (Evidently he wanted to talk about the unsurrendered ego.) But the little English word *I* turned out to be *watakushi,* a four-syllable word in Japanese. Another American evangelist, preaching in Africa, explained at the outset of his sermon that he was going to preach on the "Four Ships." The interpreter translated it literally, using the local word for "ship" or "boat." Then the speaker went on to discuss the "four ships"—relation*ship,* fellow*ship,* partner*ship,* and steward*ship.* Of course, when the interpreter translated these words into the African language, none of them ended with "ship."

Idioms are difficult to translate. A guest preacher in Japan, in the course of his sermon, used the expression "He was tickled to death." The interpreter, unacquainted with this English idiom, translated it literally, "He was scratched until he died." The use of alliteration also poses problems, for words that rhyme or begin with the same letter in one language may not necessarily do so in another.

Some sermon outlines and forms that we use in English cannot be used effectively in Hindi, or Swahili, or Korean, or some other languages. One of my favorite missionary sermons is entitled "The Great Omission." The main idea is that when we drop the *c* out of *commission,* it then becomes *omission.* And what does the *c* stand for? (1) Our *conviction* that all men are lost and need a Savior; (2) our *concern* for the spiritual needs of people; and (3) the *consecration* of our personnel and money. When we lose these three ingredients, then the Great Commission becomes the Great Omission. It is a catchy outline for a sermon, but it is based on the genius of the English language, and loses its force when translated into some other language. So we have to put aside some of our neat English outlines and develop a whole new set of outlines that are based on the genius of the language in which we are communicating.

Sometimes there is a discrepancy between the *encoding* and the *decoding* of the message, merely because of the difference in the connotation of words. The same word or phrase may have an entirely different meaning for the speaker and the listener. A missionary in the Philippines was preaching on the theme "Get thee behind me, Satan," but he used a word for "getting behind" which implied, "follow me and be my helper."[1] When the phrase "whose sins are covered" (Rom. 4:7) was translated literally into the Hiligaynon language of Mindanao in the Philippines, it did not carry the intended meaning of forgiveness, but simply meant that the sins are hidden from God's view.[2] In the First Epistle of John, the writer says: "Whoso hath this world's goods, and seeth his brother have need, and shutteth up his bowels of compassion from him, how dwelleth the love of God in him?" (1 John 3:17, KJV). But in the Chol language of southern Mexico, the phrase "close up his bowels" means to become constipated. When the translators tried "close up his heart," as found in the RSV, they discovered that this was a Chol idiom meaning "to have epileptic fits." Finally, they simply used, "He does not give him anything," which, after all, conveys the original meaning of the writer.[3]

In making such communicative adaptations to the receptor, our fear is that we shall lose the content of the message in the process, which is a legitimate concern. It is easy to twist the message out of recognition by using forms which do not fit it. True adaptation is not a *compromise* in the truths and claims of the gospel. It is an *adjustment* of the message in relation to the background of the people, in order that the meaning may be correct and intelligible to the listeners.

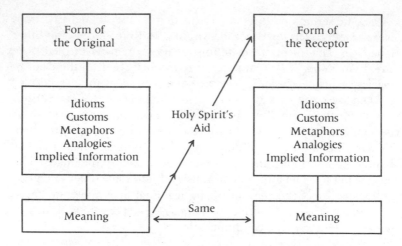

Fig. 1. The message of the original source has to be sifted from the language forms of the Scriptures and then filtered through the language forms of the receptor so that the meaning may be identical.

An even more serious problem arises when the language of the people does not possess words for some of the basic concepts of the gospel, such as repentance, faith, love, sin, salvation, and sanctification. In the language of the Motilones, a primitive tribe in Colombia, South America, there is no word for "sin." One has to name specific wrong deeds, such as lying, stealing, killing, etc. The only way to express "love" is to say, "My stomach is hungry for you—I want to eat you." "Conversion" is described as "leaving the devil's trail and starting in God's trail." "Faith" or "believe" is translated "to walk on God," which really describes the "faith" that a Motilone must exercise when he walks across a stream on a slippery log-bridge. When a Motilone becomes a Christian, "he gets a new language"; "he has Jesus talk in his mouth." This means he has received a new life.

In the language of the Dogons, a tribe in Mali, West Africa, there is no word for *conscience*. Missionaries have had to coin a word— *heart-knowledge*. There is no word for "love," so John 3:16 has to be translated, "You are important to God, so God gave His Son."

The Usarufa mountain people of Papua New Guinea do not have a noun form of the word "love." They have only a verb form, and it always demands an object. This creates problems for the translation of the great love chapter, 1 Corinthians 13, where the abstract noun is used throughout. The translators must use the verb form and decide what is the object in each case, as: "If I speak in the tongues of men and of angels, but do not love God and/or others, I am a noisy gong or a clanging cymbal." (By the way, the Usarufas do not have gongs or cymbals, so something else has to be substituted.)

"Repentance," which connotes a profound transformation involving a change of mind, will, and heart, is translated into Kekchi (of Guatemala), "It pains my heart." In Baouli, West Africa, the same concept is expressed as "It hurts so much I want to quit." In the northern Sotho language of South Africa, it is described as "It becomes untwisted." The Chols of southern Mexico speak of "My heart is turning itself back." In all of these adaptations, we can readily see the main idea of the concept "repentance" is retained, which, after all, is the important issue.[4]

The important word "faith" is not found in many languages and has to be described by an appropriate phrase. In Tzeltal, a language of southern Mexico, one can speak of "faith" as "hanging onto God with the heart," while in Valiente, a language of Panama, one must say, "To lean on God." On the other hand, the Anuaks of the Sudan say faith is "putting oneself in God's hands," and the nearby Uduks to the north claim that faith is "joining God's word to one's body."

A missionary who was working among the Bambara people of West Africa was finding great difficulty in expressing the truth that "God redeemed us," until his African helper suggested that the best equivalent would be "God took our heads out."[5] Seeing the puzzled look on the missionary's face, the man went on to explain that this expression came out of the days of slavery, the memories of which were still vivid in the minds of the Bambara people. He described the long lines of lash-driven men and women trudging wearily along to the coast, each with a heavy iron collar around his neck and with a chain leading from one slave to another. At times, as these lines of condemned slaves passed through the villages, it so happened that a local chief might see some friend being led away to the block, and he would want to redeem him. This he could do by paying the Arab trader enough gold, silver, brass, or ivory. In thus redeeming the friend he would literally "take his head out of the iron collar."

Missionaries to the Bambaras, as they tell of God's redeeming love in Christ Jesus today, explain to their eager audiences that God saw us in slavery to sin and self, being driven under the lash of Satan. So He sent His Son to pay the price for our salvation by His death on the Cross. Thus He redeemed us; literally, "He took our heads out."

And furthermore, the missionaries explain, just as in ancient times a redeemed slave, out of sincere gratitude, often volunteered to serve the one who redeemed him for the rest of his life, so we, too, may become the love-slaves of Jesus Christ.

In his book *Message and Mission,* Dr. Eugene Nida tells us that in Nilotic Shilluk of Africa, the only way to express "forgiveness" is literally, "God spat on the ground in front of us." This idiom arises from the practice of plaintiffs and defendants having to spit on the ground in front of each other when finally a case has been tried, punishments have been meted out, and fines paid. The spitting symbolizes that the case is terminated, that all is forgiven, and that the accusations cannot come into court again.[6]

All of this reemphasizes the point that we have made previously, that is, how important it is for the Christian messenger to master the language of the people whom he seeks to serve. Each language possesses its own distinctive genius which can become the vehicle of transmitting God's Word in man's vocabulary. We must make use of all the idioms, thought patterns, and descriptive powers of any particular language in order to more effectively communicate the truth of God's revelation.

Each language has its own forms of alliteration and poetic beauty. I shall never forget the sermon outline that an evangelist used in the Hindi language in India on one occasion. His two main points were:

(1) *Ao—Lo* (come and take)

(2) *Jao—Do* (go and give)

These two components, he emphasized, are the main characteristics of the Christian life. The four words form a rhythmic, poetic verse that is pleasing to the ear (euphonic) and easy to remember.

On several occasions in India I preached on the text "How shall we escape if we neglect such a great salvation?" (Heb. 2:3). I asked the question, Why is this so great salvation?—and then suggested three reasons. The Kanarese language of Karnataka State offers a wonderful chance for alliteration in three simple words. This is a great salvation because of its great:

(1) *Bele*—(cost)

(2) *Bali*—(sacrifice)

(3) *Bala*—(power)

Years after preaching this message, people would meet me and remind me of the sermon; they never forget the three important words!

Another distinctive feature of any language is its fund of proverbs or wise sayings. I was always grateful that I was required to memorize scores of Kanarese proverbs when, as a missionary in India, I was preparing for my third and final examination in the language. They came in very handy in illustrating spiritual truths. The proverb "Tinsel on the outside, but worms within" helped greatly to reinforce the fact that "man looks on the outward appearance, but the Lord looks on the heart" (1 Sam. 16:7). "Speak of money and even a corpse will open its mouth" beautifully illustrated the spirit of greed prevalent among mankind. The proverb "To return evil for good is devillike; to return good for good is manlike; to return good for evil is Godlike" was appropriate in explaining Christ's teaching, "Love your enemies" (Matt. 5:44).

*b. Nonverbal communication.* We cannot leave this discussion on linguistic adaptations without saying something about the importance of nonverbal communication in the form of gestures and signs. The same gesture may have different meanings for people of different cultural backgrounds, and thus cause misunderstanding between speaker and receptor.

In India the nodding of the head from side to side does not mean a negative response, but affirmation or agreement.

To the Chols of southern Mexico laughter does not necessarily signify a feeling of joy. It is customary for the Chols to laugh when they receive tragic news. When they first heard the story of the beheading of John the Baptist, to the astonishment of the missionary, they broke out in riotous laughter. They explained that they felt so sorry for John the Baptist they just had to laugh in order to keep from crying![7]

Once while preaching through interpretation in Colombia, South America, I wanted to give an illustration about myself from my boyhood days. I said to the group of young people gathered in the rural school, "Now when I was a boy about that tall," and I reached out my hand with palm facing downward to show how tall I was at the time. To my surprise the students all laughed, and I couldn't understand why. After the service my interpreter explained that that sort of gesture was used only in reference to animals. As a human being, I should have turned my hand sideways, with palm facing the audience.

Among the Matabele people in Rhodesia, the palm-down gesture signifies that the subject referred to cannot grow; the palm-up gesture means it has stopped growing; while the palm-up, with bent fingers, means the subject is still growing.

Thus the missionary must not only learn the meaning of the spoken words in his adopted language, but also the meaning of the nonverbal gestures and symbols; otherwise he can make some embarrassing mistakes.

Differences in language can certainly provide many problems for the Christian messenger, but through mastery of the language and wise adaptation of words and phrases, these barriers can be overcome and effective communication be achieved.

## 2. Overcoming Cultural Barriers

Cultural differences, arising from variations in customs, lifestyle, attitudes, mores, etc., are ever-present barriers to communication.

The Bambaras of West Africa cannot understand the apparent disrespect of Moses when he announced to his father-in-law, Jethro, his decision to return to Egypt (Exod. 4:18). The Bambara would not think of leaving without first asking the permission of his parent-in-law. Likewise the Kpelle people of Liberia are shocked at the record of people putting palm branches in the path of Jesus when He rode triumphantly into Jerusalem (Matt. 21:8). Whenever any Liberian dignitary comes to town, the Kpelles make sure that the road is swept clean of all branches and leaves. [8]

The words of Deut. 8:5—"As a man disciplines his son, the Lord your God disciplines you"—is difficult for many tribal people in Africa to understand; for in their societies it is not the father but the uncle (mother's eldest brother) who disciplines the children in any family.

To the Usarufa people of New Guinea, the Lord's words of judgment to Adam in the garden—"In the sweat of your face you shall eat bread" (Gen. 3:19)—do not appear as a punishment, but something to be desired. Sweat is a thing of beauty and manliness to the Usarufa men. They spend days in a steaming hothouse so that their bodies will glisten with beads of perspiration mixed with soot.

Cultural differences should be reduced as much as possible by an effective use of cultural equivalents. This is especially true in regard to the many similes and analogies that are used in the Bible. Among the tribal people in the mountains of New Guinea there is no such thing as bread. They have no word for "bread." The staple food of these people is the sweet potato, which they eat two or three times a day, day in and day out. So the words of Jesus, "I am the bread of life" (John 6:48), are translated as "I am the sweet potato of life." This, of course, conveys the real meaning of the words of Jesus and makes sense to the people of New Guinea. Likewise, in the statement of Jesus, "No one who puts his hand to the plow and looks back is fit for the kingdom of God" (Luke 9:62), the word "plow" has to be changed to "hoe," for these mountain people have never seen a plow. They do make use of a crude hoe in their gardening.

The Barundi tribe of Africa have no idea what a "yoke" is, so the words of Jesus, "Take my yoke upon you, and learn from me" (Matt. 11:29), don't make sense to them. The Bible translators had to substitute the word *ingata,* which is a doughnut-shaped object, made out of banana bark, to place on the head to carry heavy loads.

We Westerners talk about the emotional focus of the personality as the "heart." A young man says to his girl friend, "I love you with all my *heart.*" But this is by no means a universal practice. In some parts of the world the young man would have to say, "I love you with all my *stomach,*" or "with all my *liver.*" In a number of languages in Africa, John 14:1 is translated, "Let not your *livers* be troubled." The Usarufa people of New Guinea speak of different emotions arising from different parts of the body. Fear centers in the ear ("my ear is burning"); sorrow in the liver ("my liver is drowning"), anger in the intestines ("my intestines are bad"); and happiness in the liver ("my liver is good today"). To express satisfaction the Usarufa would say, "My stomach is dancing," while the expression "My shoulder is burning" is an idiom meaning "I'm tired of it." To the Usarufa, faith is progressive—"my ear hears," "my intestines hear," and finally, "I hear from my liver" (that is real faith).[9]

Differences in the value system, life-style, and attitude often make it difficult for people of other cultures to understand parts of the Bible that are very meaningful to us. The parable of the prodigal son which Jesus narrated is probably one of our favorite stories and certainly a wonderful subject matter for a sermon. But to the Usarufa people the parable poses problems. In their culture a son does not ask for his inheritance. Furthermore, even if he received his inheritance, there would be no place to where the Usarufa youth could run and spend his money in riotous living.

To orthodox Hindus in India, the parable is very appealing except for the end of the story. Hindus consider the cow as sacred, so killing the "fatted calf" in celebration of the prodigal's return is repulsive to them. A feast of delectable Indian dishes can easily be substituted, thus bringing the parable to a beautiful climax rather than a tragic letdown.

Among the Zanaki people of Tanzania, only thieves knock on doors. They approach a house in the middle of the night, knock on the doorposts, and then hide in the bushes to see if there is any movement within. If the people are at home, they dash off into the darkness. If there is no response, they stay and plunder the house. An honest man will stand outside the house and call out the names of the people inside. Thus Rev. 3:20 has to be translated, "Behold, I stand at the door and call" (not knock); otherwise the Zanakis would look upon Jesus as a thief.[10]

By adapting the Christian message to the cultural patterns of a people, the missionary can achieve effective communication. What is actually involved here is not the altering of the essential content of the biblical message, but the encasing of this message in a culturally relevant verbal form. We have no right to change the content of the gospel—that would be a betrayal of our trust—but we have the obligation to fit the same content into such culturally meaningful forms that the message will be intelligible to the hearers. In fact, because of cultural differences, there are times when the form of the message *must* be different, if the content of the message is to be equivalent.

Milk can be delivered in a variety of containers. It may be in a tin can, a glass bottle, a cardboard carton, or a plastic bottle. The type of container is not so important, as long as the milk is pure milk—not soured or watered down. The only condition in which the container might become an important item is when the buyer has a strong personal preference for a particular type of container. He may refuse to buy milk in a tin can, but be most willing to purchase it in a cardboard carton. In the same way, the Christian messenger has no right to water down the content of the gospel—it must be the truth —but he certainly must present it in such a form that will be meaningful to the listener.

What happens when we consider only the words of a language and not their cultural connotations? The results of such a process became evident to a group of linguists who were experimenting with electronic computers designed to translate from one language to another. The sentence "The spirit . . . is willing, but the flesh is weak" (Matt. 26:41) was fed into a computer, translated into Russian, and then back into English. It came back as "The liquor is good, but the meat is rotten." The same process was followed with the headline

"Mary Suspended for Youthful Prank"; and it came out as "Mary Hung for Juvenile Delinquency." "Life, liberty, and the pursuit of happiness" was translated through Japanese back into English. The result was "license to commit lustful pleasures." "Out of sight, out of mind" went into Japanese and returned to English as "invisible, insane." Communicators of the gospel must never forget that the spiritual truths they seek to proclaim are fed into minds that are precomputerized to think in ways compatible with the hearers' language patterns, cultural forms, and life experiences.

Effective communication takes place when the meaning intended by the speaker and the meaning interpreted by the listener are equivalent as shown in figure 2.

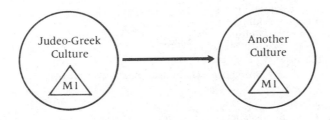

Fig. 2—Effective communication (M means "message.")

This is the ideal, but it is not as easy as it looks. For the biblical message comes to us encased in Judeo-Greek cultural forms, then becomes enculturated in our European and American culture, and finally encounters a totally foreign culture represented by the receptors. It is essential for us to understand the cultural background of the biblical revelation in order to interpret the message correctly. Then we carefully separate the essential gospel from our own cultural overhang, and encase the truth in forms the listener can understand. At times the gospel we present suffers from many Western cultural additions, or the gospel that is accepted by the non-Christian becomes tainted with unchristian features of his culture. So the result is somewhat like the situation portrayed in figure 3. To avoid this tragedy we need the guidance of the Holy Spirit in all our communication, and those who receive our message need the Spirit's guidance in the cultural expression of the gospel.

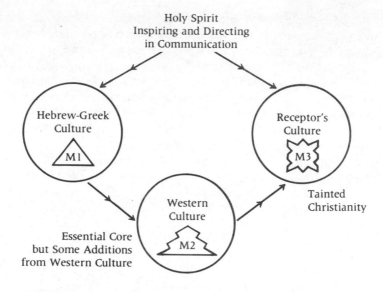

Fig. 3—Faulty communication and its remedy

*a. Cultural adaptations of the gospel.* Every culture possesses certain features that can become effective vehicles for the communication of the gospel. The Christian messenger needs to be constantly on the lookout for these. For example, in the Valiente language of Mexico the difficult term "sanctification" is expressed by the phrase "to wash and to keep clean," which is drawn from the practice of the Indian women who wash their clothes in the jungle streams and then put them in special baskets reserved for clean clothes.[11] The phrase beautifully expresses both the crisis and the process aspects of the sanctifying grace of God.

The Toba people of Argentina are a seminomadic group of Indians whose social structure is based on the practice of "sharing," rather than that of individual ownership. Every Toba feels obligated to share with all his clan and neighbors almost everything that he has. So the missionaries decided to present the gospel in terms of "sharing." God so loved the world that He shared His Son with mankind. The Son shared His teaching, His energy, even His life with all men, not only by dying for them, but also sharing with them His Spirit. All those who put their trust in Christ share in His life and nature, and thus belong to the tribe of God. All those who have received this new life must share with one another in this new fellowship of the faith. As a result of such preaching, today a large number of Tobas are disciples of Christ.[12]

The doctrine of the atonement can be presented in different ways to different people, by selecting from the total message of the Cross that feature which is culturally significant within the immediate context relevant to people's lives. For Zoroastrians, who believe strongly in the continual battle between righteousness and unrighteousness, the atonement can effectively be described in terms of the *great conflict* between Christ and Satan, in which, through the Cross and empty tomb, Christ gained the victory over Satan and death. To Muslims, who emphasize the sovereignty of God, this same approach would be useful. For many tribal people, who offer animal sacrifices to the gods or spirits, Christ can be presented as "the Lamb of God" who took upon himself our sins and died in our place as a *substitute sacrifice.* In some cultures the practice of *mediation* is a common, everyday affair. The simple, illiterate villager would never think of approaching an illustrious government official in person. He will always seek for an intermediary, a person of influence and ability, to plead his case. Such people can be reminded that "there is one God, and there is one mediator between God and men, the man Christ Jesus, who gave himself as a ransom for all" (1 Tim. 2:5-6). Through Christ we all have access to the Father. In areas where people live under the perennial burden of *debt* and are at the mercy of unscrupulous moneylenders, the good news would be that, through the Cross and Resurrection, Christ has *paid the debt* of our sin and set us free. He has "forgiven us all our trespasses, having canceled the bond which stood against us with its legal demands . . . nailing it to the cross" (Col. 2:13-14). For those persons who are keenly aware of the tragic conflicts that divide and alienate untold millions of people, the presentation of the atonement in terms of *reconciliation* is more meaningful, for in this way they can understand more readily how God was in Christ, "reconciling the world to himself" (2 Cor. 5:19).

Perhaps the finest illustration of evangelizing a people by applying spiritual truth to their own cultural patterns is found in the story of the Sawi tribe of Irian Jaya, West Irian, as narrated by missionary Don Richardson in his fascinating book *Peace Child.* When Richardson studied the culture of this stone-age tribe, he soon discovered here was a people who idealized treachery as a virtue, a goal of life. They not only were cruel but honored cruelty. Their highest pleasure depended upon the misery and despair of others. They were not satisfied with overt killing—suddenly pouncing upon and slaying a lone warrior from another tribe who had carelessly wandered into their territory. They practiced a more sophisticated style of treachery, carefully and artfully carried out over a period of time. They would gradually win the trust of the intended victim by showering him with praise and gifts, and inviting him to several feasts in their homes. Finally one day, while the unsuspecting warrior was eating and laughing merrily, the Sawi men would pounce on him with their stone axes and spears, and with shouts of glee slaughter him. They would cut his body into pieces with sharp bamboo knives, cook it, and eat it. This whole process was called "fattening with friendship for the slaughter."

Thus it happened that as the missionary was narrating the details of the life of Christ to the Sawi people, when he came to the description of Judas Iscariot's betrayal of the Son of God, he noticed that they listened with unusual interest and admiration. They chuckled with glee, whistled birdcalls, and touched their chests in awe. Suddenly Richardson realized *they were acclaiming Judas as the hero of the story!* In *their* thinking, Judas had done nothing wrong; in fact, he was a super-Sawi! They had never heard such a fantastic tale of *fattening with friendship for the kill.* And Christ, the object of Judas' treachery, meant nothing to these men.

The missionary was dumbfounded. How could he possibly get the Sawis to understand the significance of the death of Christ? How could he reverse their whole thinking in the light of their particular world view?

But one day God showed Don Richardson the way.

Because of the helpfulness of Don and his wife, who was a nurse, two Sawi clans had built villages close to each other in order to benefit from the medical and technical skills of the missionaries. But as time went on, they began to fight with each other, and several lives were lost. Finally, when their hostility came to a climax and it looked like a full-scale battle would ensue, Don Richardson called the leaders of the two clans together and announced that he and his wife had decided to leave, in order to make way for the clans to separate from each other and stop the killing. The stunned leaders went off into a huddle; and after a tumult of discussion, they returned and said to the missionary, "Don't leave us. We're not going to kill each other any more. Tomorrow we are going to sprinkle cool water on each other [that is, we are going to make peace]!"

The following morning, the missionary couple witnessed this unusual and perplexing ceremony. The leading warriors of both factions gathered in the clearing of the jungle, facing each other from a distance. Behind each group of men stood their women and children. The atmosphere was fraught with tension and excitement. Suddenly one of the men from one side grabbed his baby boy from the arms of his wife. The mother screamed and tried to hold on to the child, but the father ran toward the other side. When the man reached the other group, he handed his baby over to one of the warriors and said: "I give you my son and with him my name. Plead the words of my people among your people. Let us live in peace!"

The other man gently received the child and answered back, "It is enough! I will surely plead peace between us." Then all the members of the clan filed by, one by one, and laid hands upon the child, sealing their acceptance of the peace bargain.

The identical scene was repeated from the other side. One of the warriors wrenched his six-month-old son from the arms of his terrified wife, ran across the opening, and handed him over to the enemy. Then both parties carried off the newly adopted sons to their respective villages to decorate them for the peace celebration. Meanwhile young men stuck feathers in their hair, brought out their drums, and began to dance.

All the while, the missionaries looked on in horror and amazement. They thought, What will happen now? Will the two babies be chopped into pieces, cooked, and eaten? Don Richardson called one of the warriors aside and asked, "What are they going to do? What does all this mean?"

Exuberantly, the Sawi warrior answered, "Missionary, you have been urging us to make peace. Don't you know it's impossible to have peace without a *peace child?*" Then he went on to explain that if a man would actually give his son to his enemies, that man could be trusted. It was an unquestionable proof of his goodwill, his sincere desire for reconciliation and peace. And everyone who laid his hand on the son was bound to live in peace with those who gave him, as long as the son lived. To kill the *peace child* would be the crime of all crimes. The man assured the missionary that the two babies would not be harmed; in fact, both villages would guard the lives of these children even more zealously than they protect their own offspring.

When he heard this, Don Richardon's horror suddenly turned to excitement. The living peace child was a culturally built-in antidote to the Sawi idealization of violence. This was the key he had been praying for! Two months later, after he was convinced that the peace treaty was working effectively, he called the elders of the clans together and addressed them:

"You are right! You can't make peace without the painful giving of a son. But long before you discovered this truth, God knew it. So because He wants all men to find peace with Him and with each other, He decided to give His only Son, Jesus, as a *Peace Child* to the world. To reject God's Peace Child is the greatest of all sins. But when we accept Him, we can live at peace with God as long as the Son is alive—which means forever!"

For the first time the light of the gospel broke into the darkness of the Sawi mind. The hero ot the gospel narrative was no longer Judas, but Jesus! Jesus was God's *Peace Child,* and Judas had planned His death. The Sawis thought, We must be careful not to commit the same sin!

What was the result? After a few months of further instruction and prayer on the part of the missionary, these two entire clans of the Sawi people "laid their hands on God's Peace Child" and sealed their acceptance of His gift. Today they are all disciples of Christ, worshipping in their dome-shaped sanctuary and singing the praises of their Redeemer.

Don Richardson ends his story of the conversion of the Sawi people with this magnificent conviction—*that God, down through the centuries, has been building into the culture of every tribe and people redemptive analogies for the effective communication of the gospel!*[13] Herein lies the key to their hearts and to their conversion. And so God is looking for messengers who are willing to go and live among these people, identify with their struggles and aspirations, learn their language and culture, and discover the redemptive analogy that will enable them to understand the matchless love and grace of our blessed Redeemer.

Now it is our turn to get excited!

## 3. Overcoming Religious-Concept Barriers

Of all the barriers to communicating the gospel to non-Christians, the religious-concept barriers are certainly the most difficult to overcome.

Sometimes a difference in the connotation of an important religious term or concept can lead to a serious discrepancy in the "encoding" and "decoding" of the message. To the Christian the word *sin* means a transgression of God's moral law or anything that is contrary to His essential nature; to the Hindu it may mean a transgression of the social or caste regulations. The term *new birth* for the Christian means "a new life in Christ" while for the Hindu it means "reincarnation." *Salvation* according to Christian Scriptures denotes "deliverance from the guilt and power of sin" and "reconciliation with God"; to the Hindu or Buddhist it means "release from Karma and from the cycle of birth and rebirth."

In Spanish-speaking Latin America, such words as *confession, saint,* and *Mary* have quite different conceptual values to Protestants and Roman Catholics. These three words mean to Protestants confession of guilt in prayer to God, biblical heroes of the faith, and the honored mother of Jesus respectively. To Roman Catholics they mean confession to a priest, images in a church, and a divine protectress. "To receive Christ" to the Roman Catholic does not carry the idea of personal commitment to Christ, but means "to receive the wafer of the Eucharist." If you ask a Catholic in Latin America, "Do you know Jesus?" he is quite likely to respond, "Yes, I know him. He lives just down the street." ("Jesus" is a fairly common name in some parts of the continent.)

This means we cannot take for granted that the listener will ascribe the same meaning to words which we use so frequently. We may have to phrase things a little differently, or we may have to define our terms more accurately, in order to make our intended meaning clear.

Sometimes there are teachings and concepts in the non-Christian religious systems which are contrary to the teaching of the Bible and therefore make it difficult for the people to understand or accept the truth of the gospel. When the Muslim hears the phrase "the Son of God," he thinks of a physical relationship, with physical procreation involved, and this to him is blasphemous. When he hears about the Trinity, he thinks of three gods, and this to the Muslim is idolatry. Furthermore, the Cross is a scandal to him, for he claims that God cannot die. When the Hindu hears of the Cross and forgiveness, this to him is foolishness, for according to the law of *Karma* everyone *must* suffer by himself for his own sins—there is no place for vicarious suffering or forgiveness.

These problems will be discussed more in detail in Chapters 10—13, when we deal with each religion separately and seek to find the best approach to its teachings. All of the theological questions have to be faced frankly, intelligently, and prayerfully. With the help of the Holy Spirit they are not insurmountable.

# 9

# Communicating in an Indigenous Mold

While I was serving as a missionary in India, I received a letter from the president of a mission board in the United States, that specialized in the production of Christian literature. He enclosed five tracts in the letter and requested that I have them translated into the Kanarese language. He promised to pay the printing bill, if I would see to the proper distribution of the tracts. I read the tracts and found them to be good as far as the content was concerned, but they were slanted entirely to the Western mind. They would be good for Americans in the U.S.A., but of little value to Hindus and Muslims in India. So I wrote to the gentleman, explaining the situation, and asked him for permission to get some competent Indian Christians to write a new set of tracts geared to the mind-set of the Hindu and Muslim. I expressed my strong belief in the use of good tracts, and my hope that he would be willing to pay for the printing of these new tracts in India. The gentleman wrote back stating that we must use the five tracts that he had sent or the deal was off. So I dropped the matter.

A good deal of the ineffectiveness of gospel communication in other lands is the result of the missionary's own insensitivity and thoughtlessness. Barriers are sometimes created by the Western mind-set of the speaker, and not from the different cultural patterns or religious concepts of the listener.

While in India I often tuned in to Radio Ceylon and listened to the Christian programs that were sponsored by American mission organizations. It was the only radio station in all of southeast Asia where one could buy time and put on religious programs. Many of these programs were tapes of sermons preached in some tabernacle in America to Christian audiences, and were completely irrelevant for non-Christian listeners in India. The results were pathetically meager in terms of the expenditures involved. There was one group, however, that used tapes of sermons and music produced in India by national Christians, and these were much more effective.

## 1. Indigenous Sermons

The missionary evangelist needs to develop an indigenous style of preaching that will fit the background and life-style of his audience. Sermon topics and illustrations should be taken right out of the life of the people.

*a.* The late Rev. M. D. Ross, veteran missionary to India, was an expert in this type of approach. To this day I vividly remember certain of his sermons that he preached over 40 years ago. One of these was his "Sermon on Wells," using the text Isa. 12:3—"With joy you will draw water from the wells of salvation." In his introduction he talked about the importance of the well in the life of an Indian village, and the necessity of water to sustain life. He compared water with God's gift of salvation. He then went on to describe the various types of wells that he had seen in the villages of India, and how each of these represented a different type of Christian life. His outline was as follows:

(1) The **dry** well. Strongly built with stone and cement, equipped with pulley and rope; but without water. Represents the nominal Christian who has all the outward appearances of Christianity, but has not received the water of salvation.

(2) The **monsoon** well. Full of water during the rainy season, but dry during the summer. Represents the unsteady Christian, who is full of zeal at times and indifferent at others.

(3) The **closed** well. Once it was a good well, but later was filled in and closed. Represents the backslider, who once knew the Lord but has allowed sin to come into his life and crowd out the water of salvation. What is needed is to clean out the well and allow the water of salvation to flow in again.

(4) The **caste** well. Has plenty of water, but people of another caste are not permitted to draw from it. Represents the selfish Christian, who has received the water of salvation but does not share it with others.

(5) The **artesian** well. Always full of fresh water, in season and out of season. Represents the Spirit-filled life, which draws on all the resources of God and brings rich blessing to the lives of others.

*b.* The same missionary had an appealing sermon on "God's Bazaar," using Isa. 55:1 as the text. In India (and many Eastern countries) the weekly market is very important to the rural people. It is where they sell their products and buy what is needed for the following week. The speaker described the differences between God's and man's bazaar, such as:

(1) God's bazaar is open day and night, every day in the week.
(2) There is no bargaining in God's bazaar.

Then he went on to describe the "produce" that God has to offer, and the "price" that he requires. God offers:

(1) Forgiveness—the price is repentance and faith.
(2) Peace—the price is our willingness to forgive others.
(3) Power—the price is obedience to God's will.
(4) The Holy Spirit—the price is self-surrender.

*c.* An Indian evangelist, who passed away several years ago, often held his audience spellbound with his sermon on "The Sheep and the Goats" (text: Matt 15:31-33). Realizing that his rural listeners were well acquainted with the characteristics of these two animals, he would point out the differences between their habits and then show the differences in the character of God's people and the devil's crowd.

Here are some of the points he emphasized:

(1) *Note the head* of the two animals. The sheep usually goes around with its head down, but the goat with its head high in the air. The sheep stands for humility; the goat for pride. God's people are humble and meek in spirit; the devil's followers strut with their heads in the air, proud, arrogant, self-conceited.

(2) *Note the horns.* The horns of the sheep are usually curved and blunt; those of the goat are straight and sharp. Sheep are generally harmless, while goats love to prance around butting one another. In the same way, God's people are peaceful and loving; Satan's followers are stubborn and quarrelsome.

(3) *Note the grazing habits.* Sheep generally keep together in a huddle. Where one goes, all go. Thus it is easy for one shepherd to take care of a large flock of sheep. As for the goats, each one goes its own way. This makes it hard for the owner to look after them. And so among God's people there is found unity and fellowship. They will readily follow the Shepherd. As for the devil's crowd, each one is for himself. There is often confusion, division, and strife. This makes things difficult for the pastor.

(4) *Note the flesh of the animals.* The meat of the sheep is tender; that of the goat is tough. The believer is tenderhearted; he quickly responds to the gospel message. The sinner is hardened in mind and heart. He is rebellious and obstinate.

(5) *Note the hair of the animals.* The sheep grows long, soft wool; goat's hair is short and stiff. The sheep works for 365 days in the year, gives us beautiful wool to provide blankets and clothing. Goat's hair is useless. Children of God are generous and bring blessing to others, while children of Satan are selfish and live only for themselves.

*d.* The words of Hos. 7:8, comparing Ephraim to "a cake not turned," is translated into the languages of India as "a *chapathi* not turned." The *chapathi* is a type of unleavened bread in the shape of a pancake, made out of wheat or milo flour. To be properly done it must be cooked on both sides. So the verse makes a good text for a sermon on "Half-Baked Christians," while the context describes in what ways one can be half-hearted in his Christian life, namely, in his separation from the world, his devotion to God, and in his prayer life.

*e.* A missionary to Zaire shared with me a couple of sermon outlines that he uses, taken out of the African scene. The first is based on the cabbage, one of the main vegetables of the people. Illustrating the development that takes place in the Christian life, he describes the development of the cabbage from *seed,* to *plant,* to cabbage *head.*

The second sermon is based on the palm tree which is found everywhere and serves to illustrate many spiritual truths in the Christian life:

(1) The life of the palm tree is in the heart of the tree.
(2) Its taproots go 2-300 feet into the ground.
(3) It grows under difficult circumstances.
(4) It cannot be grafted.

(5) It bears fruit every day of the year.

(6) Every part of the tree is useful.

We must not overlook the fact that many of the incidents in the Bible have an Eastern setting and therefore have great potential for communicating gospel truth in many countries of Africa and Asia. In areas where the leper is a common sight, the story of Naaman, the Syrian general, can portray vividly the tragedy of sin and the gracious remedy provided by God. In places where blindness and spirit possession are common occurrences, the narratives of the healing of Bartimaeus and the man called Legion provide valuable sermon material for the evangelist. In rural areas where the women gather at the village well daily to draw their water supply, and where men often carry their relatives to the hospital on simple homemade cots, the narratives of the Samaritan woman and the paralytic are powerful vehicles to describe the healing and transforming power of the Lord Jesus Christ.

## 2. Indigenous Illustrations

Not only should our sermon outlines be indigenous, but our illustrations as well. How often an American-style illustration has been unintelligible to the listener abroad and therefore has fallen flat, simply because it was taken out of experiences and customs completely foreign to his own. Each culture provides an abundance of fascinating illustrations out of the storehouse of its own stories, folklore, and human experiences. The following are just a few samples:

  a. *The guilty servant* (India). There was a theft in the king's palace one day. Someone stole a set of his majesty's silver vessels. Suspecting an inside job, the king called all his servants before him and questioned them individually, but each one declared his innocence. The king then ordered that a stick of exactly the same size be given to each servant. "Bring your stick back with you tomorrow morning," he ordered. "By then the culprit's stick will have grown three inches longer, and he will be caught and severely punished." When the thief heard this, he became afraid, went home, and cut three inches off his stick. The next day when he stood before the king, his stick was shorter than anyone else's, so he was pronounced guilty and sent to jail.

  b. *The wise young boy* (China). Many years ago in China, the people in a certain town made a large bell which they wanted to hang in the center of town so that all could hear its beautiful tones. The bell was so heavy, however, that they were unable to lift it off the ground and hang it on the crossbar. While the elders all stood around arguing what to do, a young lad stepped forward and said, "Why don't you just fasten the bell to the bar while it is lying on the ground and then dig the earth out from underneath it?" (A Chinese evangelist used this story in connection with the narrative of Jesus as a boy of 12 confounding the wisdom of the elders in the Temple.)

c. *Sin and its cure* (Africa). There is a certain plant, called the *jipkomone*, that grows everywhere in the interior of Zaire. When it is young and quite tender, cattle will eat it. But in maturing, it becomes a thorny hedge, and cattle will have nothing to do with it. In the same way, sin first looks attractive but later proves to be harmful.

There is another plant which grows in the wilds of Africa, the milk of which, if it gets into a person's eyes, will produce temporary blindness. The only cure is the blood of a sheep applied to the eye.

d. *The responsibility of the pastor* (West Irian). A young Christian from one of the hill tribes of Irian Jaya left his house, garden, and pigs to go away on a year's ministry to another valley. Some of his Christian friends were talking about it. "What did he do with his pigs?" asked one. Another answered, "He left them, of course. Jesus isn't going to ask him what he did with his pigs. Jesus will ask him, 'Where are your sheep?'"

e. *The way to escape temptation* (Hmar tribe, north India). A tribal preacher said to his young son:

"Suppose a big rogue elephant chases you. What could you do?

"First, you must remember that all elephants are left-handed. So if an elephant chases you, run straight ahead, then make a sharp turn to the right, run straight again, then take another right turn. Do this four times and you will be back on your original course. Since elephants cannot turn quickly to the right, if they try they will fall to the ground, and it takes a long time for one to get up.

"Something else you must remember, my son. Satan is left-handed too. He is the enemy of your soul and would like nothing more than to lead a 10-year-old boy into sin. If you

144 / Tell It Well

are tempted to evil while far from your parents, turn to the right by reading the Word of God. Tell Jesus about this rogue, and He will tumble him on his back."[1]

f. *Deliverance from the evil giant* (Malaysia). Jacob Samuel, convert from Hinduism, now a Christian evangelist, uses the following mythological story from Hinduism to point to Christ as the great Deliverer.

Many years ago there was a giant named Narahasuran, who was going about the land torturing and killing people by the hundreds. The entire population was afraid of him and sought for a deliverer who could rescue them out of his hand. They began to call upon their gods for help. Then there came a man from an unknown world, with no beginning or end, who fought with the giant and slew him. The people rejoiced in their new freedom and celebrated with a "festival of lights." To this day the people still celebrate the festival known as *Theebavali.*

In the same way, the devil goes about as a fierce giant, deceiving and enslaving people all over the world with the chains of sin. Men are powerless to get out of his control. In order to rescue us, God sent His Son into the world, who, through His death on the Cross and the Resurrection, has defeated Satan and delivered us from the power of sin. Christians today celebrate this deliverance at the festival of Christmas.

## 3. Indigenous Methods of Evangelism

We need not debate the point that our message is always the same, but our methods change from time to time and from place to place. This is a generally accepted truth. Even a quick look at the New Testament will reveal the fact that the early Christians had but one message—Christ, crucified and risen—but they used a variety of methods to proclaim the gospel. In the New Testament we find *person-to-person evangelism* (as Christ speaking to the Samaritan woman at the well), *mass evangelism* (Peter addressing the multitudes on the Day of Pentecost), *spontaneous evangelism* (Paul and the Philippian jailer), *systematic evangelism* (Paul in his missionary journeys), and *literature evangelism* (Paul's letters to the churches). Down through the years the Church has constantly sought for new ways to tell the old, old story.

*Fixed in message; flexible in method* is a good rule for the Christian messenger to follow. It is so easy, however, to become wedded to one's customary methods and transplant these methods into other cultures, oblivious of any adverse effects. Methodists in south India soon discovered that the common use of the "altar call" was impractical for rural people attending "jungle camp meetings." When the call was given, everyone came forward, because "they did not want to disobey the missionary's command." So it was impossible to tell who were genuine seekers and who were committed Christians. Missionaries found the best way was to invite the penitent to go out under the trees and pray. Then the missionaries would seek them out and counsel and pray with each one.

Many evangelists in Japan have discovered that asking people to "raise your hands" can be very misleading in recording statistics. The Japanese people are very polite; and if requested to raise their hands, they will do so, for they do not want to offend the speaker!

Bruce Olson, pioneer missionary to the Motilones of Colombia, South America,[2] quickly discovered that to gather a group of Motilones together and address them in public produced a negative reaction among the listeners. In their culture only deceivers follow such a format. He learned that the proper way to communicate is to wait until all have climbed into their hammocks for the night, then give out "the news" from this lying-down position. The next night the chief would comment on the message given, and then all would feel free to discuss the subject. When Bruce Olson wanted to take the message of Christ to the neighboring Shayliliko tribe, he took along a sheaf of arrows, slapped them on the ground and broke them, then asserted his authority as a messenger and went on to announce the "good news." In this way the Shaylilikos recognized him as an official messenger and listened with respect.

Sometimes an ordinary method may turn out to be a wrong method in a particular culture, and, unknown to the evangelist, became a serious barrier for the acceptance of the gospel. For over 20 years two lady missionaries in Kenya, East Africa, labored untiringly to bring the gospel to a certain primitive tribe. They used flannelgraphs, music recordings, slides, and other audiovisual materials to present the story of Christ. The women and children seemed interested and would gather around to listen, but the men never attended the services. Finally one day someone asked one of the men why they were so indifferent to the Christian message. He answered, "We are not against the message, but those lady missionaries are very disrespectful. *They stand up and teach! If a woman wants to say something to a man, she should sit down!"* And 20 years had passed by without a convert among the men![3]

It is wise for the evangelist working in a foreign culture to ask the question, How do these people communicate with one another? The answer will often give him a clue to the most effective ways of preaching the gospel. Among the Sumbanese people of Africa it is the custom for a person to give a feast and then to spend most of the night telling the people just why the feast has been given. It may be that the host wants to announce the birth of a son, or tell about some unusual experience he has recently gone through. Some Sumbanese Christians have now adapted this social pattern as a means of evangelizing their neighbors. Here in the leisurely evening hours and at the happy occasion of a feast, people can listen to the simple witness of their host and ask questions. Furthermore, the guests get the impression that this new faith must be important, or the host would not have gone to so much trouble and expense in order to tell them about his spiritual experience.[4]

Among Hindus in India the *kalakshepam* (north) or *kirtan* (south) is one of the most popular means of narrating the mythological stories of the gods. The *kirtan* is a lengthy epic poem set to music and sung by a religious teacher to the accompaniment of *harmonium* (small hand-pumped organ), *thabla* (drum), and cymbals. The whole performance, interspersed with rest periods, may last for three or four hours—late into the night. Some Christian musicians have composed *kirtans* based on sections of the life of Christ, and go from village to village giving performances. Non-Christians turn out by the hundreds and sit with their families for hours, listening attentively to the story of Christ. Ordinarily they would never sit through a three-hour sermon.

From a very successful Indian evangelist[5] I learned a new talk-sing type of preaching that revolutionized my ministry among village people. The evangelist speaks for a while, and then suddenly starts singing a well-known gospel lyric that fits into the point he is emphasizing at the moment. Immediately the audience joins in the singing, clapping their hands and playing cymbals. Then the evangelist continues his sermon and a little later breaks out in song again. In this way he is able to hold the attention of his audience more easily and for a much longer period of time. To say the least, it is an excellent way to keep the audience awake!

About 15 years ago Dr. Evyn Adams, missionary to Japan,[6] initiated a special type of radio program (HOREMCO) on the island of Hokkaido, which continues effectively to this day. The program, which lasts for only 10 or 15 minutes, begins with a fanfare of trumpets and an announcement. Then follows a capsule story, usually in dialogue form, depicting a typical, everyday human problem, such as a quarrel in the home or the temptation to cheat. Finally, the announcer says, "The New Testament is the Book that tells you how to deal with this problem. Would you like to have a copy?" In this way contact is made with hundreds of inquirers, and this is followed up with a personal visit from a Christian volunteer living in the vicinity. (The program now appears on television also.)

Another missionary friend of mine recently told me of a new type of "campfire evangelism" that his gospel team is using in Zaire. They discovered that the Africans love to sit around a bonfire at night and sing and tell stories. So his team arrives at a particular village about dusk and lights a huge bonfire a short distance outside the hamlet. They start playing their instruments and singing. Before long a good crowd has gathered, and then the team members start witnessing and doing personal work.[7]

Mrs. Margaret Moore, missionary to Korea who has a master's degree in drama, has made effective use of Christian drama in the form of the shadow play so popular among Koreans. She has written a play on the life of Christ, called *The Prince of Peace,* which has been presented by a troupe of Korean Christian actors many, many times in the capital city of Seoul and all across the country. Special performances have been given in prisons and to the armed forces. The play has been highly acclaimed by Christians and non-Christians, by government officials and artists, and by the public in general. Recently the troupe went on tour through several Asian countries such as Thailand, the Philippines, and Taiwan—and was received with great enthusiasm everywhere. During the Christmas and Easter seasons the group also presents shadow plays on the birth and resurrection of our Lord. The spiritual impact of all this has been more than one could anticipate. (One of their most popular presentations is entitled *Jesus and Women.*)

In Taiwan and Japan, missionaries have developed a new form of evangelism in response to the widespread desire to study the English language. Both the Chinese and Japanese realize that English is used throughout the world and therefore are anxious to gain a working knowledge of the language. Missionaries are now teaching English to thousands of people in private classes and over the radio, using the Gospel of John as a textbook. In this way the students are exposed to the Word of God, and many show an interest in knowing more of the Christian faith. Word has now come that the government in mainland China is inviting 500,000 teachers from abroad to come to China and organize a crash study program in the English language!

Other illustrations could be cited from many countries across the world, but these are sufficient to demonstrate the wide variety of evangelistic methods that can be used in presenting the gospel to different people in different cultures. As messengers of Christ we must be constantly on the lookout for methods that have maximum communicative value and appeal for our listeners. This will add new dynamic and freshness to our ministry. It is exciting to know that we not only have a good story to tell, but we have so many good ways to tell it well!

# PART 3

# Communicating the Gospel
# to Non-Christians

# 10

# Communicating the Gospel to Hindus

Hinduism is an ancient religion with a history of over 4,000 years. It claims about 550 million followers, most of whom live in India. There are smaller groups of Hindus living in Sri Lanka, Burma, Malaysia, Bali (Indonesia), East and South Africa, and the Fiji Islands in the Pacific. In recent years, Hinduism has made forays into Western nations, in the form of the Hare Krishna movement, Transcendental Meditation, Yoga, and Vedanta philosophy.

Of all the world's great religions, Hinduism is the most difficult to define. It does not have any one founder. It is not a credal religion, like Islam and Christianity. It is more a league of religions than a single religion, and can easily absorb new ideas and new deities. Herein lies the strength of Hinduism as well as its weakness.

## 1. The Hindu Scriptures

The Hindu scriptures were written in Sanskrit over a period of more than 2,000 years and cover a wide variety of religious beliefs and practices. At different periods in the history of Hinduism, various philosophical schools and religious movements have taken their inspiration and authority from selected portions of these scriptures. The main collections are as follows:

*a. The Vedas* (1500-500 B.C.) are collections of hymns, prayers, rituals, and magical formulae. They depict the worship of a variety of gods by means of ritual sacrifices. Most of the gods are personifications of the powers of nature, such as the sun, moon, fire, storm, air, and rain. The theological concept of atonement for sin is most clearly and frequently emphasized.

b. *The Brahmanas* comprise the sacrificial ritual and act as a manual for priest and worshipper.

c. *The Upanishads* (500 B.C.—A.D. 500) provide the basic philosophical concepts of Hinduism (often in dialogue form). They describe the search after the ultimate secret of all existence and the way of release from endless transmigrations.

d. *The Ramayana and Mahabharata,* two great Hindu epics, expound the principles of the Vedas by interpreting the exploits of the great national heroes (notably Rama and Sita).

e. *The Bhagavad Gita* ("Song of the Lord"), a portion of the Mahabharata, is the best-known and best-loved scripture of modern Hindus. It consists of a conversation between Arjuna, the warrior-prince, and his charioteer Krishna, who is the disguised incarnation of Vishnu. It calls for unselfish action in doing one's duty according to one's status in society.

f. *The Puranas* are a collection of myths and legends about the several incarnations of Vishnu, seeking to evoke religious devotion among the masses.

## 2. The Caste System

The caste system is peculiar to Hinduism and has been the basic structure of Hindu society for centuries. Its origin lay largely in the primitive color bar between the fair-skinned Aryan invaders and the dark-skinned, Dravidian aborigines. Economic divisions, along occupational lines, also played an important part in the formation of the caste system, while religion played a key role in its continuation, since one's caste was held to be the result of his *karma* (deeds in a previous life). The four main divisions of caste are as follows:

a. The Brahmans (priests and religious teachers)

b. The Kshatriyas (kings and warriors)

c. Vaisyas (traders and merchants)

d. Sudras (cultivators and servants)

Outside the four castes are the "untouchables" or "outcastes," whose occupations rendered them unclean. Untouchability has been a blot on Hindu society, and several reform movements have sought to eliminate it. Mahatma Gandhi called the outcastes *Harijans,* or "the people of God." The constitution of India rules against discrimination on the basis of caste, and the government is granting special benefits to members of the low castes.

## 3. Philosophical Hinduism

*a. Monism* (Brahman). The foundation of Hindu philosophy or religion is *monism,* the idea that there is but one unified reality in the universe. This one Eternal Being is called *Brahman,* the Absolute One, or *Paramatman,* the World Soul. Brahman, the source and embodiment of all real being, is impersonal, and is usually referred to with the neuter pronoun "It." Brahman is *Nirguna,* without attributes, for the Hindu philosopher believes that to ascribe characteristics to the One Reality is to limit It. Brahman is *neti-neti,* that is, "neither this nor that." It is unlimited. Brahman is also passionless, relationless, unsearchable, unknowable. In this respect the Hindu is an agnostic of a profound type.

This sort of impersonal Being, devoid of qualities and incomprehensible to man, is no comfort to humanity. It is a nonentity to the worshipper. Brahman is shrouded with mystery and is pushed into a far-off realm beyond human ken. This has led the Hindu to seek to bring the eternal Reality a little closer and make Brahman somewhat more approachable. So from the *Nirguna-Brahman* (without attributes) he turns to the *Saguna-Brahman,* or Brahman *with* attributes, with descriptions, with relationships. It is this Being, known as *Isvara,* which we may now call "He," who creates, preserves, and permeates the world, and controls its dissolution at the end of time. He is all-wise, all-powerful, and omnipresent. This Saguna-Brahman we may well term "God" in Hinduism. It is as Isvara that most of India knows God, with his functions, his relationships with the world and with human beings.

*b. Pantheism.* Now if there is only one reality in the universe, then the question arises, What about creation and what about man? According to Hindu thought, Brahman is never the Creator of the universe in the Hebrew and Christian sense. Brahman always creates out of something or out of himself, never out of that which did not exist. The general teaching of the Upanishads is that the universe emanates from ultimate Reality as sparks emanate from fire, or a spider's web flows from the spider itself. The world has no beginning or end. It has come from the Brahman and to the Brahman it will return.

Thus out of the monism of Hinduism there emerges a type of pantheism which identifies Brahman with the sum total of creation. Everything we see is really a part of Brahman. The Hindu insists, therefore, that the world around, the world of sense, is nothing but *maya,* or illusion. To think that it is real is sheer *avidya,* ignorance.

The same is true of man. His body is a part of the great illusion, and for him to think of himself as a separate being is again the result of ignorance. But within man is the *atman* or the divine self which is really identical with the *Paramatman* or World Soul. As the air within a jar, though enclosed, is one with the air outside, so the soul within man is one with the soul everywhere. Whoever realizes this—"I am Brahman"—becomes the All.

   *c. Polytheism.* From its basic monism and resulting pantheism, Hinduism easily slips into a form of *polytheism,* or belief in many gods. It proceeds from the Brahman without attributes to the Brahman with attributes, then on to the Hindu Triad and countless lesser deities. The Triad consists of Brahma, the Originator or Creator of all visible things; Vishnu, the Preserver; and Shiva, the Destroyer (sometimes the Regenerator). As for Brahma, since his work has already been accomplished, he no longer needs worship. Little attention is paid to him. Vishnu and Shiva, on the other hand, are exceedingly popular and are worshipped in many forms. Vishnu has come down to earth in 9 *avatars,* or "descents," in order to preserve humanity from impending calamities. These incarnations are the fish, the tortoise, the boar, the man-lion, the dwarf, and 4 fully human forms including Krishna and Buddha.[1] A 10th incarnation, Kalki, is yet to come. Riding on a charger with a sword in his hand, he will come to destroy degenerate mankind and build up a new world.

   Each member of the Triad has a wife, who is an important goddess in the Hindu pantheon. Brahma's wife, Sarasvati, is the goddess of all creative arts; Lakshmi, the wife of Vishnu, is the goddess of prosperity; Shiva's wife, Parvati, is known by various names, is widely revered and has an independent cult of her own. Her son, Ganesha, the elephant-headed god of wisdom, is one of the most popular figures in Hinduism. Besides these principal deities, there are innumerable gods in the Hindu system, commonly estimated at 330 million.

   Since everything is a part of Brahman, anything can become sacred to the Hindu. There are sacred rivers (as the Ganges), sacred animals (the cow, the monkey), and sacred trees (the banyan and the pipal). Besides, there is Naga, the snake god, and Garuda, the man-eagle. The peacock is also revered.

   The worship of these innumerable deities, coupled with incantations and rituals, festivals and pilgrimages, form the basis of popular Hinduism in India. Many animistic features are also introduced, such as the use of charms and mantras (magical words), and the practice of black magic and spirit-possession.

The Hindu explains the existence of this vast array of deities as but emanations (or extensions) of the One Absolute Reality, and as manifestations of the different attributes of Brahman. He justifies the use of images with the argument that the ordinary person cannot conceive of God as mere Soul without attributes and needs to have something tangible before him to make God real. The Hindu philosopher will insist that he is really worshipping the one invisible God through the use of visible gods; but it is quite evident that, for the common man at least, the creature has taken the place of the Creator, and the worshipper's mind is more on the image in front of him than on God who is above him. However, the growth of the Hindu pantheon bears testimony to the craving of the human soul for a God who can satisfy its wants and realize its deepest longings.

d. *Karma and Samsara.* Belief in the doctrine of *Karma* is distinctive of the Hindu outlook on life. Karma literally means "action" or "doing," and stands for the principle of necessity operating in the ethical life of an individual. It extends the relation of cause and effect from the physical sphere to the moral sphere. Just as every occurrence in the physical sphere is conditioned by certain antecedents, everything that happens to an individual in his life is determined by previous actions of his own. As a man sows, so shall he reap. Bad actions reap suffering and bondage to human existence. Good actions lead to happiness and freedom from this bondage.

Karma operates as an inescapable law of justice, independent of the decrees of God or the gods. Thus the individual himself is made responsible both for his happiness and misery. Nothing unmerited can happen to an individual, and whatever happens to him is merited by him. So the individual should accept the blame for his misfortunes and not try to throw it on others or God.

Belief in the law of karma carries with it the doctrine of *samsara,* or transmigration of the soul. For what is done in this life must be reaped in a future life. A person may be reborn as a god, as a member of a higher or lower caste, or as an animal, according to his every thought, word, and act. Thus each individual carries with him his past and at the same time is creating his future. The law of karma, therefore, explains all the inequalities, injustices, and sufferings of life, as well as the distinctions of the caste system. Why is a man born intelligent or into a high caste? Why does he become prosperous in life? It is because of his good karma. Why is a man born into a low caste, or is poor? Why does he suffer calamity in life? It is his bad karma.

*e. Moksha* (salvation). Sin for the Hindu is not the personal moral guilt that it is for the Christian. It is not considered to be a transgression of the moral law of God, involving our relationship with Him. Sin is defined more as ignorance of the truth, and false ideas about reality and one's self.

The aim of Hinduism is to escape from the wheel of samsara and from karma itself. The Hindu longs for release from the cycle of birth, death, and rebirth, and from the chain of cause and effect. *Moksha* (salvation) is deliverance from the body-soul bondage and from the universe of time and space, for both are governed by the law of karma. In the end—after many reincarnations—the soul will be liberated from its prison house and be reunited with Brahman, the one Reality. Just as a drop of rain, falling into the ocean, ceases to be an individual drop of water and becomes a part of the great ocean, so the individual soul, when it is released, loses its separate existence and is absorbed into the one World Soul.

There are three main *margas,* or paths, to salvation. Each is valid, so the individual may take his choice. There is first the way of disinterested action *(karma marga).* Action performed with the desire for rewards binds the soul to the wheel of existence. Action done without any attachment to its results, however, leads to spiritual freedom. This path is followed by performing *dharma,* one's prescribed moral, social, and religious duties; or by performing *yoga,* certain disciplinary exercises which produce control of mind over body and perfect poise. Hereby every desire is subdued, all activity stilled, no fresh round of karma is set in motion, and so release comes.

The second path to salvation is that of exclusive devotion to God *(bhakti marga)*—reciting sacred formulae, repeating the name of a god, visiting the temples, etc. Devotion may depend on external aids, such as ritualistic worship, or it may be on the higher level of direct communion with God.

The third path to salvation is the path of higher knowledge or spiritual insight *(jnana marga).* It is for the inellectual few. It leads to release from the bondage of ignorance and to complete union with God. The worshipper is finally able to say, "I am Brahman."

## 4. Points of Contact with Christianity

There are several concepts and practices in Hinduism that afford a point of contact in presenting the gospel to Hindus.

*a.* The Hindu emphasis on the primacy of spirit and the spiritual world is in keeping with scriptural injunctions to "seek . . . first the kingdom of God, and his righteousness" and to "set your minds on things that are above, not on things that are on earth" (Matt. 6:33, KJV; Col. 3:2).

*b.* The emphasis on devotion to God *(bhakti)* is a basis for the biblical command to "love the Lord your God with all your heart, and with all your soul, and with all your mind" (Matt. 22:37).

*c.* The spirit of renunciation found in Hinduism is in keeping with the biblical admonition to deny oneself and to renounce the world (16:24; I John 2:15).

*d.* The practice of meditation and silence lays the foundation for a strong personal devotional life. ("Be still, and know that I am God" —Ps. 46:10).

*e.* The practice of yoga (mind control) lays the foundation for the disciplined Christian life—self-control through the Holy Spirit.

*f.* The Triad of Hinduism (Brahma, Vishnu, and Shiva) makes it easy for the Hindu to accept the Christian doctrine of the Trinity (unlike the Muslim).

*g.* Since there are supposed to be 10 incarnations of Vishnu, the Hindu has no problem in accepting the fact of God incarnate in Jesus Christ.

## 5. Points of Contrast with Christianity

*a.* The Hindu system is basically monistic, recognizing the existence of spirit alone. Christianity is dualistic, accepting both the spiritual and material worlds.

*b.* In Hinduism, God is impersonal, without attributes. In Christianity, God is a Person, with infinite attributes, with whom man can have relationship.

*c.* In Hinduism, the universe is an illusion. The material world and man are mere emanations of God. The Christian faith contends that this is a very real world, the arena of decision and eternal destiny. Man is created in the image of God, is fallen indeed through disobedience, but has the capacity for fellowship with God.

*d.* In Hinduism, the basic problem is intellectual—ignorance. In Christianity it is a moral problem—sin.

*e.* In Hinduism, the purpose of incarnation is to destroy the wicked and protect the righteous.[2] The purpose of Christ's incarnation is "to seek and to save the lost" (Luke 19:10).

*f.* In Hinduism, salvation is release from the wheel of existence and the bondage of karma (action), and is achieved through self-effort. In Christianity, salvation is deliverance from the guilt and power of sin, and is the free gift of God, received by faith in Jesus Christ.

## HINDUISM AND CHRISTIANITY COMPARED

| HINDUISM | | CHRISTIANITY |
|---|---|---|
| 1. No founder | GOD | 1. Founded on Jesus Christ |
| 2. *Monism*—one existence or reality. All else is illusion and the result of ignorance. | | 2. *Dualism*—God and the world are separate; God and man are distinct. Spirit and matter are both real. |
| 3. *Brahman*—is impersonal, unknowable, relationless, without attributes (It)  *Isvara*—personal, knowable, with attributes (He)  *Pantheon of gods* and goddesses in popular Hinduism (330 million deities) | | 3. God is One, personal, knowable; holy, just, loving; man can enter into relationship with Him. |
| 4. Triad (one person with three heads)—Brahma, the creator; Vishnu, the preserver; Shiva, the destroyer | TRINITY | 4. Father, Son, and Holy Spirit; Three in One |
| 5. Ten incarnations of Vishnu in various forms, animal and human. Purpose: to destroy the wicked. | INCARNATION | 5. One Incarnation: Jesus Christ, the God-man (divine and human). Purpose: to redeem the unrighteous. |
| 6. Mythological figures: legends of gods and heroes | | 6. The Incarnation was real, rooted in history. |
| 7. Variously defined as *avidya,* ignorance of the truth; *maya,* attributing reality to personhood; *mala,* the feeling of individuality | SIN | 7. A wrong relationship to God; transgression of moral law; disobedience to God; unfaith. Sin brings guilt and condemnation. |
| 8. *Karma*—good and bad deeds and their consequences; an impersonal system of justice; no possibility of forgiveness or vicarious suffering. | ACTION | 8. Moral law: action and results. "You reap what you sow." There is a personal Lawgiver and Judge. Christ took our *karma* on himself; forgiveness is possible. |
| 9. *Samsara*—reincarnation according to past karma. Cycle of birth and rebirth. | REBIRTH | 9. There is one life. New birth (spiritual life) is possible through Christ. Resurrection of the body to come. |
| 10. *Moksha*—release from the cycle of birth and rebirth; absorption in Brahman  *By works*—way of knowledge, way of action, way of devotion | SALVATION | 10. *Redemption*—deliverance from the guilt and power of sin; gift of eternal life. God living in us.  *By grace* through faith. Results in knowledge of God, good deeds, devotion to God. |

## 6. Karma and the Cross

The basic theological barrier to Christianity in Hinduism arises from the Hindu doctrine of Karma when it is pushed to its farthest limit. The fact that "a man reaps what he sows" is a universal principle and is fully acceptable. But the problem arises when the Hindu insists that "a man *must* eat the fruit of his deeds," that there is absolutely no escape from the results of karma. This means there can be no forgiveness for our bad actions or our sins. And when the Hindu insists that all the injustices and tragedies of life are the result of one's own karma, and no man can pass his karma on to someone else, this completely rules out the possibility of vicarious suffering. It means the innocent cannot suffer for the guilty. If a man suffers, it is a sign he is guilty.

A Christian evangelist in India was once preaching in a public marketplace. He was describing the humiliation, the physical agony, and the mental anguish that Jesus suffered in Pilate's judgment hall and on the Cross. A Hindu listener stepped forward and said, "Sir, this Jesus must have been a very wicked man in his previous life in order to suffer so much in this life!" He was not trying to be sacrilegious, but was merely looking at the Cross through the spectacles of karma. According to karma, if Jesus suffered, He alone was responsible. He must have been guilty. This, of course, cuts across the whole idea of the atonement.

We must point out to our Hindu friends that the statement "Each man reaps what he sows" is only a half-truth. Other people also reap what we sow—good or bad. During World War II 6 million Jews died at the hands of Adolph Hitler. Can we say that the tragic death of so many people was strictly the result of their own evil karma performed in some previous existence? Or was their death the result of the madness of Hitler himself? Then again, the lives of countless millions have been saved through the process of immunization discovered by Louis Pasteur, the French chemist and bacteriologist of the 19th century. Can we attribute the benefits thus received to our own good karma? Or were they the result of another man's beneficence? We observe all around us that often one man sows and another reaps. If the parent sins, the children and society suffer. If the parents are good, the children benefit. Our deeds affect the family, society, and the world.

This fact opens the door to vicariousness. Suppose one man, the most significant person in history, organically connected with the whole world, sowed himself on the Cross. Could the whole world reap the benefits? If Jesus were only a man, He could not pass on the benefits to the whole race. His death would only be a martyr-dom. But suppose God would sow. Could He pass on the results to all mankind? This is possible! Jesus was the Son of Man and the Son of God. He was the God-man—God in human flesh. He deliberately went to the Cross and laid down His life. Can we, then, reap what He sowed and not what we have sown? If so, this opens up great possibilities—forgiveness, freedom, life!

"But," our Hindu friends may contend, "it is unjust for the innocent to suffer for the guilty!" This is the argument that seems conclusive and would nullify all our hopes and reasonings on the subject. But let us look at the objection more closely. Does it fit the facts of life?

Here is a mother with a son who is breaking her heart. She had splendid hopes for him, but now he is spending his days in reckless folly and evil. You go to that mother and say, "It is unjust for you to suffer in this way on account of your son. You are innocent and he is guilty. It is unjust." She would look at you with a pained expression and say, "To suffer for my son is unjust? It is the very thing that motherhood within me wants to do. My heart longs to do it." Could we in the name of justice deny to that mother the privilege of suffering for her son? The privilege of being noble?

Suppose you would say to her, "You must deal with your child after the manner of strict justice. Whatever he gives to you, you may give in return—no more, no less." Would she obey you if she were a real mother? Would you really want her to do so? A family founded on strict justice alone would become like a marketplace where goods are bargained for and paid for in the coin of similar deeds. The finest thing in life would die, namely, *sacrificial love.*

This law of sacrifice runs through life, from the lowest to the very highest of life. In any realm of life those who save others cannot save themselves trouble, sorrow, yes, sometimes even death. The seed gives itself and dies in order to produce a harvest. The mother bird throws herself into the jaws of the serpent in order to save her young. The human mother goes down into the valley of death to bring a child into the world. The young patriot, with all his life before him, takes his one life into his hands and marches out against the bayonets of the enemy, in order to save his home and country. This spirit of sacrifice is the most noble thing in life.

Now if this is a universal law—and it seems to be—then when we come to God, the highest Being, we would expect to find in Him the greatest and noblest expression of sacrificial love in the whole universe. Otherwise the creature would be greater than the Creator. A worm would be greater, a bird, an animal; they give themselves, but not God. It is unthinkable that God would write a law of saving by sacrifice throughout the universe and be empty of it himself. If there is not a loving, sacrificing God in the universe, then there ought to be! The highest in man and the universe calls for it.

But the Cross shows that there is such a God. When Jesus was suffering untold agony on the Cross, the people mocked Him and said, "He saved others; he cannot save himself" (Matt. 27:42). Strange as it may seem, the mocking phrase of those hatred-crazed enemies became the central truth of Christianity. He was saving others and, therefore, could not save himself. Here we see sacrificial love at its highest. For here was the God of the universe sacrificing himself for lost humanity; the Divine suffering for the human, the innocent for the guilty, the sinless for the sinful.

Thus the Cross reveals that God is not only a God of *law* and order (as the doctrine of Karma shows), but He is also a God of *love* (as the law of sacrifice shows). The Cross reveals that God is not only zealous to uphold the moral order of the universe and to do something about wrong action and sin, but He is also zealous to uplift the one who has gone against the moral order and to redeem the sinner. So in the Cross the justice and the love of God meet. There we see that God loved justice too well to forgive lightly, and loved man too well to be indifferent.

There was a great religious and military leader in the Caucasus, by the name of Shamyl, who died in 1871. Bribery was so rampant in his kingdom that he made a penalty of 100 lashes for anyone taking or giving a bribe. One day a culprit was brought before Shamyl. He turned pale. It was his own mother. What would he do? Lightly forgive? He was too just for that. Would he do nothing to save her? He was too loving for that. So he ordered the lash. First came 1 blow—then 2, 3, 4, 5. Then suddenly he cried out, "Halt!" He knelt in his mother's place and took the remaining 95 lashes. Some exclaimed, "How just!" Others, "How loving!" Actually, it was both. Shamyl kept the law, but he saved his mother. Two things came together—justice and mercy, law and love. From this the followers of Shamyl caught a vision of how deeply just their master was. He would not change his laws, and yet he saved the guilty.

In the Cross we see that God is both just and merciful. He is so just that the penitent soul is inflicted with a punishment more severe than any other—the pain of having wounded love, God's love. But He is so merciful that the penitent soul is set free and goes through life with a song. He is forgiven, redeemed. God's love is a principled love.

Does the Cross then repeal the law of karma? No. It merely introduces a higher law. In the universe every law is restrained by a higher law. The *centrifugal* force is restrained by the *centripetal;* otherwise our earth would fly into space, a runaway world. The law of gravity, if it were not restrained by other laws, would pull everything to earth and there would be total collapse. The law of aerodynamics overcomes the law of gravity and enables a plane to fly. In all of life we can overcome one law by the introduction of a higher one. We do not do away with the lower law; we simply suspend its operation for the moment. Gravity is still there when I take advantage of the law of muscular strength and raise my arm.

The law of sowing and reaping (karma) underlies the moral sphere, as gravitation underlies the physical realm. God introduces man to a higher law in the cross of Christ—the law of sacrificial love. If we take hold of that law and let it operate within our lives, we suspend the old law and are lifted above it. We do not do away with it; for as soon as we cease to take advantage of the highest law, the lower comes into operation again, as gravity operates as soon as we cease to take advantage of the law of aerodynamics. "The law of the Spirit of life in Christ Jesus has set me free from the law of sin and death," cried the apostle Paul (Rom. 8:2). The introduction of the higher law of life in Christ made him free from the lower law of sin and its consequence, death.

So whereas the law of karma reveals a *principle,* the *Cross* reveals a *person.* Karma is something impersonal and systematic; the Cross reveals Someone very personal and sympathetic. Whereas the law of karma reveals to us that sin is against ourselves and brings us pain, the Cross reveals that sin is basically against God and brings Him pain. Whereas the law of karma reveals God to be a God of justice, the Cross reveals Him to be also a God of love.

It is interesting that when Mahatma Gandhi was assassinated in India in January, 1948, the people of India did not apply the principle of karma to his death. They might have said that his tragic, untimely death was the result of his own bad karma. But they loved and respected Gandhi too much to do that. They looked upon him as the father of their new nation. So instead, Hindus all across the country began to compare Gandhi with Christ. It happened that, like Christ, Gandhi was killed on a Friday and by one of his own group.

So this made the comparison all the more real. Pictures appeared by the thousands, showing Gandhi slumped over from the bullet wounds, and in the background Christ hanging on the Cross. Hindus began to say: "Just as Christians have been telling us that Christ was innocent and died for others, so Gandhi was a good and innocent man, and gave his life for his country." When I heard this, I felt that India for the first time was beginning to understand the meaning of the Cross and vicarious suffering.

### 7. The Vedas and the Cross[4]

In the Hindu scriptures there are a number of verses where sacrifice is spoken of as the only means of salvation. In the Vedas, for example, we find such statements as:
"Sacrifices are the foremost of our first duties."
"It is sacrifice that bestows all things."
"Sacrifice is the bark [boat] that enables one to live well."
"Only by means of sacrifice did the gods attain heaven."
"Afford deliverance through the path of sacrifice."
The Bhagavad Gita also affirms the importance of sacrifice:
"Thus spoke the Lord of Creation when he made both man and sacrifice: 'by sacrifice thou shalt multiply and obtain all thy desires'" (Gita 3:10).
"All those know what is sacrifice, and through sacrifice purify their sins. Neither this world nor the world to come is for him who does not sacrifice" (4:30-31).
"Works of sacrifice . . . should indeed be performed; for these are works of purification" (18:5).
In other places the Hindu scriptures declare that the sacrifices performed do not themselves confer salvation, but they are the type or shadow of a great salvation-giving sacrifice.
"Ye gods, sacrifices are like the timbers of a bark; there is no doubt that they are unsound."[5]
"It is a sacrifice that saves. What is being performed is the shadow of sacrifice."[6]
"He whose shadow and death become nectar shall, by his shadow and death, confer the spirit and strength."[7]
Even more significant are those verses in the Hindu scriptures that speak of God himself being the sacrifice:
"Prajapati [Lord of all creatures] himself is the sacrifice."[8]
"God would offer himself as a sacrifice and obtain atonement for sins."[9]

"God became half mortal and half immortal."[10]

What is evident from these above verses is that the true and great redeeming sacrifice would be the one performed by the Sovereign Lord of this world, who, becoming incarnate as God-man, would offer himself as a sacrifice to redeem mankind from their sins. All this has been fulfilled, once and for all, in the incarnation and death of our Lord Jesus Christ.

## 8. The Gospel for the Hindu

At the heart of the Hindu religion is the all-consuming desire to know God. We have seen how the Hindu moves from the impersonal God to the personal God, then on to the divine Triad and numerous gods, and finally to images of the gods—all in the attempt to make God real and bring Him close. So in our approach to the Hindu, we must meet him at the point of this magnificent obsession.

This means that we must begin with the person of Christ. If we begin with God, we begin with only our false ideas about God. If we start with man, we start with a problem. So we begin with the God-man. Christ Jesus is the one true *avatar*, or incarnation, of God. His descent into this world is not a myth but a historical fact. At a certain point in history, God took upon himself the form of a man and became a member of the human race. Jesus was Immanuel, "God with us." He was God at close range. In Jesus we see the true nature of God. We learn that God is absolute holiness, absolute justice, and absolute love. We know Him as Creator, as Judge, and Redeemer. We discover that He is a seeking God, reaching out to man and bringing him back into fellowship with himself. All that we need to know about God is found in Jesus Christ. We can think of nothing higher or nobler; we dare not think of anything less.

In Christ not only do we see God, but we see ourselves. In His presence all our self-righteousness and good deeds appear as filthy rags. We realize how far short of the glory of God we have fallen. For Christ is perfect Man, and we are sinful men.

This brings the Hindu face-to-face with his karma. The Bible clearly states that "whatever a man sows, that he will also reap" (Gal. 6:7). It also declares that all men have sown bad karma, for "all have sinned," and "the wages of sin is death" (Rom. 3:23; 6:23). Thus all men stand as sinners, guilty before God. Hindus recognize the sinfulness of man, for they talk about the "six enemies of the soul—lust, anger, avarice, fascination [with the world], pride, and jealousy."[11] Even Shankaracharya, the most famous exponent of Hindu philos-

ophy who lived in the eighth century, cried out in a prayer of peni-
tence: "I am a sinner, a sinner by deed, a sinner in spirit, a sinner by
nature. O God, have mercy on me."

This is true *self-realization*—the recognition that we are sinners in
the sight of God. The "self-realization" that leads to the alleged discovery that "I am God" is, in fact, the great universal lie which Satan
himself has concocted. We must reject this great lie and confess that
we are not God, but mere men and sinful men at that. We must bow
the knee to the one true God and cast ourselves upon His mercy.

Having brought the Hindu thus far, we are now ready to introduce him to Christ the Savior. The Vedas say that "it is sacrifice that
saves," and the Bible declares that "without the shedding of blood
there is no forgiveness of sins" (Heb. 9:22). The Vedas state that
"Prajapati [Lord of all creatures] himself is the sacrifice," and the
Bible proclaims that Jesus is "the Lamb of God, who takes away the
sin of the world" (John 1:29). Jesus is the final and perfect Sacrifice
for sin, of which all other sacrifices are mere shadows. In Jesus on
the Cross, God laid His love alongside the sin of man. He took our
karma upon himself. He now offers full and free pardon for all our
sins, and deliverance from bondage of sin. He offers us eternal life.
Salvation is possible *here and now*, the moment we accept God's free
gift.

Our karma, therefore, is in one of two places. Either it is on
Christ, or it is on us. If we repent and believe on Christ as our Savior,
then our karma is rolled on Him and taken away. If we do not repent
and believe, then our karma remains upon us, and "we will have to
eat the fruit of our deeds." If we live under the law of sacrificial love,
we will find freedom and life. If we continue to live under the law of
karma, we will find bondage and death. The choice is ours.

To those who respond in faith, God grants the special gift of His
Spirit. This means that through the presence of the Holy Spirit, God
himself will dwell in us, transform us, and enable us to live in a
manner pleasing to Him. This makes God very real, and personal,
and closer than hands or feet. He is no longer just God *above* us, or
God *with* us, but God *within* us.

Christ is thus the Fulfillment of the noble aspirations of Hinduism. He says to the Hindu: "I am the Way"—the *Karma Marga*, the
method of acting; "I am the Truth"—the *Jnana Marga*, the method of
knowing; "I am the Life"—the *Bhakti Marga*, the object of devotion
(see John 14:6). The Jnana Marga is devotion to an idea; the Karma

Marga is devotion to a code; the Bhakti Marga is devotion to a person. Jesus is that idea become Fact; the code is now a Character; the person is now the Supreme Person.

Christ is also the answer to the fervent prayer of the Hindu, expressed in the Vedas:

> "From the untruth lead me to the truth;
> From darkness lead me to light;
> From death lead me to immortality."

Christ clearly says: "I am the truth. If you know Me, you know the Father; you are in touch with reality. I am the Light of the World. If you follow Me, you will no longer walk in darkness. I am the Resurrection and the Life. If you believe in Me, you will never die" (see John 14:6-9; 8:12; 11:25-26).

# 11

# Communicating the Gospel to Buddhists

Buddhism came into existence almost 600 years before Christ. It is the offspring of Hinduism and of India, and was the first of the great world religions to become international. Today the Buddhist world stretches from central Asia to the Far East, and claims anywhere from 250 to 500 million followers.

Buddhism is not a homogeneous system, but presents a variety of doctrines and practices. It knows the rival trends of conservatism and liberalism, of orthodoxy and revolt, the tension of sects and parties, the corrupting influence of other systems and cultures, and the recurrent return to the original fountain of the faith. There are tendencies toward atheism and theism, monism and dualism, enlightenment by faith and enlightenment by works, salvation as the bliss of nothingness, and salvation as the bliss of paradise. However, there are certain basic ideas that persist throughout.

The canon of orthodox Buddhism, called the *Three Pitakas,* is a voluminous collection about 11 times the size of the Christian Bible. Written in the Pali language, it is reputed to contain the teachings of the Buddha, although they were not committed to writing until several centuries after his death.

## 1. The Life of Buddha

The founder of the Buddhist religion was Siddhartha Gautama (about 563-483 B.C.), a prince of the Kshatriya caste of Hinduism. He was born in north India near the border of Nepal, about 100 miles north of Varanasi (Benares). His dates make him a contemporary of Confucius and a younger contemporary of Ezekiel. Gautama was reared in the palace in the lap of luxury and was shielded from some of the grimmer aspects of life. One day, however, in spite of every precaution, on his way to the royal park he saw an old man, a sick man, a dead man, and a begging monk. So deeply was he affected by the hard realities of the world that he began to ponder hard and long on the problem of human suffering. Finally, at the age of 29, he stole away from the palace one night, leaving his sleeping wife and infant son and abandoning wealth and prospects, in order to seek the answer to the riddle of life. At first he put himself under the instruction of two famous Brahman hermits, but he was unable to find satisfaction in their teaching. Next he turned to a life of extreme asceticism in the jungle, living on a few grains of rice each day, until his body was reduced almost to a skeleton. Still he was unsatisfied. Accordingly he turned from the extremes of asceticism and self-mortification to a simple life of intense mental activity.

Eventually, as the culmination of prolonged meditation, while Siddhartha Gautama sat under a bodhi tree, he suddenly received the answer to his questions and became the *Buddha*, the Enlightened One. This was the turning point in his life. The seeker had not only solved his own burning problem, but he possessed a message which the world must hear. So Buddha began to teach others the way that he had found. He preached his first sermon and gained his first disciples in a deer park at Sarnath, on the outskirts of Varanasi, the holy city of the Hindus. Until his death at the advanced age of 80 he was an itinerant preacher, instructing all who would listen. The insights that Buddha gained from his enlightenment became the essential message of Buddhism and can be summarized in the following four truths.

## 2. The Four Noble Truths

*a. The fact of suffering.* Existence entails suffering. Suffering (mental and physical) is universal and is involved in the very nature of life. All forms of existence are subject to it. It is inseparably bound up with individual existence. To exist is to suffer.

*b. The cause of suffering* is desire, the thirst for possession and selfish enjoyment of every kind, but particularly the craving for separate individual existence.

*c. The cure for suffering* is the extinction of all desire. Suffering ceases when desire ceases, when this selfish craving for pleasure and life is renounced and destroyed.

*d. The way to be emancipated* from desire is to follow the Eightfold Path:

(1) *Right views.* This involves a knowledge of the four truths and such beliefs as are implicit in them. Among these beliefs is the rejection of the existence of the self, or soul. There must also be a rejection of unworthy attitudes and acts, such as covetousness, lying, and gossip.

(2) *Right aspirations.* By this is meant the renunciation of pleasures, abstaining from malice, and doing harm. The thoughts are to be free from lust, ill will, and cruelty.

(3) *Right speech.* This includes abstention from slander, lying, harsh words, and foolish chatter. Speech must be gentle, soothing to the ear, penetrating to the heart, useful, and rightly timed.

(4) *Right conduct.* The devotee must not kill any living being and must abstain from stealing and from unlawful sexual intercourse.

(5) *Right means of livelihood.* The follower must avoid any occupation that brings harm to any living thing. He must take up work which will give scope to his abilities and make him useful to his fellowmen.

(6) *Right effort,* which includes the effort to prevent wrong states of mind from arising, the effort to overcome evil, the effort to develop meritorious conditions (such as detachment and concentration), and the effort to bring these conditions to maturity. The climax of this achievement is universal love.

(7) *Right-mindfulness.* The devotee must be master of his body and of himself. He will be aware of his own feelings and the feelings of others, and will do nothing heedlessly, but only purposefully.

(8) *Right meditation.* This means concentrating the mind on a single object, all hindrances having been overcome. Such arduous mind-development leads on into trances where the individual is purified from all distractions and evils and filled with peace and rapture. Finally he transcends all sensation and consciousness and attains full enlightenment.

### 3. Nirvana

The ultimate goal of the Buddhist Path is *nirvana*, a state which is most difficult to describe. In the West nirvana has traditionally been equated with annihilation, as nothingness, "the state of the snuffed-out candle." And so it has been said, Buddha would have us get rid of the problems of life by getting rid of life itself; he would have us get rid of our headaches by getting rid of our heads.

This interpretation, however, has been challenged by Buddhist scholars. What is extinguished, they insist, is not life itself, but the craving for, and vain attachments to, life. Nirvana is sheer bliss—a consciousness of peace and rest; a perfect, passionless happiness. It is an ethical state, a condition which eliminates any future rebirth, the extinction of all craving, the final release from suffering. And yet, while rejecting the idea of total annihilation, the Buddhist at the same time frowns on the notion that nirvana means continued existence.

It is not entirely certain just what the Buddha believed nirvana to be. Clearly it is the end of desire and the wearisome round of births and rebirths. But is it the end of individual existence? On that point Buddha appears not to have been specific. He persistently refused to give a plain answer to the inquiries of his disciples whether he would or would not, enjoy any kind of existence after death. Almost certainly he thought the question to be unimportant. What to him was primary was attaining to the state in which the thirst or desire that is the bane of human existence has been extinguished, and therefore the suffering that is its fruit has come to an end.

The modern Buddhist scholar insists that a true description of nirvana is impossible. How can any human, he argues, grasp a concept that is beyond himself? It's like a frog trying to tell a tadpole what land is like. The frog may say, "It's not water; it's not wet; it's not a liquid," etc.; but that's as far as it can go. For tadpoles only understand things according to their environment. In the same way, the concept of nirvana does not fit into human categories, so it is difficult for men to understand it.

Buddha taught that salvation is an achievement of the individual. One must not look to any external source for help. It is true that the teaching and counsel of those who have already attained nirvana may be a help to the seeker, but actually he must work things out for himself. Prayer to unseen beings is of no avail. Buddha did not deny the existence of gods or spirits, but he thought of them as being, like men, caught up in the long chain of births and rebirths, and believed that in future incarnations they may no longer be gods or spirits. Thus they are unable to help man in his struggle toward nirvana.

Gautama himself shunned all claims to divinity. He professed to be only a man who sought the way and found it; a teacher who pointed out the way to others. But it is for every man to do the walking on his own. Hendrik Kraemer, the Dutch theologian, described Buddhism as a "non-theistic ethical discipline." It is purely man-centered, a system of self-training, stressing ethics and mind-culture to the exclusion of theology. Buddhism as taught by its founder is in no sense a system of faith and worship as understood in the Christian view. Buddha left no room for prayer or praise; he offered neither forgiveness nor heaven; he warned of no judgment and no hell. It must be pointed out, however, that the followers of Buddha have turned him into "God," to whom they offer homage and supplication.

## 4. Buddhism and Hinduism

In certain respects Buddhism was a revolt against Hinduism. Buddha reacted against the Vedic sacrificial system and against the leadership of the Brahmans, either as experts in religious ritual or intermediaries between gods and men. He also reacted against the caste system, and welcomed into his society anyone who was willing to pay the price of following the Eightfold Path. In a sense, Buddha was a layman, and the movement he started was a laymen's revolt against the Brahmans.

*a. Like Hinduism,* Buddhism accepts the concepts of karma (action-reaction) and samsara (death-rebirth). The law of cause and effect is an unbroken chain through the ages. You are what you are and do what you do as a result of what you were and did in previous incarnations. Similarly, your future rebirths will be determined by what you are and do in your present life. Thus differences in birth are attributed entirely to one's karma, not chance, environment, or some Creator. It is not possible to cancel the effect of evil deeds by performing good deeds. Good will bring its reward; evil will bring its reward. The two operate independently of each other.

*b. Unlike Hinduism,* Buddha rejected the concepts of the World Soul and the individual soul. He substituted the state of nirvana for the World Soul, and he replaced individual soul with the doctrine of *anatta* (no-self, non-ego). Buddha taught there is nothing eternal inside a man's body such as a soul. He denied the existence of the self as a separate entity. There is no permanent ego. In fact, everything is in a state of change or flux. The "soul" is a series of mental states; man is a combination of *skandhas,* or aggregates. Buddhism, therefore, stresses the idea of "rebirth" rather than "transmigration," for it rejects the notion of a soul forming the connecting link between successive incarnations. What lives on after death is not some inward and invisible part of the individual, but simply karma, the results of what has happened before. It is like a man lighting a lamp from another lamp, and not like an electric current that runs through the entire line. If this all sounds confusing to the reader, don't worry; it is confusing to the writer as well!

### 5. Two Main Streams of Buddhism

As time passed, Buddhism developed in two main directions— Mahayana, meaning the Greater Vehicle; and Hinayana, the Lesser Vehicle. Hinayana Buddhism is generally closer to the original teachings of the founder and accepts only the original Pali scriptures for its authority. It is found in Ceylon, Burma, Thailand, Cambodia, Laos, and Viet Nam. It stresses the monastic way of life as the way to nirvana, and teaches that each man must work out his own salvation. Those seriously seeking to attain nirvana join the Order of Monks or the Order of Nuns, accept the life of a mendicant, and vow to observe the "Ten Precepts." These precepts are abstinence from destroying life, stealing, impurity, lying, intoxicants, eating at forbidden times, dancing (music and theaters), garlands, high or large beds, gold or silver. Outside the Orders stand the Buddhist laymen, who do not seek for nirvana now, but aim by good living and almsgiving to improve their chances of attaining it in a future rebirth.

Mahayana Buddhism is noted for is adaptability and radical departure from the original teachings. It is prevalent in Japan, China, Korea, Nepal, Tibet, and Indonesia. It offers salvation to the laity as well as to the monks, and has as its goal the ultimate salvation of all living beings. Buddha is worshipped as the Divine Being or as an incarnate Savior, along with an innumerable company of *Boddhisattvas.* These are men, sometimes purely mythical, who have attained nirvana but postpone its enjoyment in order to help others achieve it. The way of salvation has become faith in Buddha and the Boddhisattvas, and prayer is addressed to them. Images are used to aid the illiterate, and idolatrous polytheism has supplanted Gautama's original atheism. Heaven and hell in afterlife are vividly portrayed, and individual immortality is the hope set before the devotee.

## 6. Buddhism and Christianity

### a. *Points of contact:*

(1) Both Buddhism and Christianity emphasize *the fact of impermanence.* As we look at life in general, one thing is self-evident—the fact of change. Nothing is permanent. The grass withers; the flowers fade; kingdoms rise and fall; peoples wax and wane. Even every achievement of man is touched with mortality. Life goes on constantly changing, and for every man ends in death.

(2) Both faiths uphold a *high standard of ethics.* They command truth-speaking, chastity, purity of mind, and charity. They denounce murder, dishonesty, sensuality, lying, gluttony, and drunkenness. In the Ten Precepts and Eightfold Path of Buddhism there is a basis for the Ten Commandments and ethical system of the Christian faith.

(3) Both faiths place a strong emphasis on *meditation* and *self-discipline.*

(4) Both faiths commend *compassion for others* and *reverence for life.*

(5) Buddhism speaks of the *elimination of all desires.* Christianity speaks of the *sublimation* of our natural desires, and *cleansing from unholy, selfish desires.*

(6) Mahayana Buddhism, with its *belief in heaven and hell* with future rewards and punishments, seems singularly akin to Christian views of the future life.

(7) Buddhism's teaching about those who have postponed entering nirvana to make possible the salvation of others somewhat resembles the Christian doctrine of *vicarious suffering* and the practice of *unselfish evangelism.*

(8) Both faiths speak of *inner peace.*

### BUDDHISM AND CHRISTIANITY COMPARED

| BUDDHISM | CHRISTIANITY |
|---|---|
| **FOUNDER** | |
| 1. Gautama Buddha. Disclaimed divinity. A human teacher who shows us the way. | 1. Jesus Christ, God Incarnate. He said: "I *am* the way." *Who* Christ is is even more important than His teachings. |
| **GOD** | |
| 2. *Atheistic* in its original form. God and gods not necessary. In popular Buddhism, Buddha is worshipped as the Divine Being or as incarnate Savior. | 2. *Theistic.* There is one God, omniscient, omnipotent, omnipresent; Creator, Redeemer, and Judge. Christ is the Savior of the world. |

MAN'S PROBLEM

3. Starts with problem of pain and suffering; concerned with the cause of, and cure for, suffering; goal is to be delivered from suffering; is man-centered.

3. Starts with sin, moral evil; concerned with the holiness of God, the sin of man, and man's deliverance from sin; is God-centered.

MAN AND SOUL

4. There is nothing eternal inside man's body; there is no permanent ego; separate individual existence is really an illusion.

4. Man has an eternal soul; individual existence and selfhood are real.

ACTION AND RESULTS

5. *Karma*—action and reaction; law of cause and effect; attached to cycle of birth and rebirths; karma lives on.

5. Moral law: you reap what you sow; but forgiveness is possible and offered by Christ; results in new birth and new life.

SALVATION

6. *Nirvana*—state of passionless happiness and peace; release from karma and suffering; cessation of separateness and becoming

6. Redemption from sin, its guilt and power; eternal life; victory over suffering and death through the vicarious death of Christ

WAY OF SALVATION

7. By elimination of all desire; system of self-deliverance; pure humanism

7. By grace through faith in Christ, who suffered for us and triumphed over suffering and death. Man is unable to save himself; God takes the initiative and provides redemption as a gift.

REFUGE

8. The Buddhist says: "I take refuge in Buddha, the Dharma, and the Sangha."

8. The Christian says: "I take refuge in Christ, the Word, and the Church."

*b. Points of Contrast:*

(1) Orthodox Buddhism leaves God out of the picture *(atheistic).* The Christian faith begins and ends with God *(theistic).* God is both First Cause (in time) and Final Cause (in purpose).

(2) Buddha steadfastly shunned any claim to divinity. He said, "I have found the way, and now *I show you the way."* Jesus claimed to be the Son of God, one with God. He said clearly, "*I am the way!"*

(3) Amidst the *impermanence* of the world and life (that Buddhism stresses), there stand the *unchangeable Christ* and the *unshakable Kingdom* (as the Bible affirms).

(4) Buddhism *centers on man*—his needs, his efforts. Christianity *centers on God*—His purpose, His provision.

(5) Buddhism claims there is nothing eternal or immortal inside a man's body. There is no permanent ego. Christianity claims that man has an eternal soul. Individual existence and selfhood are real.

(6) The basic problem in Buddhism is that of *suffering*. The basic problem in the Christian faith is *sin*.

(7) Salvation to the Buddhist is *release from suffering,* deliverance from the endless chain of birth-death-rebirth. It is *extinction of life.* Salvation according to the Christian Scriptures is *deliverance from* sin and reconciliation to God. It is the *expansion of life* through a single new birth.

(8) In Buddhism each individual works out his own salvation by his own self-effort. Salvation is achieved through meditation, good deeds, and knowledge. The Christian faith declares that no man can save himself. Salvation is the gift of God. The sinner is saved "by grace . . . through faith" (Eph. 2:8).

## 7. The Gospel for the Buddhist

Perhaps it is with the Buddhist that the Christian messenger has the hardest task of all. For the Buddhist there is no God; therefore there is no sin against God, and no need of deliverance from sin. Suffering is the great evil, and desire the cause of suffering. Take away desire, and suffering will come to an end. Love is a form of desire; therefore, when Christians say that love is the highest quality of all, they are tying men down to the very thing from which they should seek to be free. How is this to be answered?

Perhaps the best way to approach the Buddhist is through the gospel of "The Four Noble Truths" and "The Eightfold Path." The Four Noble Truths are:

*a.* Suffering is a fact of life.

*b.* The cause of suffering is sin.

*c.* The cure for sin is the suffering of Christ.

*d.* The way of deliverance is through faith in Jesus Christ.
The new life in Christ is expressed in the Eightfold Path:

(1) Right views
(2) Right desires
(3) Right speech ·
(4) Right conduct
(5) Right mode of livelihood
(6) Right effort
(7) Right meditation
(8) Right awareness

Let us now examine the "Four Noble Truths" of Christianity more closely:

*a. The fact of suffering.* It is an indisputable fact that life involves suffering of all sorts—mental suffering: failure, disappointment, separation, grief, loneliness, anguish, fear, anxiety; physical suffering: disease, disability, discomfort, pain, and death. Suffering is no respecter of persons; it lays it hand upon young and old, rich and poor, educated and uneducated, European and Asian. It is a universal experience. No one can escape suffering in this life.

*b. The cause of suffering.* Buddhism declares that desire is the cause of suffering, and so we need to get rid of all desire—particularly the craving for life itself. But not all desires are evil. There are certain desires that are God-given and therefore legitimate, such as hunger, thirst, the sex drive, ambition, and love. It is only when we allow these desires to get out of control, or try to satisfy them in the wrong way, that they become evil. The Bible makes it clear that the root of suffering goes deeper than mere desire. Desire is just a symptom of the real disease. The disease is sin.

Life's basic problem is not sorrow but sin. Sin is more than just a wrong relationship to our fellowman; it is more than just an immoral deed, like lying or stealing. Sin is primarily a wrong relationship to God. It is that attitude of rebellion and disloyalty which we have toward God who is the Ground of our being, the final Cause of the world, and the purpose which gives meaning to life. It is the spirit of self-centeredness and self-sufficiency; the unconscious or conscious assumption that we hold within ourselves the clue of life's meaning and can of ourselves discover and obey that clue. The effects of this wrong vertical relationship with God can be seen in the wrong acts that we commit against our fellowmen. Just as we reject or try to use God, so we also reject or try to use other people. We forget that they, too, receive their selves from God and belong to God as uniquely as we do.

The essence of sin, then, lies in its relation to God. It is more than just breaking the rules of an ethical code, which is common to all men. It is an offense against God's redeeming love. It is an act of ingratitude and disloyalty. It is specifically disobedience to God's will as He reveals it to me by His Spirit with respect to the choices and decisions of my life. Sin means to miss the mark, to live at random, not to fulfill the purpose of God for oneself.

It is not enough, therefore, that I seek to walk in the middle path of discipline, or follow a teacher who will show me that path.

My need is for a Savior who will do for me what I cannot do for myself, who will take away from me that rebellion in my nature so that I can come to live naturally and spontaneously in God. It is I who am the problem and not the world; it is my sin and not the world's sorrow that needs primary attention. The Bible makes it clear that the suffering of this world—fear, anxiety, pain, disease, death—is all due to man's sin, his fallen state. So sin is life's basic ill.

   c. *The cure for sin.* As we have seen, sin is an essential wrongness in man which only God's power and love can make right. "It is not an imperfection that time will set right, or a disease that the psychotherapist can heal, or just ignorance which education will enlighten."[1] It is a condition which must be radically changed.

   The Bible clearly reveals that God has acted in response to man's need; He has taken the initiative. He is not One who stands aloof from the human predicament, unconcerned, indifferent. He is One who cares deeply and involves himself fully in the human situation.

   It was a dangerous thing for God to create man with freedom of will. For man might go wrong and bring sorrow to His heart. But God took that chance. And the moment man sinned, a cross was formed in the heart of God. Long before Christ carried a cross on His back, God carried it on His heart. That is why Jesus is spoken of as "the Lamb slain [before] the foundation of the world" (Rev. 13:8, KJV). The Cross was inherent in creation. The moment man sinned, God began to suffer. This was inevitable, inherent.

   Then how could we know this fact? We couldn't know it unless God showed us the inner, unseen cross through an outer, visible Cross lifted up at a point in history. So God, through the person of Jesus Christ, entered into the stream of human history and identified himself with the sin and suffering of the world. He identified himself with our humanity—He was born of a woman. He identified himself with our poverty—He was born in a stable. He identified himself with our toil—He worked at a carpenter's bench. He identified himself with our physical needs—He hungered and thirsted. He identified himself with our temptations—He "was in all points tempted like as we are" (Heb. 4:15, KJV). He identified with our sin and death—He died on a cross.

   Amy Carmichael, well-known missionary in India, had 300 girls in her rescue home and school. One girl wouldn't respond to the spirit of the institution. She was hard and rebellious. Miss Carmichael did everything to change her attitude. Finally she took the girl into her room and bared her arm before the girl. "I'm going to pierce my arm with a needle," she said.

"It will hurt," said the girl.

"Not nearly as much as you are hurting me," answered the missionary. "To let you know the pain in my heart, I am going to thrust this needle into my arm." She did so and the blood ran. The girl began to weep, and through her tears she cried, "I didn't know you loved me like that." She was changed, changed through that blood.

Did something like that happen in history? Yes, I look up through the wounds of Christ and see the heart of God, and cry out, "I didn't know You loved me like that!"

Back of everything is redemptive love. God cares, cares enough to do something about my need.

And so Christ took our karma, our sin, upon himself and bore it away. He took suffering—mental anguish and physical agony of the worst kind—and turned it into our redemption. He took the greatest tragedy—death on a cross—and turned it into the greatest triumph.

Many objections might be raised against this plan of redemption as described in the Bible The Buddhist may ask, "Why all this long process from Abraham to Calvary? Why all this untold suffering and agony on the part of Christ?"

And the Christian answer is factual. It simply says, "It is so." We cannot give reasons why God chose to act in a particular way; all we can do is to try and understand the full consequences and implications of His actions. After all, what is important for us is to understand the nature of the salvation that He offers without speculating as to why He adopted the methods He did.

*d. The path to salvation is through faith in Jesus Christ.* Buddhism has been well called "the most radical system of self-deliverance ever conceived in the world." It claims that man can be, and indeed must be, his own savior. The Bible, on the other hand, clearly states that man is a sinner and absolutely incapable of saving himself. If there is to be any salvation for man, it must come from God's side. He alone can save. He must take the initiative and act.

The "good news" of the Bible is that God *has* taken the initiative; He *has* acted. *Man's need became God's deed.* He acted in a Person. Jesus is God's act on man's behalf. So whereas Buddhism says to us, "Here is a set of teachings to follow; here is a system of discipline to perform," the Bible says to us, "Here is a Person; believe in Him; follow Him."

As was already pointed out, Buddha never made any claims to divinity. He confessed he was only a man, a seeker after truth. He said clearly, "I have sought and found the way; now I show you the way."

Jesus, on the other hand, declared openly, "I am the Son of God. . . . I am the light of the world. . . . I am the way, and the truth, and the life; no one comes to the Father, but by me. . . . He who has seen me has seen the Father" (see Mark 14:61-62; John 8:12; 14:6, 9). So Jesus was fully God and fully man; He was the God-man. As such He is the Mediator between the infinite, holy God and finite, sinful man.

We readily recognize that Gautama the Buddha was indeed one of the greatest sons of Asia, and that he has had a profound influence on the lives of countless millions and on the culture of many nations. He dedicated his life to rescuing men from the despair and disillusion into which contemporary Hindu religion had led them. His was a protest against the fruitless salvation promised by the practices of formal religion. The Buddha had a tremendous mission in his contemporary scene—hence the strength and charm of his life. But in spite of all this, he was only a man; a great man, but not a redeemer.

We recall a story from the life of Buddha, as told by his followers. Once a mother stood before him with the body of her dead child in her arms. She said to Buddha, "You have attained enlightenment. Please restore the life of my child."

The Buddha shook his head and replied, "As we come into this world, so we must leave. The child is dead. There is nothing I can do."

Contrast this story with the narrative of Jesus found in Luke's Gospel (7:11-18). As Jesus entered the city of Nain, he saw some people carrying out a dead man, the only son of his mother, who was a widow. Jesus had compassion on the woman and said to her, "Do not weep." Then He touched the bier and said softly, "Young man, I say to you, arise." And the dead son sat up and began to speak!

In Christ God has acted decisively and finally. He has done for us what we could not do for ourselves. The gospel is not merely that "God is love," but, "God so loved." He loved us so much that He did something about it. He sent His Son, and the Son gave His life. God now offers to us salvation as a gift. He offers us forgiveness for the sins of the past, and cleansing from the sins of the inner heart and mind. He reconciles us and restores us to fellowship with himself. He grants to us eternal life.

The Buddha saw that life was meaningless in itself and set out to rescue men from this meaninglessness. Jesus, on the other hand, saw that life could be meaningful in God and set out to call men to share that meaning. Jesus said, "I have come that you might have life and have it more abundantly" (see John 10:10). So the Christian faith is life-affirming, not life-negating. It offers salvation *in* life and *to* life, rather than salvation *from* life. So the truth is that the *craving for life,* about which Buddha spoke, is not destroyed but satisfied!

This does not mean that because we are redeemed from sin, we are automatically delivered from suffering and death in this life. There will still be pain; there will still be death. But Christ has taken the sting out of suffering and death. He has taken suffering and turned it into our redemption, and now He gives us power to face suffering victoriously and even use it for His glory. He has conquered death through His death and resurrection, so we no longer need to fear death; it is only the door into His eternal presence. God has entered into history, challenged the prince of this age in his domain, and routed him. The evil, suffering, and death that we now deal with have been exposed and defeated. Christ doesn't command us to strive for victory; He invites us to share in a victory already won. Therefore, we work, not *toward* the victory, but *from* the victory.

The salvation, however, that we enjoy in this life is only a foretaste of the salvation yet to be. The time will come when sin and suffering and death will be no more, and our human life will be resurrected into life eternal!

It is true that God has freely provided this salvation, but man must appropriate it. God has acted in response to man's need; now man must act in response to God's deed. The basic question of the gospel is this: *What have you done about what God has done for you?* Have you given life for life, love for love, devotion for devotion? I can either accept God's gift or reject it. If I reject the salvation that is in Christ, and persist in my sin, then the curse of suffering haunts my whole life. I have sorrow in my earthly existence and greater sorrow in the life to come. But if I repent—change my attitude to myself and to God—and trust in Christ as my Savior, then I receive forgiveness and life. I have peace in my earthly life—peace which the sorrow of this world cannot take away—and perfect peace in my experience of eternal life.

*The Eightfold Path.* In Buddhism, the path of discipline and ethical behavior is the means by which deliverance from desire and suffering is to be achieved. But in the Christian faith, it is the path to be trod after one has been reconciled to God and delivered from the power of sin. Discipline and ethics are not in order to merit salvation; they are the result of having entered into the experience of salvation already. To offer our morality, our good deeds, to God as the "price" of our salvation is to refuse to meet God at the place where He has come to meet us. It is essentially an act of self-assertion, which is the essence of sin. It is possible for man to be moral, good, and decent, and yet a sinner. The question still remains for every man: *What have you done about what God has done for you in Jesus Christ?* In the face of that question, moral excellence and spiritual enlightenment are irrelevant. The point simply is this—the very morality we boast about may become the ground of our self-assertion (sin), when it ought to be the fruit of our love for Him who gave himself for us.

Of course the saved life is a life of morality and good deeds. Salvation makes ethics obligatory, for "faith without works is dead" (Jas. 2:26, KJV). It also makes ethics possible. God doesn't command us to live the ethical life without enduing us with the power to do it. That would make our situation desperate. Instead God gives us the gift of the Holy Spirit, who lives within us, takes us over and makes us over, and enables us to be the kind of persons we ought to be. Ethical living then becomes God's requirement as the fruit of the experience of His saving act.

Now we can outline the eightfold duty of the Christian ethical life:

(1) *Right views.* This involves acceptance of the Four Noble Truths described above, and the acknowledgment that truth is found in Christ and His Word, not in our speculations about God.

(2) *Right desires.* Our natural desires must be controlled and satisfied in ways God intended them to be. We now have one supreme desire in life, that is, to become like Christ and to please Him.

(3) *Right speech.* "Putting away falsehood, let every one speak the truth with his neighbor" (Eph. 4:25). "Let your speech always be gracious, seasoned with salt, so that you may know how you ought to answer every one" (Col. 4:6).

(4) *Right conduct.* "Put to death . . . what is earthly in you: immorality, impurity, passion, evil desire, and covetousness, which is idolatry. . . . Put on then, as God's chosen ones, holy and beloved, compassion, kindness, lowliness, meekness, and patience, forbearing one another and . . . forgiving each other" (Col. 3:5, 12-13).

(5) *Right mode of livelihood.* Each person must take up work which will use his God-given talents and make him useful to his fellowmen. He should make his living honestly and avoid a life of luxury.

(6) *Right effort.* "Forgetting what lies behind and straining forward to what lies ahead, . . . press on toward the goal for the prize of the upward call of God in Christ Jesus" (Phil. 3:13-14).

(7) *Right meditation.* Be still before God and know His presence. Meditate on His Word every day. Pray constantly.

(8) *Right awareness.* Be aware of the burdens and needs of your fellowmen; share your resources with them. Also be aware of the spiritual needs of people across the world, and be involved in God's world mission.

## 8. The Bodhi Tree and the Tree of Calvary[2]

The tree is a significant symbol in both Buddhism and Christianity.

*a. Buddhism.* Buddhists venerate the bodhi tree because Gautama attained enlightenment while meditating under it. The story of his renunciation is one of the world's greatest stories. Having severed all ties of family, society, and nation, Gautama renounced the world and went in search of the truth. Toward the end of his spiritual quest he sat under a bodhi tree where he spent his time day and night in meditation, until he reached a state of knowledge and attained salvation for himself. Thus the bodhi tree signifies three things:

(1) It signifies *the perfection of knowledge. Bodhi* means "knowledge" or "wisdom."

(2) It signifies *the attainment of self-salvation.* What the Buddha attained under the tree was for himself. By his enlightenment he did not claim to save others.

(3) It signifies *detachment from the world.* One can gain salvation for himself only when he renounces the world.

*b. Christianity.* The Cross, the tree on which Christ died (Acts 5:30; 10:39), is the most significant symbol in Christianity. While the Buddha sat *under* the tree in *meditation,* Jesus died *on* the tree as an *expiation.* Thus the Cross signifies three things that stand in contrast to what the bodhi tree stands for:

(1) It signifies the *perfection of love.* It is not the quest for knowledge but His love for man that drove Jesus to the Cross.

(2) It signifies *universal salvation,* for Christ died for all.

(3) It signifies *involvement*, not detachment. It was not by renouncing the world, but by getting involved in the world that Christ became the Savior of the world.

If Jesus had renounced the world, detached himself from life, and spent His time in meditation and mental culture, He would have become a great philosopher; He would have reached great mystical heights; He would have become a great religious teacher pointing the way to others; but He never would have become the Savior of the world. Through detachment one might gain personal satisfaction for himself, but one cannot love and remain isolated. Love leads to involvement and identification.

It is this sacrificial love that we see on the Cross. There on the tree Jesus laid down His life not only for His friends, but also for His enemies. Through love He identified himself with humanity in order to save the world. Jesus said, "And I, when I am lifted up from the earth, will draw all men to myself" (John 12:32).

The Buddhist says: "I take refuge in Buddha;
            I take refuge in the dharma [teaching];
            I take refuge in the sangha [monastic
               order]."

The Christian says: "I take refuge in Christ;
            I take refuge in His Word;
            I take refuge in the fellowship of the
               Church."

# 12

# Communicating the Gospel to Animists

The term *animism* is derived from the Latin word *anima*, meaning "breath" or "soul." It is the belief in the existence of spiritual beings, including the spirits of the living and the dead as well as those that have no human origin. It is the doctrine that places the source of mental and even physical life in an energy independent of, or at least distinct from, the body. Most commonly animism has been defined simply as "spirit worship," distinguished from the worship of God or gods.

Animism is a very ancient religion. Apart from revealed religion (in the Old Testament), some form of animistic belief has preceded all the major historical religions. The forefathers of those who today call themselves Hindus, Buddhists, and Muslims were, at one time, all animists. Before the spread of Christianity, Europe was a center of animistic faith.

Animism in some form or other is found in practically every continent. It is the prevailing religion of all the tribal peoples across the world who are yet unevangelized; all the way from the Indian tribes of North and South America, to the tribes of Africa and southeast Asia, the aborigines of Australia, and the hill tribes of New Guinea. In addition, underneath the forms of the "higher religions" there is an unmistakable animistic substratum, which, in many situations, is actually the most important element in the religious life of the people. Among Buddhists one finds such animistic features as prayer wheels, spirit houses, and the fear of ghosts—practices which would have been utterly unacceptable to Buddha himself. In popular

Hinduism we find such elements as black magic, spirit-possession, and "auspicious days." Similarly, many Muslims may claim that they believe only in the will of Allah; but at the same time they wear charms to protect themselves, seek to placate the malicious *jinns* (spirits) in various ways, and offer sacrifices to propitiate the village spirits. Even "Christians" in the U.S.A. are not free from the trend toward animism. Witness such superstitions as "Friday the 13th"; "Don't walk under a ladder"; "Watch out for that black cat"; etc.; also the growing interest in fortune-telling, seances, and the use of the horoscope.

However, as a predominant religious force, animism is found primarily among the traditional tribal societies of the world, comprising anywhere from 200 to 300 million people. These tribes differ from our modern societies in that they lack a written language and a literary tradition and are undeveloped in scientific knowledge, technological skills, and economic life. They also have a simpler social organization, are smaller in scale, and self-contained; some may number only a few hundred people, others a few million. Tribal societies are not critical of their own sensations; there is no process of self-analysis or self-judgment.

The Christian movement has had its greatest success among animistic peoples. Tribal society is characterized by a strong group consciousness and communal solidarity. The people usually decide and act as a group. They exhibit a strong resistance to change, especially at the beginning, but once a movement toward Christ commences, it has the possibility of becoming a "people movement" and bringing the whole tribe to the feet of the Savior. Some of the greatest indigenous churches in Christendom are found among peoples who once followed animism, such as the Karen church of Burma, the Batak church of Sumatra, the Naga church of Assam in India, and the Fijian church of the South Pacific. Millions of animists in Africa are today followers of Christ and constitute the largest block of Christendom outside the Western world. The impact of scientific knowledge, education, and the disruption of village life by industrialization and urbanization have all contributed to the rapid disintegration of animism in many parts of the world.

Animism cannot be considered a single, homogeneous religion, for there are as many varieties as there are tribes. This makes generalizations difficult. Each tribal society expresses itself in its own distinctive religious forms, and each must be studied in its own right by the discerning missionary. However, there are certain common principles and features that run through the entire animist world, so we will attempt to make a summary of these.

## 1. Underlying Principles of Animism

Edward G. Newing, former Australian missionary to Kenya, suggests there are five such principles.[1]

a. *The holistic view of life.* The animist does not fragment or departmentalize life. He does not distinguish between secular and sacred, between the spiritual and the material, between public life and private life. Everything is interconnected so that every activity from birth to death—and beyond—is interpreted as belonging to a religious whole. The animist's world is a rhythmic whole permeated with vital spiritual forces. This is why it is so difficult to separate the social structure, the culture, and the religion of tribal people. They are all interwoven.

b. *The spiritual view of life.* The animist lives in close relationship with a world which he believes is inhabited and dominated by an infinite variety of spiritual beings. To him the spiritual forces are primary. Thus in every happening he looks not for the normal relation of cause and effect, but for the spiritual forces that control the outcome. In every event—illness, injury, accident, death—the animist will see the hand of some spirit at work. Even if he accidentally stubs his toe on a stone in the path, he will attribute the cause to some malicious spirit. This spiritualistic interpretation of their world dominates the thinking of animist peoples.

c. *The mythical view of life.* By means of myths all the great moments of life and death are given interpretation and meaningful expression. The animist has a myth for everything important—the origin of the world, the origin of the tribe, the origin of life and death, the tribe's relationship to God and/or the gods. All the fundamental beliefs are set out in mythical forms. Myth is the means by which a tribal people express their faith in the reality of life.

d. *The ritualistic expression of life.* Great importance is given in tribal societies to the observance of rituals. Some of these are expressions of the tribal myths; others are connected with the events of everyday life. The animist tends to look upon life as a rhythmic cycle. There is the seasonal cycle of seedtime and harvest, wet and dry season, winter and summer. Then there is the human life cycle of birth, puberty, marriage, and death. For all of these seasons and events, rituals have been developed and are carefully observed. In addition, there are rituals for such trivial matters as eating, cooking, house building, departing and arriving, buying and selling, and so on.

e. *The cyclic view of time.* An important aspect of the rhythmic principle is the animist's view of time. For him time is a cyclic and not a linear process. Time is not a continuous flow, moving toward some future moment. It is a series of regular events that take place routinely, in accordance with the seasonal pattern. The past is important because it provides the way of response in the present; the future is unimportant because it is nonexistent; the present is all-important.

## 2. Major Characteristics of Animism

a. *Hierarchy of spiritual beings.* To the animist the spirit world is very real. He believes in a variety of spirits, all the way from the spirits that inhabit the stones and the trees to the Great Spirit of the sky.

Every known tribe recognizes the existence of a Supreme Being, a Creator, with varying mythological views of his character and the story of creation. But this "God" is deemed to be afar off, aloof, and uninvolved in the daily affairs of men. He is content to play the part of a disinterested observer. Furthermore, he is considered to be benevolent and thus harmless, so the animist feels he does not need to pay any attention to him. He does not worship him, pray to him, build shrines in his honor, or do sacrifices to him. In fact, he has practically forgotten him.

Many tribes—by no means all—also believe in the existence of gods other than the Supreme Being. These are usually an array of nature-gods and goddesses, personifications of the powers of nature-gods and goddesses, personifications of the powers of nature—the earth, sun, moon, thunder, lightning, fire, volcano, etc. There is little or no attempt at material representation of these divinities, and therefore idolatry is not an important feature in the worship. Of all the gods, the most popular is usually the goddess of fertility (here lies the mystery of birth, the future of the race, and the supply of food).

Closer at hand is the innumerable multitude of spirits which populate the realm of nature. A few of these are good spirits, such as the tribal ghosts which watch over the welfare of the people; but for the most part they are malevolent. They dwell in all sorts of places, such as trees, rivers, rocks, caves, mountain passes, river crossings, animals, and so on. They are quite unpredictable, and people are always most careful not to offend them and to pay proper respect by making small offerings of food when they pass by their supposed dwelling places. It is with this vast array of spirits that the animist is chiefly concerned.

An important part of the spirit world are the ancestral spirits or the "living dead." For most tribal peoples there is a continuing relationship between the living and the dead. They believe strongly in the existence after death of the spirit of the human being. A person once dead is believed to be both in the Land of the Dead and able to cause mischief to those whom he has left behind. For this reason the mortuary rites are of the utmost importance and must be carefully carried out, otherwise the soul may return and cause harm to the family. In addition, offerings of food and drink are regularly made to these ancestor spirits in order to keep on their good side. Failure to do so may result in illness or a variety of mishaps.

This then is the hierarchy of the spiritual forces recognized by the animist, and with which he has to contend in his daily life.

*b. Prevalence of spiritual power (mana).* All animist societies recognize the existence of an impersonal, mysterious life force which pervades everything. The Melanesian word *mana* has been adopted by scholars to describe this sacred power. Mana may concentrate in certain things such as stones, plants, trees, animals, and people with varying degrees of intensity. A person's success or position in the community depends largely on the amount of mana he possesses, so its acquisition and manipulation are of extreme importance to him. Mana can be gained by wearing certain charms, by performing certain rites, and by eating the flesh or drinking the blood of an animal (such as the lion). The practice of cannibalism, no doubt, found its origin in this same idea. The warrior believed that by eating the flesh of his enemy, the victim's strength would be added to his own.

*c. The shaman and magic.* The belief in spirits and spiritual forces leads to the development of magic and the religious expert, in order to appease or control the vast array of spirits, and to gain or manipulate mana. Magic can be used for a beneficent end, to strengthen the individual or bring good fortune. For example, there is imitative magic—rolling a stone downhill, beating on a drum and shouting, "Boom, boom"—in order to produce rain for the crops. Or one may wear fetishes or amulets to ward off evil and bring good luck. It is not claimed that the charm is inhabited by a spirit, but that it is the container of a harnessed, pervasive evergy. As long as it brings good fortune, the owner will keep it. Otherwise, he will discard it and look for another.

For the most part, however, magic is employed to inflict harm upon an enemy. There is *contagious magic,* for example, which connects an individual's welfare with something that is severed from him, such as a lock of hair, nail parings, or even his excreta. If such things can be obtained from an enemy, they may be used for revenge without even going near him. The fear of "black magic" is so intense that when a person discovers someone has put a spell on him, it often leads to extreme vomiting, convulsions, and/or sometimes to his death.

The *shaman,* or religious specialist, is an important and powerful personage in animist society. He is medicine man, priest, and mediator. He is able to discern and influence offended spirits; he cures sickness, directs the communal sacrifices, and escorts the souls of the dead to the other world. He is supposed to have the ability to leave his body and observe events in distant places.

*d. The observance of taboo.* Where a belief in magic and mana exists, utmost caution will be used in securing protection from invisible attacks of one's enemies. This gives rise to the common practice of taboo. One way to keep out of trouble is to avoid it. Hence, where mana is concentrated in a particular person or thing, one must not touch or come near it or him. It is considered dangerous; it is taboo. A whole range of people, things, and places are thus prohibited: sacred persons (like the priest); the dead and all that belongs to them; menstruation and sickness; sanctuaries like sacred groves and spirit houses; certain animals, plants, and insects. Many taboos are associated with women in childbirth; with infants when born; with seasons of sowing, planting, and harvesting; with house building; and especially with funerals. It is true to say that the life of the animist is governed by taboo from birth to death, by day and by night, and is one of the important controlling forces in his daily activity.

## 3. Inherent Weaknesses in Animism

This section uses material from the book *Introducing Animism.*[2]

*a. No fundamental moral basis.* Though the animist believes that certain acts are right and others are wrong, he lacks a moral basis for judgment and a definite ethical system to guide him. Behavior is not related to a moral being or a moral law. Good and evil are judged by a very simple rule—whether or not it does harm to the well-being of the community. Actions are good if they preserve the harmony of life and ensure the blessings of the Divine; they are evil if they threaten communal harmony and bring calamity. Customs and taboos are the binding factors in society. Sin is offending against tribal custom or taboo, and what is morally evil may be regarded as good if it does not transgress tribal law.

*b. No satisfactory answer to life.* Animism provides no satisfactory answer to the question of the meaning of life and the significance of history. With the overriding emphasis on spirit beings and the dead and the enforcing of tribal customs, the entire orientation of society becomes focused on the past. When people are asked why they do things in a particular way, the only real answer they can give is, "Our fathers and grandfathers did it that way." This approach will not bring satisfaction for long to people who are confronted with new opportunities from the outside world. Merely looking back does not provide opportunity for progress or inspiration for the future.

*c. No power to meet life's crises.* Though the animist, with the aid of his religious rites, may feel he has some sort of control of his environment, yet he is unable to overcome his fears and effectively solve the problems of life. He gets rid of one set of fears only to be faced with a whole new array of fears. Natural fear gives way to spritual fear— fear of the spirits themselves. There is nothing or no one the animist believes he can trust or depend upon, so he feels insecure in an unpredictable, dangerous world.

*d. Lack of constructive leadership.* Often the religious leaders among animistic people—shamans, sorcerers, or mediums—are the lunatic fringe of society. They are often psychotic, mentally deranged, emotionally unstable. They are men to be feared, or used for one's benefit, but not persons to be trusted and followed. They maintain law and order, but they stifle initiative and progress.

## 4. The Tragic Effects of Animism

*a. Fear is dominant.* Fear is the outstanding characteristic, the moving power, of animistic religion. The animist lives in constant fear. He is surrounded by evil spirits who are constantly out to "get him." All his energy is expended in the effort to appease or manipulate these spirits.

Take, for example, the mental state of the Iban people in Sarawak, northern Borneo (now part of Malaysia), before the gospel was proclaimed to them. The men believed that if they had a bad dream at night, it was a warning not to go to the fields the next day, for the evil spirits were after them. (Many of the Ibans were heavy drinkers and naturally they had bad dreams at night.) Even if a man were on his way to the field, but a black rodent ran across the path, that was a warning to turn back, for evil spirits were after him. Or if he heard the cry of a hornbill bird, that was a further warning to stay away from the fields. And because there were many black rodents and hornbills in Sarawak, only about one-third of the working force ever got to the fields on any given day. Food was therefore scarce and many Ibans suffered from hunger and malnutrition. They were not really lazy; they were simply afraid. Fear is the dominant emotion in the breast of the animist.

*b. Hope is absent.* There is a complete absence of the conception of love on the part of the spirit world or the spirit worshipper. This deprives the individual of any of the consolations of religion. For the old and infirm, life has few comforts; they are considered useless to the tribe, so their existence is only tolerated. For the living, death holds only terror, for it is a passing into the darkness of the unknown. There is no certainty of meeting again the loved ones left behind on earth. The animist is without hope.

The manner of life beyond the grave bears no relation to the quality of life here on earth, whether good or evil. Misfortune is due, not to personal choices, but to external forces beyond control. All the events of life are predetermined and in no way dependent on the character of the individual. This naturally leads to a fatalistic outlook on life that precludes belief in a merciful God.

*c. God is distant.* Though every tribe recognizes the existence of a Supreme Being, there seems to have been a universal departure from the worship of the Creator. The common essence of animism is not a denying of God, but an ignoring of Him in the worship of natural powers and demonic spirits through magical sacrifices and ceremonies. It is because the animist has turned from the worship of a Life Giver that he finds himself a slave, in bondage to fear of evil spirits. In forsaking the light he once possessed, he has dragged himself into the darkness of despair, from which he is unable to escape. Now God has become distant, unknown. As Paul so clearly described in his letter to the Roman Church: "Although they knew God they did not honor him as God or give thanks to him, but they became futile in their thinking and their senseless minds were darkened" (Rom. 1:21).

## 5. The Gospel for the Animist

The Christian missionary must approach the animist with empathy and love. He should never look down on him. The animist may be uneducated and illiterate, but he is not stupid. He has a logic and psychology of his own. His faculty of memory has been sharpened to a high degree. Given the same opportunity, he will prove himself to be as intelligent and alert as anyone else.

The animist should be treated as a person; yes, even more—a person for whom Christ died. He is not simply a "pagan" or "heathen." He is more "spiritual" than many secular-minded, materialistic Westerners, who live only for the temporary things of life, without any reference to God and His will. The African in particular, when he has been approached with the gospel of Jesus Christ, has shown an unusual capacity for spiritual understanding and devotion.

The missionary who lives among animists in an undeveloped society must be willing to adopt a simple life-style and identify himself with the people. Bruce Olson, pioneer missionary to the Motilones of Colombia, South America, was willing to live with the people in their "round house," sleep in a hammock high off the ground, and eat the food they ate—including grubs and insects. No wonder the Motilones consider him a member of their clan and are willing to listen to his message.

It is also essential for the missionary to master the language and thought patterns of the people, to know their customs and culture, and to understand the particular form of animistic belief they have developed. This will enable him to discover the points of contact and the redemptive analogies which will serve as effective bridgeheads in presenting the gospel of Jesus Christ. Once this has been done, the missionary is better prepared for the task of evangelism.

Providentially, the animist has not been without a witness. Through the mysteries of nature he has some sense of the existence of a Creator, and through the voice of conscience he has some concept of right and wrong. He has also been the object of redemptive love through the silent, mysterious working of the Holy Spirit. He has been the recipient of prevenient grace. As Don Richardson has pointed out, down through the years God has been building into the cultural and religious patterns of every tribe and clan certain redemptive analogies that serve as a preparation for the gospel. It is up to us to discover these analogies and use them for the communication of eternal truth.

As a general approach to animist peoples we suggest the following progression of basic truths which may effectively lead them to a genuine experience of salvation in Jesus Christ.

a. *The truth about God the Father.* As has already been pointed out, every tribe has some concept of the existence of a Supreme Being.

The animist makes a clear-cut distinction between his own skill and technical know-how on the one hand, and the supernatural on the other. When he plants his garden, he knows how to go about it—how to recognize a suitable location, cultivate and irrigate, and recognize the time for harvest. But he realizes that many other factors are beyond his control, such as the productivity of the soil, the rain and sun, and fruiting of the crop. Whether he turns to magic or religion in dealing with these forces, he recognizes there is a supernatural on whose goodwill he depends. It may be a friendly god whose aid he seeks, or an evil spirit who has to be placated in some way. He feels the presence, though he does not understand. Somewhere out there is "the unknown God," if only he can discover how to know Him.

Descriptions of the Motilone's search for God are pathetic indeed. He will dig a hole in the ground about six feet deep, then lie on his stomach and shout into the hole, "God, God, come out of the hole." Or he will climb to the top of a tree, stuff leaves into his mouth and try to chew them, while shouting at the top of his voice, "God, God, come from the horizon."

For most animists God is very distant. He has gone off somewhere and is uninterested in the daily affairs of men. He is not considered to be a troublemaker, so He can be ignored most of the time. The animist is more worried about the innumerable evil spirits that are all around and playing tricks on him.

The first task of the Christian messenger is to give the animist a new concept of God. He must present God not merely as Creator and Lawgiver, but as Redeemer and Father as well. He must bring God close to the people. It must be emphasized that though man has forgotten God, God has not forgotten man; that God is deeply involved in human affairs and that He cares for and loves the individual.

Often the mythology of a tribe offers a marvelous point of contact for the missionary to emphasize man's estrangement from God, and affords an opportunity to call the people back to God. The Shona tribe of Rhodesia tells the story that God and man once walked together; but in the course of time man became so wicked that one day when they came to a river, God walked across the water and left man standing on the bank.

In West Africa a variety of myths are told in an attempt to explain this strange aloofness on the part of God: (1) A woman was pounding grain and reached so high with her pestle that she struck God in heaven who, in anger because she refused to stop, got up and left. (2) People kept wiping their dirty hands on the sky, which was much lower in those days, so God left in disgust. (3) People used to insist on sending smoke up into God's eyes, and He just could not stand it.[3]

The good news in all these cases is that God has not gone off in anger and left us stranded. But in love He has returned in the Person of His Son to redeem us and reconcile us to himself. This brings us to the second great truth.

*b. The truth about Christ the Son.* The only way to make God real to the animist is to present Jesus Christ, God incarnate in human life. Through the Son the animist can know the character of the Father. So we must tell in a simple manner the story of the life of Christ, emphasizing His miracles and parables, His death and resurrection. We must emphasize Christ's purity and goodness, His compassion and love, His concern for the poor, the needy, the sick, and the sinful. The story of the Cross will bring a new sense of sin to the animist, which is often lacking in his religion. Then the forgiveness of Christ can be made clear.

In seeking to communicate the significance of the Incarnation to the Motilones, missionary Bruce Olson discovered a wonderful tool in one of their legends. According to the story, a Motilone sat on the trail after a hunt one day, and he noticed some ants trying to build a home. He wanted to help them make a good home—like that of the Motilones—so he stooped down and began digging in the dirt. But because he was a stranger and so big, the ants became afraid and ran in all directions. Then, quite miraculously, the Motilone became an ant. He looked like an ant, thought like an ant, and spoke the language of an ant. He lived with the ants and they learned to trust him.

One day he told them he was not really an ant, but a Motilone, who had once tried to help them build their home, but had scared them. The ants said their equivalent of, "No kidding? That was you?" And they laughed at him because he didn't look like the fearful giant who had stooped to help them that day.

But at that moment he was turned back into a Motilone and began to move the dirt into the shape of a Motilone home. This time the ants recognized him and let him do his work, because they were no longer afraid of him.[4]

Using this legend as a background, Bruce Olson proceeded to explain to the Motilones that the only way God could reveal His love and will to us was for Him to become a man, live among men, and talk to us in our own language. So by looking at Christ we can see what God is like.

*c. The Book of Truth.* The Christian faith is based on *revealed religion* as opposed to *natural religion.* God has revealed himself to us through His Son, and the record of that revelation is found in the Bible. The only way we know the truth about God and the truth about Christ is through IIis written Word. Thus is is very important that we give the Bible to animist people in their own language. We must emphasize that "God talks" to us through His words.

Since each tribe has its own unwritten language, the task of getting the Bible to the people is indeed a difficult one. It means that someone must live among the tribe, "crack" the language—learn the sounds, vocabulary, grammar, and syntax—then reduce it to writing, and translate the Scriptures into meaningful, cultural forms. This requires, on the average, about 12 years of concentrated effort on the part of a trained linguist.

The American and British Bible societies and Wycliffe Bible Translators are doing magnificent work in this area. The latter group in particular has as its goal the translation of the Bible—at least portions of it—into every known language of the world. At present, Wycliffe Bible Translators has about 4,000 members on its staff and is working in approximately 830 different languages. But it is estimated there are still close to 3,330 languages that are untouched.

The animist is very impressed by the fact that God can speak his language. When he reads the words of God in his own mother tongue, they become personal and alive to him. And sometimes the coming of "the Book" is the answer to the longings of the tribe expressed in its legends. For example, in the case of the Karen people in the hills of Burma, they believed that originally they had received a written language and books. But somehow their ancestors had allowed a surly dog to come along and snatch away their books. Since that time they had no writing and no books. But someday, their prophets had assured them, white-faced strangers from across the seas would come and bring back the Book of God which they had lost. When that time came, they were to be ready to listen and obey. Thus when George Boardman, the first American Baptist missionary, arrived in their midst with a Bible, they felt this was the fulfillment of their hopes, and they listened to the gospel with glad hearts. Today the Karen church in Burma numbers about half a million and is one of the most outstanding indigenous churches to be found anywhere.

The Motilones of Colombia had a legend about a prophet who would come carrying a banana stalk, which would tell them about

God. When Bruce Olson arrived with his Bible, and they saw him flipping through the pages, the Motilones were excited. One of the men walked over to a banana tree nearby, cut off a section, and then split it in half. Leaves that were still inside the stalk, waiting to develop, started peeling off. They looked like pages from a book. Then, pointing to the Bible, they said: "This is it! This is God's banana stalk. It will tell us about God." And God's banana stalk, through the mouth of the missionary, began to speak to the Motilones that day clearly, meaningfully, redemptively.[5]

*d. The truth about sin.* Though there is no moral foundation in animist religion, the people do have some concept of right and wrong, and a sense of estrangement from the Supreme Being. All the tribal, mythological stories about the Fall, however crude they may be, have one basic idea in common—the separation of man from God. Man has done something that has brought displeasure to God, so God has walked off and left him. So the animist knows something is wrong.

The animist's view of sin may be somewhat superficial, nevertheless he does regard certain acts as offenses. Social offenses are sins against the deified ancestor, because he is responsible for harmony in society and will punish the offender. This accounts for the ambivalent attitude of fear and affection to the ancestor. The tribal deity, as judge and preserver, is regarded in the same way, and with this goes the notion of right and wrong behavior—approval of the former and punishment of the latter. In a society without gods, this guiding and correcting role may be assigned to spirits, which may be friendly or hostile. The common denominator is the notion of right and wrong action, with corresponding results. Having accepted the idea of the supernatural, this notion makes it possible for the animist to see himself as a sinner in need of a Savior.

The animist's understanding of sin and its guilt will develop along with his increased understanding of the gospel. When he learns of the death of Christ on his behalf, and that he himself was indirectly involved in the tragedy of the Cross, he will begin to see the awfulness of his sin and his need for forgiveness. As the truth of the Word is preached, the Holy Spirit will convince the individual of "sin and righteousness and judgment" (John 16:8).

*e. The truth about salvation.* Although both the deity and the tribe are displeased with the offender, the animist always has hope for some way of escape from punishment. This inner compulsion leads him to magic on one level and religion on another. Thus basically, the animist is salvation-oriented. It is interesting to observe all the atonements and sacrificial remedies for human offenses that animist societies have developed on their behalf. Here are a few illustrations from the past and present:

(1) The Tahitians of Oceania, after war, put into a canoe certain offerings (a model house, a basket of food, and the effigy of a man) and pushed it out into the Pacific Ocean. As the priests sought forgiveness from the gods, the sin offering was symbolic of the taking away of the sin from the land.

(2) The Ulawans of the Solomon Islands annually drove a dog out to sea as a sacrifice to take away the sins that brought sickness upon the people. (This is akin to the scapegoat of the Hebrews.)

(3) In a certain Fijian mountain village there used to be a large stone, called the Rock of Refuge, on which a manslayer could take refuge from the avenging chief.[6]

(4) Among the Yali tribe of Irian Jaya, when an offender is slain, the priests kill a pig, catch its blood in gourd containers, and sprinkle it for atonement wherever some of the culprit's blood might have soaked into the ground unnoticed.[7]

(5) Among the Motilones of Colombia, after a hunt for wild boars, the leader cuts the skin from the animal and puts it over his head to cover his ears and keep out evil spirits.[8]

All of these rituals are symbolic expressions of the necessity of a remedy for sin and find their perfect fulfillment in Christ and His atoning death at Calvary. It should be emphasized to the animist that God himself has provided the final sacrifice, and now He no longer demands from us any kind of animal sacrifice. Instead we are to accept His sacrifice.

In addition there are the many and varied tribal rituals performed to bring reconciliation between man and man; such as the sacrifice to a tribal deity, drinking the ceremonial beverage, eating salt together, smoking the pipe of peace, offering the peace child, and so on. All of these ceremonies lay the foundation for the concept of reconciliation between God and man, which has been effected by Christ as our Mediator.

*f. The truth about freedom.* Fear is the dominating factor in animism—fear of evil spirits, the forces of nature, death itself. The Christian evangelist must emphasize that God is Sovereign, the Lord of Creation, that He has power over the forces of nature, is stronger than the spirits, and is Victor over death. The narration of the miracles of Christ—healing the demoniac, calming the sea, healing the blind and leper, raising Lazarus—will convince the animist that Christ is Lord of all.

Mention has already been made of the Iban tribe in Sarawak, Malaysia, and how they lived in constant fear of bad dreams, black rodents, and the hoot of the hornbill bird. The turning point in the life of these people came when they made contact with some of the Chinese Christians who had migrated from southern China to Sarawak following the Boxer Rebellion in their homeland. The Ibans noticed that these Christians walked the forests, rowed the rivers, and worked their fields unafraid. They lived well and had plenty to eat. So the Ibans began to question these newcomers. "Aren't you afraid of the evil spirits all around you?"

"No," replied the Chinese Christians. "We worship a living God who is gracious and loving and more powerful than all the forces of this world."

As a result the Ibans became interested in the Christian faith. Shortly afterward, Methodist missionaries from the United States, together with missionaries from nearby Indonesia and the Philippines, arrived on the scene to assist in the evangelization of these people. Today thousands of the Ibans are Christians. If anyone were to ask them, "What has Christ done for you?" no doubt their first reply would be, "He has delivered us from our fears."

It is difficult for us to imagine the tremendous sense of relief and freedom that comes to the animist as a result of his new life in Christ Jesus.

The animist's belief in spirit possession lays a foundation for the concept of the indwelling presence of the Holy Spirit, who cleanses and empowers us for daily living. The true *mana* is the power of God made available to us, sustained by prayer, meditation, and obedience.

In response to the animist's fatalistic outlook on life, the consolations of the Christian faith must be emphasized: the peace of God, the joy of the Lord, the comfort of the Holy Spirit (the Comforter), the gift of eternal life, the hope of Christ's return, and the hope of heaven.

There is always an expression of anxiety in the ritual of the animist; there is emotion, excitement. The emotions of the Christian life, the excitement of being a Christian, must be portrayed. There must be cultural substitutes for all the former animistic practices that are eliminated by the gospel. Christianity must become indigenous, and the new Christians must be free to express themselves in their own cultural patterns.

The animist tribe now becomes the Christian tribe—the "clan of God"—the fellowship of God's people in the Church of Jesus Christ!

# 13

# Communicating the Gospel to Muslims

### 1. The Life of Mohammed

Islam, the latest of the great world religions, was founded by Mohammed, who was born in Mecca, Arabia, in A.D. 570. An orphan at the age of six, he was brought up first by his grandfather and then by his uncle. Little is known of his early life. Traditions tell us that he spent his boyhood among nomad tents; that at the age of 12 he went with his uncle to Syria, where he met a Christian monk named Bahira. He later found employment with a rich widow named Khadija, who put him in charge of her caravan. His economic and social status changed for the better, when, at the age of 25, he married Khadija, who was 15 years his senior.

The adult Mohammed soon showed signs of a markedly religious disposition. He would retire to a cave for seclusion and meditation; he frequently practiced fasting; and he was prone to dreams. Profoundly dissatisfied with the polytheism and crude superstitions of his people, he appears to have become passionately convinced of the existence and transcendence of one true God. There is little doubt that he was influenced in this regard by contacts he made with Jews and Christians from time to time.

It was at the age of 40 that the first revelation of the Koran is said to have come to Mohammed. These visions went on for about 2 years. While contemplating in a cave one day, he felt himself called to be a prophet of the one true God, Allah. Encouraged by his wife, Khadija, he began to proclaim the message of Allah, the one true God, and to warn of the Day of Judgment. But the response in Mecca was small, and opposition began to grow. So in A.D. 622 Mohammed took the decisive step of withdrawing with his small band of followers to Medina, to which he had been invited by a party of its citizens. This withdrawal, or *Hijrah*, proved to be the turning point in Mohammed's career, and has been appropriately chosen as the beginning of the Muslim era. In Mecca he had been the rejected prophet, but in Medina he at once became the statesman, legislator, and judge —the executive as well as the prophet of the new theocracy. He was soon able to gain a large number of followers and to build an army with which to engage the forces of rebellious Mecca. After a somewhat chequered career, Mohammed entered Mecca in triumph, smashed the idols which surrounded the Kaaba (a shrine containing a black meteorite), and established the city as the center of the Islamic faith. By the time of his death—Medina, A.D. 632—he had established Islam, nominally at least, throughout the greater part of the Arabian peninsula. Within the next hundred years his followers had planted the sign of the crescent throughout the Middle East and all across North Africa, and even in Spain and southern Europe. The Muslim army was finally turned back at the strategic Battle of Tours in southern France in the year A.D. 732.

Today Mohammed's followers number about 700 million, and the Islamic world stretches all the way from Morocco in North Africa to Indonesia in Southeast Asia, with minority populations in North America, Europe, Russia, China, the Philippines, and the Fiji Islands in the South Pacific.

## 2. The Six Articles of Faith

There are six fundamental articles of faith that must be held by every Muslim:

*a. Allah.* God is One and is Creator and Judge. He is all-seeing, all-knowing, all-powerful. His transcendence and sovereignty are particularly emphasized, to the tragic neglect of His holiness and love. There is a list of 99 "beautiful names" for God that are known to Muslims.

*b. Angels.* There is a hierarchy of angels who are created of light. The most important ones are Gabriel, who transmitted the Koran to Mohammed; Asrafel, who will sound the trumpet on the Day of Judgment; and Azrael, the angel of death. Shaytan or Iblis (Satan) was put out of the Garden of Eden when he failed to comply with God's command to bow down to Adam. There are also spirits called *jinns* created from fire. For the most part they are evil and cause all sorts of trouble.

*c. Holy books.* The Old Testament is considered sacred, and is usually spoken of as two books—the Torah or Book of the Law, and the Zabur or Psalms. Muslims claim that the New Testament or Injil "descended upon Jesus," but insist that the original was taken back by Christ when He ascended into heaven, and the copy now in the hands of Christians has been changed. The Koran is God's final revelation to man, and therefore supersedes all former sacred books. Muslims claim it is the copy of the original Koran in heaven. The angel Gabriel dictated the Koran to Mohammed, and he merely repeated it word by word (a verbal inspiration of the most mechanical sort).

*d. Prophets.* There are six eminent prophets: Adam, the chosen of God; Noah, the preacher of God; Abraham, the friend of God; Moses, the speaker of God; Jesus, the Word of God; and Mohammed, the apostle of God, who is the last and greatest of all the prophets, and supersedes all those who came before. It is not really the Koran but later traditions that have glorified the figure of Mohammed as one who existed before the creation of the world, the worker of all sorts of miracles, the ideal character, and the sinless one (in spite of the fact that in the Koran he prays for the forgiveness of his sins).

*e. Predestination.* According to Muslims, everything that happens, either good or bad, is foreordained by the unchangeable decrees of Allah, a doctrine which makes Allah the author of evil. Most Muslim theologians completely deny the free will of man, while some allow some place for free will. This leads to a fatalistic philosophy of life; even the worst calamities are often accepted by Muslims with no more than a stoic shrug of the shoulders.

*f. The Day of Judgment.* The evil and good deeds of each individual will be weighed on a special balance, as the soul crosses a bridge of enormous length, as thin as a hair and as sharp as a sword. Those who are evil will topple off into the fires of hell below, while the good will pass across as swiftly as light to paradise. This is a place of sensual delight, containing restful gardens with every manner of delicious fruits, rivers of wine that do not intoxicate, and beautiful women to be companions of the faithful.

## 3. The Five Religious Duties

There are five fundamental duties in Islam, commonly known

as the Pillars of Religion, which must be faithfully observed by every true Muslim.

   a. *Recitation of the Word of Witness,* the Muslim Creed—"There is no God but Allah; Mohammed is the apostle of Allah." It is the first speech of infants and the last word of the dying. It is recited over and over in the five calls to prayer, and on countless other occasions.

   b. *Reciting the stated prayers.* The five stated prayers are required daily of every Muslim—at dawn, noon, mid-afternoon, sunset, and after dark. The prayer is preceded by ceremonial washing of the face, hands, and feet. The worshipper faces Mecca and goes through a series of prescribed positions. On Friday noon a special service is held at the mosque.

   c. *Observing the month of fasting* during Ramadan, ninth month of the Muslim lunar year, since the descent of Koran is supposed to have taken place during the latter part of this month. The fasting is obligatory during the hours of daylight, but eating is permitted at night. The requirement includes abstinence from drinking any liquids and from smoking.

   d. *Giving the legal alms.* The Muslim is required to give 1/40 of all money received to charity, plus a certain portion of other types of income, determined by a rather complicated system. This offering goes to the poor, orphans, widows, the sick, and other unfortunates.

   e. *Making the pilgrimage, or Hajj, to Mecca.* This is required at least once during the lifetime of every pious Muslim who is physically able and can afford to make the trip. In special cases, he can send a substitute. The days of the great pilgrimage are from the 1st to the 12th of the last month in the lunar year.

## 4. Major Problems in Reaching Muslims

   a. *Historically,* there has been an unfortunate relationship between Christianity and Islam down through the centuries. To begin with, Mohammed got a false impression of Christianity from whatever contacts he had with Christians in Arabia. It is obvious that he completely misunderstood the idea of the Trinity, which he thought consisted of God and Mary and Jesus. Then as Muslim forces swept across North Africa they found a church woefully torn by division and strife, arguing over minor doctrinal matters. Later came the Crusades (1090-1290) with all of their abuses, as Christians took up the sword against Muslims to regain control of the Holy Land. This was followed by the colonial period when most of the Muslim nations were under the control of Western Christian nations. More recently, the establishing of modern Israel, particularly through the influence of "Christian" Britain and the U.S.A., has been a major source of friction between Christendom and the Islamic world. All this has left a residue of bitterness in the minds of Muslims, particularly throughout the Arab world.

The postcolonial period brought new problems. Several independent Muslim governments have forced the withdrawal of all Christian missionaries, while others have placed serious restrictions on the entry of missionaries and the preaching of the gospel.

*b.* Then there are the *cultural* barriers. Islam is not only a religion, it is also a social and political system, as we clearly see in the case of Iran. Muslims make little distinction between secular and sacred, between mosque and state. This produces a very tightly knit society that strongly opposes conversion from Islam to any other religion. Converts are ostracized, severely persecuted, and sometimes put to death.

*c.* Add to this the *religious* barriers. Muslims, for the most part, are very proud of their faith and extremely fanatical in their loyalty. They feel that Islam is the final truth and is superior to all other religions. To forsake the faith is to become an infidel. Furthermore, they have a prejudiced position against Christianity, for they believe what the Koran says about Christ, not what the Bible declares.

## 5. Points of Contact with Christianity

There are several concepts and practices in Islam that provide a common ground for our approach to Muslims.

*a.* Islam means "submission," and a Muslim is "one who submits" (to the will of Allah). The Christian is one who says to God, "Not my will, but thine, be done" (Luke 22:42).

*b.* Muslims believe in one supreme, personal God, who is Creator and Judge.

*c.* Muslims are people of a book. They believe that God is One who reveals.

*d.* The Koran speaks of Jesus as "The Word of God" and "the Spirit of God."

*e.* Many words in Islam are familiar to the Christian— *God, apostles, witness, good, sovereignty, unity, subjection.* These are words full of associations bound up with Christ, in whom, for the Christian, they find the fullness of their significance.

*f.* Many practices in Islam are also familiar to the Christian—in particular, fasting and almsgiving. These values must be preserved.

## 6. Theological Barriers in Islam

In many ways Islam appears closer to Christianity than all the other world religions. In reality, however, it is farther apart and much more difficult to confront, because it approaches the Christian faith with a preset position. Islam has certain theological ideas that cut right across the basic truths of the gospel. These teachings have to do primarily with the validity of the Scriptures, the nature of God, the person of Jesus Christ, and the doctrine of the atonement.

*a. The validity of the Scriptures.* Though the Koran clearly testifies to the authenticity of the Christian Scriptures, the Muslim is faced with a problem when he reads the Bible and discovers certain contradictions to the teaching of the Koran. If the Bible and the Koran are both revelations from God, there should be a harmony and continuity, not contradiction. To escape from this dilemma, Muslims have introduced the theory of the corruption of the existing copies of the Jewish and Christian Scriptures. To prove their position, they point to all the variations in the Greek manuscripts and the many different versions of the Bible that are in use today. Thus the Bible in its present form is unreliable, and it is the Koran that gives the true divine revelation. What the Koran says about God, Christ, and the Cross must be accepted over against what the Bible teaches.

Christians, however, should not hesitate to use the Scriptures in dealing with Muslims. If a thief and rapist broke into your home one night and you leveled a gun at him, but he just laughed at you and said, "I don't believe in guns," would you put the gun aside and give up? Just one shot fired in his direction would be enough to convince him otherwise. In the same way, just because the Muslim does not believe in the reliability of the Bible is no reason to lay it aside. It is still God's Word and acts like a two-edged sword to pierce the hearts and minds of men. It is ironical that the Muslim himself often quotes from the New Testament in order to prove his point. Actually, the Christian is in a strong position in inviting the Muslim to read the Scriptures, for the Koran does testify to their authenticity and even advises the perplexed Muslim to consult the Christians about matters of religion which he does not understand (Koran 10:94).

As for the alleged corruption of the Scriptures, it can easily be shown to be without foundation, from the simple fact that complete manuscripts of the Greek New Testament which go back more than two centuries before the time of Mohammed, are in existence today. These substantiate the text of the present-day Arabic version, and not the Koranic variant. Furthermore, we can remind the Muslim that in the early days of Islam, when variations were developing in handwritten copies of the Koran in different areas, Muslim scholars solved the problem by simply destroying all versions but one.

*b. The doctrine of the Trinity.* The Muslim is a staunch unitarian and, as such, has great problems with the idea of the Trinity in Christianity. He accuses the Christian of believing in three gods and, therefore, of practicing idolatry. The problem arises basically from a misunderstanding of the Trinity. Most Muslims think that the Trinity consists of God, Mary, and Jesus; some think it consists of Gabriel, Mary, and Jesus. Thus either God had sexual intercourse with Mary and they had a son, Jesus; or, the Holy Spirit in the form of a man (Gabriel) married Mary and by intercourse produced Jesus. Naturally, all of this appears as sheer blasphemy to the Muslim.

Our first responsibility as Christians is to clear up this misunderstanding. We must state clearly that we don't believe in three gods. The Old Testament categorically declares there is only one God, and He alone is the object of our worship (Deut. 6:4). Jesus, in the New Testament, reiterated this truth (Mark 12:29-30). We must say to the Muslim that God did *not* marry Mary. He never marries, cannot marry, has no need to marry. When the Muslim hears this, he immediately feels greatly relieved and assumes a much more relaxed attitude in conversation.

The doctrine of the Trinity is indeed difficult for anyone to understand. The fact of the matter is, when we try to explain divine mysteries in human language, we get just so far and then find we can go no farther. Christian evangelists have used various illustrations in attempting to explain the Trinity to Muslims, but each one has its limitations. Some use the illustration of the egg, which has three parts—the shell, yolk, and white—but is one single object. Others point out that a man may have three different roles—as father, son, and doctor—but he is still one person.

Perhaps the best way to explain the Trinity to the Muslim is to ask him the questions: Are you a living body? Are you a living soul? Are you a living mind? When he answers in the affirmative, ask him, "Which of the three is you?" He will naturally say, "I am all three." Then it can be pointed out that each one of us is a trinity on the human level, and yet we regard ourselves as one. Somehow, in some mysterious way beyond our comprehension, the Godhead is Three and yet One. If we deny the divine Trinity, we also deny the human personality.

Actually, the Koran quotes God as saying, "*We* created . . . *We* sent prophets," and in both cases the form of the Arabic verb that is used refers to at least three persons. There is a different form of the verb when only one subject is speaking, and yet another verb form when two persons are involved. This is equivalent to the Genesis record where God says, "Let us make man in our image, after our likeness" (Gen. 1:26). The Muslim's attention can be drawn to this fact.

In the long run, however, it is doubtful if we can ever convince the Muslim of the Trinity by sheer logic. Like the disciples of Jesus, he will have to come to an understanding of the Trinity by personal experience. The disciples, as orthodox Jews, believed strongly in one God. They were strict monotheists. But when Christ came on the scene, claimed to be the Son of God, and authenticated His claim by miracles and a sinless life, they said to themselves, "This is God with us!" Now they were faced with God the Father and Christ the Son. Then on the Day of Pentecost they experienced the indwelling Holy Spirit, purifying and empowering them, and they were forced to say, "This is God within us!" Now they were faced with God the Father, God the Son, and God the Holy Spirit—Three in One. It was sometime later that the actual doctrine of the Trinity was formulated as part of the Christian creed. First came the experience, then the doctrine. From my personal contacts with Muslims, I have observed that once they come into a personal experience with Christ as Savior and Lord, the intellectual problem of the Trinity seems to disappear. What they could not understand with their

heads, they now accept in their hearts. Bishop John Abdus Subhan, convert from Islam in India, agreed that this was the case
in his own religious pilgrimage.

    *c. The person of Jesus.* Every Muslim professes to believe in
Jesus, but it is "another Jesus" presented in the Koran. The 'Isa
of the Koran is one of many prophets and was sent solely to the
Jews. He was born of the Virgin Mary, but Gabriel was his
father, according to most Muslim interpreters. 'Isa was not the
Son of God, and he himself denied the Trinity. Like Adam, he
was created out of the dust. He performed many great miracles,
but this was only by God's permission. He foretold the coming
of Mohammed (see John 14:16). The Muslim contention is that
the Greek word *parakletos,* translated "Comforter" in the KJV,
is a corruption of the original word *periklutos,* "the praised one,"
which really refers to Mohammed. 'Isa was not crucified and
did not die; it only seemed so to men. He lives today and will
return to this earth where he will marry , have children, and die
at Medina where he will be buried beside the prophet Mohammed. He will reign for 40 years and will establish Islam in the
whole world.

    There are a number of verses in the Koran where the Son-
ship of Christ is specifically denied. "He [God] begets not and is
not begotten . . . God could not take to himself any son!" (Koran
112:3; 119:5). To call Jesus "the Son of God" is to be guilty of
*Shirk* (making anyone a coequal with God), which is the most
deadly of all sins. Furthermore, the Muslim interprets the term
"Son of God" to mean that God had intercourse with a woman,
and she bore a son called Jesus. This, he feels, is blasphemy!

    We must be careful to explain to the Muslim that Sonship
is not a physical concept. Jesus was born of the Virgin Mary
through the power of the Holy Spirit. He had no human father.
He was not created; He came from God. Thus in a special sense
God is His Father. But this is a spiritual relationship, not a
physical one.

    We can point out to the Muslim that in everyday speech
the expression "son of" is used as a metaphor to convey likeness
of character and does not imply physical relationship; as, "son
of a jackal" or "son of thunder." The Koran actually speaks of
Jesus as "the Word of God," or "Word from God."[1] In Arabic,
the prepositions "of" and "from" signify the same genus. Thus
"Word of God" and "Son of God" are identical in meaning. Just

as the word is the expression of the speaker's thought, so the son is the manifestation of the father's character. As Word and Son, Jesus reveals the nature of God. We can refer to John 1:1-4, and say: God does speak to men. He speaks through His Word, as I do. Where were my words before they came from my mouth? In my brain or in my thoughts? But if you cut open my head, you will not find them there. In some mysterious way I and my word are the same. Whatever my word does, either pleasing you or annoying you, you can say that I am doing it. So whatever the Word of God does, God himself is doing it. In the same manner, the Father and the Son are one. Whoever looks at the Son sees the Father.

The best analogy to illustrate this truth is that of the sun and its rays. God, like the sun, is the Source, the Sender. Jesus, like the rays of the sun, reflects the light and gives life. The Holy Spirit, like the rays which melt and heat, produces energy or power in the life of the individual. The three can't be separated. Jesus (the rays) is the concrete expression of the Father (the sun). The Sender has extended himself through Jesus and the Holy Spirit. God is everywhere, but we can't see God except through His manifestation. Thus when we look at Jesus, we are looking at the Father. This is exactly what Jesus meant when He said to Philip: "He who has seen me has seen the Father" (John 14:9). Because God loves and cares for us, He has removed the cloud (or the veil) that hides the Sun and has revealed himself in a human form in Jesus. The Father-Son concept expresses the spiritual relationship (not physical) between the infinite God of the universe and God Incarnate who entered the world and human history.

It is interesting to note how Jesus dealt with the Pharisees concerning the truth of His Messiahship. When they asked Him if He was the Messiah, He seldom answered directly, "Yes, I am." Because they had false ideas of the Messiah, Jesus had to convey the truth about himself in other ways, such as "I am the bread of life; . . . I am the door; . . . I am the good shepherd" (John 6:35; 10:9, 11). We must also try to convey to the Muslim something of the uniqueness of Christ without using the phrase "Son of God" until he has begun to understand. A careful study of the Book of Acts will reveal that when the apostles were preaching to pagans or Gentiles, they did not refer to Jesus as "the Son of God" but used the expression "Lord." When people believed in Jesus, then they were led on to a fuller understanding of His eternal Sonship as described in the Epistles. We can take the same approach when dealing with Muslims.

This does not mean that we are to compromise our message or tone down the truth. Eventually the Muslim will have to face the fact that Jesus *is* the Son of God. But in order to bring him to that point of faith, it is much wiser to start with terms that he already accepts than to begin with terms which he misunderstands and against which he is prejudiced.

Charles Marsh, missionary to Algeria and Chad, suggests that the Arabic word *Rabb* (Lord) conveys the thought of One who is supreme, for it is used for God frequently by the Muslims. To speak of Jesus as *Rabba na 'Isa,* our Lord Jesus, would clearly imply His deity.

When Muslims accuse us of making a man God, we must remind them that this is exactly the opposite of what the Bible declares. The Bible teaches not that a man became God, but that God became man. The Eternal Word became flesh and dwelt among us. The idea of incarnation, of course, is something difficult for the Muslim to accept, for he feels it is unthinkable that the sovereign Ruler of the universe would stoop to become a mere man. That is simply below His dignity. But if God can speak through human language—Arabic—why not through human personality? Which is the greater revelation? A book, or a life? Furthermore, if God is truly sovereign, can He not choose to become a man and reveal himself in person? Who are we to deny Him that right?

*d. The death of Christ.* The major theological barrier in Islam is the outright denial of the death of our Lord. The Koran clearly states: "They did not kill him, nor did they crucify him, but it appeared so to them" (Sura 4:158). Most Muslims believe that God took Jesus to heaven just before the Crucifixion and that a substitute, perhaps Judas, was crucified in His place.

It is on the basis of the sovereignty of God that the Muslim formulates his attitude toward the Cross. It is unthinkable that God would allow His prophet to be scourged, spat upon, and crucified between two thieves. God always vindicates His prophets with victory. So it is impossible that such a good man as Jesus should die, for God is all-powerful and would certainly have saved Him from this horrible death. Furthermore, the atonement was completely unnecessary, for God can forgive sins by His own sovereign act, by word of mouth.

Here again, it is exactly on the basis of God's sovereignty that we can take our stand as Christians. If God is really sovereign, can He not choose to make the Cross the means of our redemption? Who are we to tell Him how He should manage His affairs? Furthermore, it is because God is sovereign that the atonement became necessary. He cannot forgive sin lightly with just the wave of His hand. There would be no moral quality in such cheap forgiveness. But through the Cross He upheld His moral law and dealt radically with sin. Now He offers forgiveness in a nail-pierced hand, a forgiveness with real moral content.

We can ask the Muslim: Which is the greater victory for Almighty God? To snatch away Jesus at the last moment and rescue Him from death? Or to allow Him to die and then raise Him victoriously from the dead?

In the death of Christ we see the sovereign will of God. He planned the atonement before the foundation of the world. Through His prophets He foretold how Christ must suffer, many years before it happened. All through the Scriptures, God spoke of the death of His Son, as in Isaiah 53. When Jesus came to earth, He accepted the will of His Father. He stated clearly that no one could take His life from Him, but He would lay it down of His own free will (John 10:17-18). He could have easily summoned a legion of angels and destroyed those who sought to kill Him. He could have come down from the Cross by His own power. But out of love He suffered on the Cross to redeem us from our sins. God then approved the sacrifice that Jesus made by raising Him from the dead.

The writer of Hebrews tells us that "without the shedding of blood there is no forgiveness of sins" (Heb. 9:22). Since the Muslim accepts the Old Testament as one of God's holy books, we can demonstrate the truth of this statement by reminding him of the many sacrifices recorded in the Old Testament. The following incidents, known to all Muslims, are especially helpful:

How God clothed Adam and Eve with garments of skins
(Gen. 3:21)

Cain and Abel (Genesis 4)

Noah offering sacrifices after he came out of the ark (Gen. 8:20)

Abraham sacrificing the ram in place of Isaac (Genesis 22)[2]

The Passover lamb (Exodus 12)

The red heifer (Numbers 19)

It can be pointed out that all of these Old Testament believers approached God by the way of sacrifice. Then the importance of Heb. 10:1-18 can be explained, and the finality of Christ's sacrifice emphasized.

## ISLAM AND CHRISTIANITY COMPARED

| ISLAM | | CHRISTIANITY |
|---|---|---|
| 1. To Allah | SUBMISSION | 1. To God |
| 2. Sin of *Shirk*, making one a partner with God | ONE GOD | 2. Trinitarian (Three in One), Father, Son, and Holy Spirit |
| 3. Transcendence. Man is the *slave* of God, not a child. | SOVEREIGNTY OF GOD | 3. Transcendence and immanence. Father—love of God; man can be a child of God. |
| 4. Righteous, punishes evil, rewards the good, forgives on the basis of sovereignty (atonement not necessary) | JUDGE | 4. Holy, forgives on the basis of the atonement in Christ |
| 5. Only His will | ONE WHO REVEALS | 5. Himself (self-disclosure). Reveals His will and nature |
| 6. Not Son of God; did not die on the Cross (no Resurrection) | CHRIST Prophet, born of virgin, the Word of God | 6. Incarnation of God. God as a person has revealed himself in a person. |
| 7. God will not permit His prophet to be disgraced and defeated. Mohammed the apostle of God, the final prophet | | 7. Son of God; crucified and risen! His death necessary to reconciliation; His resurrection the greatest triumph of God! |
| 8. The Bible is corrupted. The Koran is infallible, supersedes all previous sacred writings. Torah (Law) Zabur (Psalms) Injil | SACRED BOOKS | 8. The Bible, the inspired revelation of God Old Testament New Testament |
| 9. By works, By fulfilling the five duties | SALVATION | 9. By faith in Christ. Forgiveness of sins, eternal life. |
| 10. Paradise (place of sensual delight) | FUTURE | 10. Heaven (eternal presence of God) |
| 11. To infidels and evildoers | JUDGMENT (Hell) | 11. To sinners, unbelievers |
| 12. Means of salvation | WORKS | 12. Expression of the Christian life |

## 7. Practical Suggestions for Ministering to Muslims

*a. Develop a true friendship.* The Muslim usually will not be won in a short time by a casual acquaintance. He must be reached through an extended friendship. Invite him to your home; show that you really care for him as a person. Show concern in times of illness or bereavement. The Muslim will always respond to love. In nearly every case of conversion, the Muslim has been influenced by Christian love.

*b. Maintain an attitude of sympathy and understanding.* Avoid criticism, a negative approach, prejudice, denouncement. Realize the Muslim's strong veneration for Mohammed and the Koran, and his sincere belief in one God. The Muslim is usually a very religious and God-fearing person.

*c. Start with the Bible.* The Muslim has a false image of Christ from the Koran. Expose him to the biblical account of Christ—His true character, His claims, His sinless life, His death and resurrection. Do not give the Muslim a copy of Mark's Gospel to begin with, for the very first verse speaks of Jesus as "the Son of God." Rather, give him a copy of John's Gospel, for it begins with Jesus as "the Word of God," a term that the Muslim is already familiar with. Matthew's Gospel can also be helpful, because it traces the genealogy of Christ back to David and Abraham, and describes the virgin birth of our Lord—all of which are acceptable to the Muslim.

*d. Don't argue—witness!* When necessary, answer the sincere questions of the Muslim and give him reasons for your faith. But don't allow the dialogue to become a debate. Emphasize your personal relationship with God and the forgiveness of sins through Christ. Usually the Muslim has no assurance of either one.

Remember, the Word of Witness is very important to the Muslim—"There is no God but Allah, and Mohammed is the apostle of Allah." The Christian also has a "word of witness," found in John 17:3—"This is eternal life, that they know thee the only true God, and Jesus Christ whom thou hast sent." The second and third clauses are very much similar to the Muslim Word of Witness; but the first clause is unique, and this is what makes all the difference. Christ alone is life—abundant life, eternal life.

*e. Live the Christian life.* Words alone cannot bring Muslims to the foot of the Cross. No amount of interpretation in the abstract can, of itself, convince him that Jesus is the Savior. You must show in your

214 / Tell It Well

life how Christianity is in truth the incarnation of the love of God. Most Muslims who have followed Christ have done so because of the sacrificial life and sustained love of some Christian friend.

The Muslim is indeed a difficult person to reach with the gospel; but armed with truth and love, with humility and tact, the Christian witness can effectively lead him to the foot of the Cross.

# 14

# The Power of
# the Gospel

*I am not ashamed of the gospel: it is the power of God for salvation to every one who has faith, to the Jew first and also to the Greek* (Rom. 1:16).

These are the words of the apostle Paul, the first and perhaps the greatest Christian missionary of all time. He had perfect confidence in the message he preached. He knew it was not just the words of mortal men, but the Word of the living God. He knew what the gospel could do for others, because he knew what it had done for himself. By the grace of God he had been transformed from a hateful persecutor and murderer into a compassionate evangelist and builder of the Church. Then in his own ministry he had seen the transforming power of the Word in the lives of licentious Corinthians, idolatrous Thessalonians, proud Romans, and sophisticated Greeks. He had seen Christ save from the guttermost to the uttermost. He had witnessed Christ taking the devil's castaways and making monuments of grace out of them.

The gospel is still the same today. Christ is the same today. The Holy Spirit is still at work today. All across the world we are witnessing the transforming power of God among people of all races and tribes and religions. God is working among the Bataks, Karens, Sawis, Yalis, and Motilones; among Japanese, Chinese, Koreans, Indians, Africans, Europeans, and Americans.

## 1. The Gospel Is the Power of God for Hindus

Several years ago I was invited by a group of low-caste Hindus to come to their village and tell them about Christ. These people were illiterate, uneducated, and extremely poor. I sat cross-legged on the cow-dung-smeared floor of one of their mud huts and told in simple story form the life of Christ from Birth to Resurrection. When I finished, they said, "This is a wonderful story of a Man who loved us so much that He gave His life for us. Please come back and tell us more."

So I went back several times and explained more about the Way, exhorting them to turn from their idols to the living God. Several months later they said to me, "Missionary, we now believe in this Christ. We have already buried our idols, and we want to be baptized as Christians." So we set a date, and on the appointed day I baptized seven families—about 35 people in all.

The change in the lives of these people soon became evident. All the old habits were gone. There was a new radiance and joy in their outlook on life. They said to themselves, "We may be untouchables, but God has touched us. We may be outcastes, but God has taken us into His family. We are now the children of God. We can be somebody; we can do something."

The first thing they did was to clean themselves up on the outside. They began to take more baths and wear cleaner clothes. They tore down their mud huts, one by one, and built seven new homes, a great improvement over the original ones. Then one day when I visited the village, they said to me, "Missionary, our children are growing up in ignorance. Can you send us a teacher and start a school for them?"

So I sent them a Christian teacher, and he began a primary school with the first three standards (grades). When the children finished there, they could come to the mission school at the district center and continue on through high school.

Sometime later I loaned these new Christians a few hundred dollars, and they bought some land. They worked hard in the fields, the monsoon was abundant, and soon they were becoming economically self-sufficient. One of the men opened up a small shop.

About the second year the group said to me, "Missionary, we need a church here in which to worship. We will supply the land, the burned bricks, and the unskilled labor. Can you help us with funds for the lumber and skilled labor?"

Soon the work was begun, and within a few months the church was ready for dedication. I shall never forget when my father and I went out for the ceremony. The service started late at night, after the people had come back from the fields and had eaten their evening meal; it ended about midnight. My father and I crawled into our sleeping bags in a tent erected nearby, and the last thing we remembered when we fell asleep was their joyful music and singing in the church. We awakened early in the morning and found them still singing. They hadn't gone to bed that night—they sang the whole night through. It was a momentous day in their lives.

Just recently I was back in this village for a visit, after an absence of about 20 years. The group of Christians—now about 75—gathered in the church for a special service of testimony and praise. When I arose to speak, I started reminiscing about the beginnings of the work in their midst—my first visit, their conversion, the starting of the school, the building of the church, and so on. Suddenly I was interrupted by a fine-looking young man who stood up in the back. In perfect English he said, "Sir, may I say a few words?"

I agreed, and he came forward to address the group. "Sir," he began, "I was just a boy when you first came to this village. I remember you crawling on your hands and knees to get into the mud hut where we were all gathered. I was one of the pupils in the school you started here. I helped to carry the bricks for the building of the church." Then he went on to describe the various changes that had taken place in their lives. He informed me that he and two other boys who had studied in the village school had gone on with their education and now had their M.A. degrees. Two were teachers in the mission high school; one was pastor of a city church. (The speaker was a teacher.) He told how the high-caste people in town used to despise his people but now respected and looked up to them. He invited me to visit their new homes after the service and see their bins full of grain.

When he came to the end of his remarks, the young man suddenly raised himself up to his full height and, with deep emotion in his voice, declared: "Missionary, when Christ came to this village and into our lives, *He changed us spiritually, economically, socially, and eternally!*"

## 2. The Gospel Is the Power of God for Buddhists

In an earlier chapter describing the resurgence of the non-Christian religions, I quoted several times from the book *Revolt in the Temple*, by Vijayawardhana, a Buddhist scholar. I first came across this ponderous volume of over 500 pages when I was visiting Sri Lanka in the early 60s. The remarks of the author disturbed me deeply, because he claimed that Christianity is a dead religion and Buddhism is the living religion of today. When I expressed my concern to my Singhalese host, who was a Christian, he smiled and replied, "Mr. Seamands, you will be interested to know that the author of that book passed away a year or two ago, but just recently his wife has publicly declared her faith in Christ."

Immediately I was excited and requested my host to contact the lady and ask for an interview. She responded graciously by inviting both of us to tea at her home. It was there that I learned the story of her conversion from her own lips.

Mrs. Vimala Vijayawardhana was a staunch Buddhist and for several years was minister of health in Prime Minister Bandaranaike's cabinet. Then in 1959 the prime minister was suddenly assassinated by a Buddhist monk named Talduwa Somarama. (The story of his conversion before his hanging has been described in Chapter 5.) Mrs. Vijaya[1] was arrested and imprisoned on suspicion of being involved in the assassination plot. The trial went on for about nine months.

Providentially, the matron of the prison where Mrs. Vijaya was being held was a committed Christian. She gave a copy of the New Testament to the lady; and having nothing else to do, she began to read it just to pass the time. But soon the written Word became the living Word, and the reader began to see her sinfulness and need of a Savior. The farther she read, the more concerned she became about her spiritual condition. She was under deep conviction.

At this point in her testimony, Mrs. Vijaya looked at me with tears in her eyes, and with great feeling said, "Mr. Seamands, when I came to Ephesians, chapter 2—'and you hath he quickened, who were dead in trespasses and sins' [KJV]—my faith suddenly laid hold of Jesus Christ, and for the first time in my life I knew that my sins were forgiven. That was the greatest moment in my life!"

Not long after, Mrs. Vijaya was acquitted and released from prison. She went straight out and was baptized as a Christian. Today she is still witnessing for Christ in the capital city of Colombo.

## 3. The Gospel Is the Power of God for Muslims

Abdus Subhan[2] was born in the city of Calcutta, India, of a very orthodox Muslim family. He grew up under the simple, puritanical influence of his parents. They taught him to hate doing anything or uttering any word which was not regarded as good and honorable; also to refrain from smoking, chewing betel, and using profane language.

Abdus developed a fanatical zeal for Islam early in life. He faithfully observed the hours of prayer and the days of fasting. Before he was 10 years of age, he completed reading the entire Koran and memorized large portions of it. Under the guidance of noted *Maulvis* (Muslim teachers) he started studying Arabic and Persian, and took a course in Islamics. When he read of the early conquests of Islam, he dreamed of participating in another *jehad* (holy war) and drawing the sword against all unbelievers. Seeing his zeal, his parents encouraged him to become a Maulvi.

Abdus was convinced of the truth of Islam. He felt that every other religion was an invention of the devil, and that all non-Muslims had no right to exist, for they were polluting God's fair earth. He considered the worst of God's enemies to be Hindus (who were idolaters) and Christians (who were polytheists).

When he was 13, Abdus developed a great desire to know more about God of whom the prophets spoke, so he turned to books on Islamic mysticism. The result was a growing dissatisfaction with the form of religion based on legalism. He came to realize that true inner satisfaction was not to be attained by the observance of rituals or through formal beliefs, but by an inner experience. So he became a *Sufi* (Muslim mystic). For a while he drifted into the practice of magic and use of charms, but he finally decided that to be a *Kamil* (perfect one), he must attain the true knowledge of God and live in close fellowship with Him.

About this time, a copy of John's Gospel was given to Abdus by a Muslim friend, who himself had received it from a Christian colporteur. On previous occasions he had torn such Gospel portions into shreds; for he had been warned by the Maulvis that the New Testament was not a true *Injil* of which the Koran testifies, but a corrupted form of it, and consequently contained blasphemous teachings. But this time he felt impressed to read it.

The result of his first reading of John's Gospel was startling. In the first place Abdus did not find a single sentence or clause which in any sense could be interpreted as blasphemous or satanic. On the other hand, he was greatly impressed with the high ethical teachings of the Gospel. But what attracted him most was the narration of the crucifixion of Jesus. He thought, No follower of religion would intentionally invent such a narrative which would attribute to his leader such shameful treatment at the hands of his enemies.

The second reading of the Gospel convinced the young man that it was the true Injil. It was God's Word and His revelation. Through the Gospel he had seen Christ and come to know the Father. To use his own words:

> It was sufficient. I decided to become a Christian. Christianity . . . was after all to me the only true religion. It was a great discovery, but not mine. It was God discovering His erring and wandering child. I was His creature with the possibility of becoming His child.[3]

And so at the age of 15 he was baptized as John Abdus Subhan. He had to suffer much at the hands of his relatives and friends because of his new faith in Christ. They spat on him and called him a blasphemer and infidel. His public witness caused such a stir among the students and teachers that he was asked to leave the high school. But he found admission to a Christian high school, and so went on with his education until he had completed college. He was later ordained as a minister, and for several years taught at Bareilly Theological Seminary and the Henry Martyn School of Islamics.

In 1946 Rev. John Subhan was consecrated as bishop in the Methodist Church of Southern As 1—the first and only Muslim convert to ever become a bishop in the history of world Methodism! He was *my* bishop. I will always be grateful to God for the privilege of serving under his leadership. He was a devout Christian, an excellent preacher of the Word, and a good friend. He went to be with his Lord in the late 70s.

## 4. The Gospel Is the Power of God for Animists

In the heart of Manipur State in northeast India there is a tribal people known as the Hmars. For generations they were animists and practiced animal sacrifices and head-hunting.

One of the first missionaries to make contact with the Hmars was a young Welsh missionary by the name of Watkin Roberts. He was a very compassionate and loving person, zealous to share his faith. He did not treat the tribal people of the area as other white men did. He never demanded that the people be his coolies and carry his baggage without pay. Those who accompanied him he called his traveling companions. He ate with them; he slept with them.

The British agent would not permit Watkin to enter the Hmar territory because they were regarded as an unfriendly, dangerous people. So Watkin would sneak into the area each morning and return by dark. The Hmars treated him kindly and listened to his message with interest. He preached a simple message about God's Son who died as a sacrifice for the sins of mankind. In a short while he had his first group of converts. Since he was unable to live among the people, he started a training school outside the state, and the new converts went to him for instruction. Watkin gave them a basic Bible course and impressed upon them that they should be the evangelists to their own people and leaders of the churches they established. The new converts proved to be zealous and effective witnesses for their Lord. Once head-hunters, they now became heart-hunters. Soon a "people movement" was in progress, spreading from village to village, and hundreds of families "followed the trail of Christ."

Out of this movement came a young lad by the name of Ro-chunga Pudaite,[4] a son of Chawnga, the first Hmar convert and preacher. At the age of nine, under the preaching of his father, Ro gave his life to Christ and "entered the trail." Some days later his father began to talk to him about a great need in the Hmar tribe. "My son," he said, "you know we do not have God's Word in our own language. Someone must translate it into Hmar and have copies printed for everyone. I believe you are the person to do this. You will have to get an education and prepare yourself for this task."

And so at the age of 10, Ro trudged 96 miles through the tiger- and snake-infested jungles to enter the mission school at Churcha-chandpur. This was the first step in a long and arduous journey toward his appointed goal. The next 18 years were filled with excitement, hard work, and discouragement, as Ro struggled through grade school and high school, and then on to the famous University of Allahabad in northern India. On each campus he became a spiritual leader among the Christian students and an effective witness among the non-Christians.

All during this period Ro never forgot the two main goals of his life—to serve his Hmar people and to translate the Word of God into their language. As soon as he entered the university, he began the translation work. All his spare time was given to this important task. Then on one occasion when the prime minister of India came to Allahabad, by sheer courage and persistence, Ro made his way into the presence of Pandit Nehru and placed before him the needs of his people. He pointed out that in the 4,000 square miles inhabited by the Hmars and kindred tribes, there was not a single government school or post office. The prime minister was so impressed with the sincerity of the young man that he promised to look into the matter. Not long after, Ro was invited to visit the prime minister in Delhi to explain further the condition of his people. As a result, the central government opened up four post offices in the area and granted scholarships for Hmar children to go to school.

Upon his graduation from college, the way opened for Ro to go to Glasgow, Scotland, for further studies. While there he met the manager of the British and Foreign Bible Society, who became interested in his translation work and agreed to publish the Hmar Bible upon its completion. At the same time Ro had the privilege of meeting the famous American evangelist, Billy Graham, who was holding an extended campaign in Glasgow. When Mr. Graham heard that the whole Hmar tribe in India was holding all-night prayer meetings for his campaign in Scotland, he invited Ro to come to his hotel for a visit. The American evangelist was so impressed with the young man that he offered to provide a scholarship for him at Wheaton College in Illinois. So from Scotland, Ro came over to the United States.

The next few years were some of the happiest and most fruitful years of Ro's life. He completed his master's degree, accompanied Dr. Bob Pierce of World Vision on an extended preaching tour through Southeast Asia and the Far East, and organized the Partnership Mission in order to strengthen the Hmar Christian Church back in India. By 1970 the mission was supporting 350 national evangelists and operating a college, high school, Bible institute, hospital, bookstore, and 65 village schools. During this period Ro also took unto himself a wife—the beautiful Mawii, the first Hmar girl to graduate from college.

All this time Rochunga never forgot the goal that his father had set before him as a boy. He kept diligently at the task until he finally completed the New Testament in the Hmar language. Copies were soon rolling off the press; and when they arrived in India, the Hmars held a service of jubilation in every village. When the old man Chawnga, Ro's father, held the first copy in his hands, tears of gratitude and joy streamed down his face. His dream had come true at last! Within six months the first edition was all sold out, and an order for 10,000 more copies had to be placed.

But Ro's heart continued to burn with the desire to extend his ministry for Christ. His Hmar people were now Christians, but there were still millions of people in India and the rest of the world who had not yet heard the name of Christ. Ro spent hours on his knees beseeching God to reveal a new method by which he might reach the world for Christ.

One day, while in prayer, his concentration kept being broken by the telephone slogan, "Let your fingers do the walking—let your fingers do the walking." In frustration he stopped praying. As he rose from his knees, his attention was arrested by two telephone directories on his desk. Suddenly the vision was clear. Those books listed the names and addresses of everyone in Calcutta and New Delhi who had telephones. They were the best educated and most influential people, the very leaders he wanted to reach. And most of them knew English.

That's it! he thought. We'll let our fingers do the walking. We'll mail the Gospel to everyone whose address is in the telephone directory. The Word of God has always been the best missionary.

Within a short while, with the cooperation of Dr. Kenneth Taylor, copies of the *Living New Testament* were on their way to all the telephone owners in India—a million and a half of them! The cover bore the title *The Greatest Is Love* and showed a picture of the famous Taj Mahal. The response was amazing. Ro received thousands of letters from appreciative readers, and some of them witnessed to their faith in Christ.

This was the beginning of Bibles for the World, an organization which so far has sent New Testaments to all telephone owners in Nepal, Sri Lanka, Burma, Malaysia, the Philippines, and Taiwan. The ultimate objective is to send the Word of God to all telephone owners throughout the world.

It is beyond our wildest imagination to think that God would pick out a 10-year-old lad from an unknown animist tribe in the jungles of northeast India, and use him—not only to give the Bible to the Hmar people, but to millions of people around the world.

\* \* \*

Yes, the gospel of Jesus Christ *is* "the power of God for salvation to every one who has faith." And the risen Christ has commanded us to "go into all the world and preach the gospel to the whole creation" (Mark 16:15). He has asked us to tell the Good News to every nation and every person. Let us be sure that we tell it, and that we *TELL IT WELL!*

# NOTES

## Chapter 1

1. *Christianity Today,* Nov., 1975, "World Scene," p. 76; and Feb. 13, 1976, "World Scene," p. 75.

2. K. M. Panikkar, *Asia and Western Dominance* (London: Allen and Unwin, 1959), p. 297.

3. Vijayawardhana, *The Revolt in the Temple* (Colombo: Sinha Publications, 1953), p. 502.

4. Ibid.

5. Ibid., quoted on p. 500 from *The Buddhist,* Dec., 1945.

6. M. B. Niyogi, *Report of the Christian Missionary Activities Enquiry Committee, Madhya Pradesh* (Nagpur: Madhya Pradesh Government Printing, 1956), 1:131.

7. Arnold Toynbee, *Christianity Among the Religions of the World* (New York: Scribners, 1958), p. 95.

8. J. G. Davies, *Dialogo con el mundo.* Lectures given on tour of South America.

9. Vijayawardhana, *The Revolt in the Temple,* p. 531.

10. Ibid., p. 532.

11. *Lexington Leader,* Lexington, Ky., Feb., 1960.

12. Mahmud Brelvi, *The Impact of Islam on Human Progress* (Karachi: Technical Printers, 1964). See Table of Contents.

13. W. R. Read, V. M. Monterroso, and H. A. Johnson, *Latin American Church Growth* (Grand Rapids: Eerdmans, 1969), p. 51.

14. William F. Nicholson, "Evangelical Movement Grows Strong in Latin American Nations," *Sunday Herald-Leader,* Lexington, Ky., May 22, 1977, p. F-7.

15. Jack Stowell, "Brazil's Fastest Growing Religion," *Cable* (Overseas Crusades, Jan.-Feb., 1965), pp. 1-2.

16. Dale Kietzman, "Brazil's Spirit Cults," *World Vision,* Apr., 1968, pp. 6-9.

17. John Carden, *The Ugly Missionary* (London: Highway Press, 1964), pp. 96-97.

## Chapter 2

1. Gerald H. Anderson, ed., *The Theology of the Christian Mission* (New York: McGraw-Hill, 1961), pp. 146-47.

2. J. N. Farquhar, *The Crown of Hinduism* (London: Oxford University Press, 1930), p. 45.

3. Kenneth J. Saunders, *Ideals of East and West* (Cambridge, 1934), pp. 219-24.

4. J. S. Enderlin, "The Old Way and the New to the Muslim Heart," I.R.M., Jan., 1942, pp. 112 ff. Rev. Enderlin was with the Basel Mission in Egypt.

5. Hendrik Kraemer, *The Christian Message in a Non-Christian World* (Grand Rapids: Kregel, 1956), p. 102.

6. Ibid., p. 131. For further exposition of Kraemer's theory of discontinuity, see the Madras Series, Vol. 1, *The Authority of the Christian Faith* (New York: IMC, 1939), pp. 1-22.

7. Ibid., p. 145.

8. Anderson, *The Theology of the Christian Mission*, p. 208.

9. William E. Hocking, *Living Religions and a World Faith* (New York: Macmillan, 1940), p. 254.

10. George Seaver, *Albert Schweitzer: The Man and His Mind* (New York: Harper, 1947), p. 276.

11. Arnold Toynbee, *Christianity Among the Religions of the World* (New York: Scribners, 1958), p. 95.

12. William E. Hocking, Chairman, *Re-thinking Missions: A Laymen's Inquiry After 100 Years* (New York: Harper, 1932). Seven denominations, each unofficially represented by a group of 5 men and women, joined to constitute the 35 directors of the commission. The denominations represented were Northern Baptist, Congregational, Methodist Episcopal, Presbyterian Church in U.S.A., Protestant Episcopal, Reformed Church in America, and the United Presbyterian. The inquiry was restricted to India, Burma, China, and Japan. Visits to the field were made from Sept., 1931, to June, 1932.

13. Pages on which the quotations can be found are (in order of quotation): 6, 7, 8, 16, 19, 52, 31, 33, 40, 44, 59.

14. William E. Hocking, *Living Religions and a World Faith*, p. 254.

15. Ibid., pp. 196-97.

16. Raimundo Panikkar, *The Unknown Christ of Hinduism* (London: Darton, Longman, and Todd, 1968).

17. Carl E. Braaten, *The Flaming Center* (Philadelphia: Fortress Press, 1977), p. 109.

18. E. Stanley Jones, *The Christ of the Indian Road* (New York: Grossett and Dunlap, 1925), p. 50.

19. Kraemer, *The Christian Message in a Non-Christian World*, p. 128.

20. Edmund Perry, *The Gospel in Dispute* (Garden City, N.Y.: Doubleday, 1958), pp. 217-18.

## Chapter 3

1. E. Stanley Jones, *Along the Indian Road* (New York: Abingdon, 1935), p. 116.

## Chapter 5

1. Mahatma Gandhi, *Christian Missions* (Ahmedabad: Navajivan Publishing House, 1941), p. 3.

2. M. B. Niyogi, *Report of the Christian Missionary Activities Enquiry Committee, Madhya Pradesh* (Nagpur: Madhya Pradesh Government Printing, 1956), 1:118-22.

3. Don Richardson, *Lords of the Earth* (Glendale, Calif.: Regal, 1977), pp. 228-29.

4. E. Stanley Jones, *Along the Indian Road* (New York: Abingdon, 1935), pp. 98-99.

## Chapter 6

1. David Mason, *Apostle to the Illiterates* (Grand Rapids: Zondervan, 1966), pp. 31-35, 43.

2. Eugene Nida, *Customs and Culture* (New York: Harper, 1954), pp. 212-13.

3. Stephen Neill, *A History of Christian Missions* (Grand Rapids: Eerdmans, 1964), pp. 312-13.

4. T. Stanley Soltau, *Facing the Field* (Grand Rapids: Baker, 1959), pp. 51-52.

## Chapter 7

1. William Woodard, "Japan's New Religions," *World Vision,* Feb., 1965, p. 24.

2. John R. W. Stott, *Christian Mission in the Modern World* (Downers Grove, Ill.: InterVarsity Press, 1975), pp. 44-53.

3. J. Waskom Pickett, *The Dynamics of Church Growth* (Nashville: Abingdon, 1963), pp. 82-84.

4. E. Stanley Jones, *A Song of Ascents* (Nashville: Abingdon, 1968), pp. 65-66.

5. E. Stanley Jones, *The Christ of the Indian Road* (New York: Grossett and Dunlap, 1925), pp. 7-8.

6. Ibid., pp. 9-10.

7. *Practical Anthropology* (Nov.-Dec., 1960), p. 272.

8. J. Merle Davis, *New Buildings on Old Foundations* (New York: International Missionary Council, 1947), p. 43.

9. Eugene Nida, *Message and Mission* (New York: Harper, 1960), p. 226.

10. Abraham Maslow, *Motivation and Personality* (New York: Harper, 1970), pp. 88-106.

11. James Engel and H. Wilbert Norton, *What's Gone Wrong with the Harvest?* (Grand Rapids: Zondervan, 1975), pp. 44-46.

12. Ibid., p. 46.

13. Ibid.

## Chapter 8

1. Eugene Nida, *Customs and Culture* (New York: Harper, 1954), p. 216.

2. Ibid.

3. Ibid., p. 217.

4. Eugene Nida, *Message and Mission* (New York: Harper, 1960), pp. 47-48.

5. Eugene Nida, *God's Word in Man's Language* (New York: Harper, 1952), pp. 13-14.

6. Nida, *Message and Mission*, p. 194.

7. Nida, *Customs and Culture*, p. 4.

8. Nida, *Message and Mission*, p. 220.

9. Told in person by Dr. Darlene Bee, former Wycliffe missionary to the Usarufa tribe.

10. Nida, *Customs and Culture*, p. 221.

11. Nida, *Message and Mission*, p. 180.

12. Ibid.

13. Don Richardson, *Peace Child* (Glendale, Calif.: Regal, 1974), pp. 234, 287.

## Chapter 9

1. James and Marti Hefley, *God's Tribesman* (Philadelphia and New York: A. J. Holman, 1974), p. 27.

2. Bruce Olson, *For This Cross I'll Kill You* (Carol Stream, Ill.: Creation House, 1973). See this book for Olson's complete story.

3. This information came from Rev. Uzele Mesa, evangelist in Kenya, who spoke in my class in Feb., 1979.

4. Eugene Nida, *Customs and Culture* (New York: Harper, 1954), pp. 13-14.

5. Mr. Mallappa, first a government excise inspector, who, after his conversion, became a lay evangelist in the Telegu language. He passed away in the mid 50s.

6. Dr. Evyn Adams is at present a professor in the University of Hawaii at Hilo.

7. Told to me personally by Rev. Kenneth Enright, veteran missionary to Zaire under the United Methodist church.

## Chapter 10

1. The Hindu names of the 10 incarnations are as follows: Matsya (fish), Kurma (tortoise), Varaha (boar), Narasimha (man-lion), Vamana (dwarf), and the four fully human forms of Purusarama, Dasaratharma, Krishna, and Buddha; Kalki is yet to come.

2. See Bhagavad Gita 4:7-8. "For whatever right declines, O Bharata, and wrong uprises, then I create myself. To guard the good and to destroy the wicked and to confirm the right, I come into being in this age and in that."

3. From notes taken on a sermon preached by Dr. E. Stanley Jones in India on one occasion.

4. The author is indebted for some of the ideas in this section to the late Adhyaksha Mandapaka, Telegu evangelist in Andhra Pradesh, India, who wrote a tract entitled *Sacrifice*, published by the Gospel Literature Service, Bombay.

5. Skanda Purana Yagna Vaivhava Khanda, seventh chapter.

6. Tandya Maha Brahmana.

7. Rig Veda.

8. Sathpatha Brahmana.

9. Tandya Brahmana of Sama Veda.

10. Satapadha Brahmana.

11. The six enemies of the soul *(shadvairi)* are *kama* (lust), *krodha* (anger), *lobha* (avarice), *moha* (fascination with the world), *mada* (pride), and *matsarya* (jealousy).

## Chapter 11

1. D. T. Niles, *Buddhism and the Claims of Christ* (Richmond, Va.: John Knox Press, 1967), p. 72.

2. From sermon preached by Rev. L. A. DeSilva ("The Cross and the Bodhi Tree") on Good Friday, 1969.

## Chapter 12

1. Sir Norman Anderson, ed., *The World's Religions*, 4th ed., rev. (Grand Rapids, Eerdmans, 1970), Chap. 1 "Religions of a Pre Literary Society," by Edward G. Newing.

2. Eugene Nida and William A. Smalley, *Introducing Animism* (New York: Friendship Press, 1959), pp. 56-58.

3. Ibid., pp. 15-16.

4. Bruce Olson, *For This Cross I'll Kill You* (Carol Stream, Ill.: Creation House, 1973), p. 157.

5. Ibid., p. 156.

6. Donald McGavran, ed., *Crucial Issues in Missions Tomorrow* (Chicago: Moody Press, 1972), Chapter 5, "Possessing the Philosophy of Animism for Christ," by Alan Tippett, pp. 137-38.

7. Don Richardson, *Lords of the Earth* (Glendale, Calif.: Regal, 1977), p. 73.

8. Olson, *For This Cross I'll Kill You*, p. 158.

## Chapter 13

1. Koran: "'Isa bin Mariam kalimat Allah—Jesus, Son of Mary, Word of God."

2. The Muslims claim that Abraham sacrificed Ishmael, not Isaac. Rather than argue about this, we can simply state that Abraham sacrificed *his son*, without mentioning the name.

Chapter 14

1. We have taken the liberty to use this shortened form because of the cumbersomeness of the full name.

2. For the complete autobiography see: John A. Subhan, *How a Sufi Found His Lord* (Lucknow, India: Lucknow Publishing House, 1942).

3. Ibid., p. 20.

4. For the full story of Rochunga Pudaite read: James and Marti Hefley, *God's Tribesman* (Philadelphia and New York: A. J. Holman, 1974).

# Bibliography

Ahmad-Shah, E. *Theology—Christian and Hindu.* Lucknow, 1966.

———. *Theology—Muslim and Christian.* Lucknow, 1970.

Anderson, Gerald H., ed. *The Theology of the Christian Mission.* New York: McGraw-Hill, 1961.

———. *Sermons to Men of Other Faiths and Traditions.* Nashville: Abingdon, 1966.

Anderson, J. N. D., ed. *The World's Religions.* Grand Rapids: Eerdmans, 1957.

———. *Christianity and Comparative Religions.* Downers Grove, Ill.: InterVarsity, 1971.

Anderson, Sir Norman, ed. *The World's Religions.* Grand Rapids: Eerdmans, 1977.

Arberry, A. J. *The Koran Interpreted.* New York: Macmillan, 1967.

Bach, Marcus. *Strangers at the Door.* Nashville: Abingdon, 1971.

Bavinck, J. H. *The Church Between Temple and Mosque.* Grand Rapids: Eerdmans, 1966.

Bethmann, Erich W. *Steps Toward Understanding Islam.* Baltimore: American Friends of the Middle East, 1966.

Braaten, Carl E. *The Flaming Center.* Philadelphia: Fortress Press, 1977.

Bradley, Daniel G. *Circles of Faith.* Nashville: Abingdon, 1966.

Brannen, Noah S. *Soka Gakkai.* Richmond: John Knox, 1968.

Brelvi, Mahmud. *The Impact of Islam on Human Progress.* Karachi: Technical Printers, 1964.

Chen, Kenneth K. S. *Buddhism, the Light of Asia.* Woodbury, N.Y.: Barron's Educational Series, 1968.

*Christian Witness Among Muslims.* Accra, Ghana, Africa: Christian Press, 1971. For Christians in Africa.

Cragg, Kenneth. *Sandals at the Mosque.* New York: Oxford, 1959.

———. *The Call of the Minaret.* New York: Oxford, 1964.

Davis, J. Merle. *New Buildings on Old Foundations.* New York: International Missionary Council, 1947.

deKrester, Bryan. *Man in Buddhism and Christianity.* Calcutta: Y.M.C.A., 1954.

Dewick, E. C. *The Christian Attitude to Other Religions.* New York: Cambridge University Press, 1953.

Engel, James F. *Contemporary Christian Communications: Its Theory and Practice.* Nashville: Nelson, 1979.

Engel, James F., and Norton, H. Wilbert. *What's Gone Wrong with the Harvest?* Grand Rapids: Zondervan, 1975.

Farquhar, J. N. *The Crown of Hinduism.* London: Oxford University Press, 1930.

Gandhi, M. K. *Christian Missions.* Ahmedabad: Navajivan Publishing House, 1941.

Guiness, Os. *The Dust of Death.* Downers Grove, Ill.: InterVarsity, 1973.

————. *The East, No Exit*. Downers Grove: InterVarsity, 1974. The swing toward Eastern mysticism.

Hefley, James and Marti. *God's Tribesman*. Philadelphia and New York: A. J. Holman, 1974.

Hesselgrave, David J. *Communicating Christ Cross-Culturally*. Grand Rapids: Zondervan, 1978.

Hill, W. D. P., trans. *The Bhagavad Gita*. London: Oxford Press, 1928.

Hocking, William E. *Living Religions and a World Faith*. New York: Macmillan, 1940.

————. *Re-thinking Missions: A Laymen's Inquiry After 100 Years*. New York: Harper, 1932.

Hogg, A. J. *The Christian Message to the Hindu*. London: S.C.M., 1947.

Hunter, George. *The Contagious Congregation*. Nashville: Abingdon, 1979.

Jones, Bevan. *People of the Mosque*. Calcutta: Baptist Mission Press, 1959.

————. *Christianity Explained to Muslims*. Calcutta: Y.M.C.A., 1952.

Jones, E. Stanley. *A Song of Ascents*. Nashville: Abingdon, 1968.

————. *Along the Indian Road*. New York: Abingdon, 1935.

————. *The Christ of the Indian Road*. New York: Grossett and Dunlap, 1925.

Kraemer, Hendrik. *The Christian Message in a Non-Christian World*. Grand Rapids: Kregel, 1956.

————. *Why Christianity of All Religions?* London: Lutterworth, 1962.

Latourette, Kenneth S. *Introducing Buddhism*. New York: Friendship Press, 1956.

Manikam, Rajah B., ed. *Christianity and the Asian Revolution*. New York: Friendship Press, 1954.

Marsh, Charles R. *Share Your Faith with a Muslim*. Chicago: Moody Press, 1975.

Maslow, Abraham. *Motivation and Personality*. New York: Harper, 1970.

Mason, David. *Apostle to the Illiterates*. Grand Rapids: Zondervan, 1966.

McGavran, Donald. *Crucial Issues in Missions Tomorrow*. Chicago: Moody, 1972.

McVeigh, Malcolm. *God in Africa: Concepts of God in African Traditional Religion and Christianity*. Cape Cod, Mass.: Claude Stark, 1974.

Miller, William. *A Christian's Response to Islam*. Philadelphia: Presbyterian and Reformed Publishing Co., 1976.

————. *Ten Muslims Meet Christ*. Grand Rapids: Zondervan, 1969.

Neill, Stephen. *Christian Faith and Other Faiths*. New York: Oxford Press, 1970.

Newbigin, Leslie. *The Finality of Christ*. Richmond: John Knox Press, 1969.

Nida, Eugene. *Customs and Culture*. New York: Harper, 1954.

————. *God's Word in Man's Language*. New York: Harper, 1952.

————. *Message and Mission*. New York: Harper, 1960.

————. *Religion Across Culture*. New York: Harper, 1968.

Nida, Eugene, and Smalley, William A., *Introducing Animism*. New York: Friendship Press, 1959.

Niles, D. T. *Buddhism and the Claims of Christ*. Richmond, Va.: John Knox Press, 1967.

————. *That They May Have Life.* New York: Harper, 1951.

North American Lausanne Committee for World Evangelization. *Conference on Muslim Evangelization.* Colorado Springs, Oct. 15-21, 1978. Many reports.

Olson, Bruce. *For This Cross I'll Kill You.* Carol Stream, Ill.: Creation House, 1973.

Panikkar, K. M. *Asia and Western Dominance.* London: Allen and Unwin, 1959.

Panikkar, Raimundo. *The Unknown Christ of Hinduism.* London: Darton, Longman, and Todd, 1968.

Perry, Edmund. *The Gospel in Dispute.* Garden City, N.Y.: Doubleday, 1958.

Peterson, William J. *Those Curious New Cults.* New Canaan, Conn.: Keats, 1973.

Pickett, J. Waskom. *The Dynamics of Church Growth.* Nashville: Abingdon, 1963.

Pitt, Malcolm. *Introducing Hinduism.* New York: Friendship Press, 1958.

Richardson, Don. *Lords of the Earth.* Glendale, Calif.: Regal, 1977.

————. *Peace Child.* Glendale, Calif.: Regal, 1974.

Soltau, T. Stanley. *Facing the Field.* Grand Rapids: Baker, 1959.

Stott, John R. W. *Christian Mission in the Modern World.* Downers Grove, Ill.: InterVarsity Press, 1975.

Subhan, John A. *How a Sufi Found His Lord.* Lucknow, India: Lucknow Publishing House, 1942.

Thompson, E. W. *The Word of the Cross to Hindus.* Madras: C. L. S. Press, 1956.

Thomsen, Harry. *The New Religions of Japan.* Rutland, Vt.: C. E. Tuttle Co., 1963.

Toynbee, Arnold. *Christianity Among the Religions of the World.* New York: Scribners, 1958.

Vijayawardhana. *The Revolt in the Temple.* Colombo, Sri Lanka: Sinah Publications, 1953.

Wilson, J. Christy. *Introducing Islam.* New York: Friendship Press, 1958.

————. *The Christian Message to Islam.* New York: Fleming Revell Co., 1950.

# INDEX